MEETING HUMAN NEEDS
2: Additional Perspectives
From Thirteen Countries

SOCIAL SERVICE DELIVERY SYSTEMS
An International Annual

Series Editors

DANIEL THURSZ
School of Social Work and Community Planning
University of Maryland at Baltimore

JOSEPH L. VIGILANTE
School of Social Work
Adelphi University

SOCIAL SERVICE DELIVERY SYSTEMS
An International Annual
Volume 2

MEETING HUMAN NEEDS

2: Additional Perspectives From Thirteen Countries

Editors
DANIEL THURSZ
and
JOSEPH L. VIGILANTE

SAGE Publications   Beverly Hills / London

HV
40
.M46
V.2

For information address:

SAGE PUBLICATIONS, INC.
275 South Beverly Drive
Beverly Hills, California 90212

SAGE PUBLICATIONS LTD
St George's House / 44 Hatton Garden
London EC1N 8ER

Printed in the United States of America

ISBN No. 0-8039-0590-4 (cloth)
ISBN No. 0-8039-0591-2 (paper)

Library of Congress Catalog Card No. 76-6314

FIRST PRINTING

CONTENTS

PREFACE

This volume, the second in an international series on the architecture of various national social service delivery systems, brings the number of countries thus far reviewed to a total of 22. The approach that the authors used in assembling these reports from 22 different countries was to select well known social welfare experts on each of the countries and to provide them with guidelines on how to describe the content of the social service systems of those countries. Never, however, did we fully expect or desire that each author would confine himself or herself strictly to our suggestions. In fact, in the interest of maintaining the unique flavor of each country's approach to social services, we felt that it was important *not* to attempt to limit writers to our own preconceived notions as to the relevant content of social service systems. As our own final Chapter 14 indicates, we gained in our knowledge and our perspectives on social service delivery as a result of this flexibility.

The chapters in this volume, as in the first, vary widely in the manner in which the authors describe particular social service systems. Just as we attempted to maintain a loose posture with regard to the content, so did we try to preserve the original flavor of the English language as written by authors for whom English is not a mother tongue. The authors' use of English varies widely. Thus, non-English colloquialisms and non-English professional jargon will appear. (We should say non-American.)

Future volumes of this series will emphasize specialized aspects of social service delivery systems. Volume 3 will be concerned with the use of the neighborhood as a locus of organization of social welfare services. Volume 4 will be dealing with special aspects of delivering services to the aging.

As we approach the organization of Volumes 3 and 4, we will be testing a new methodology. Because we believe that the emphasis on specialized content requires a broader method of selection, for these volumes we are soliciting articles from contributors instead of commissioning articles. We hope especially to be able to identify innovative attempts at social service delivery.

The editors have been aided by our distinguished Editorial Advisory Board. The help that was given us by the administrative staffs of Adelphi University's School of Social Work and the University of Maryland's School of Social Work and Community Planning has, once more, been invaluable. At Adelphi, we once again thank Evelyn Geddes and Maria Georgiou and graduate assistants Suzy Sonenberg, Betsy Sinks, Sharon Kaplan, and Norma Berman. At the University of Maryland at Baltimore, we thank David Stoesz, graduate assistant, Louise White, Assistant to the Dean, and both Nancy Steele and Sharon Backof, secretaries in the Dean's office.

We are indebted to Haddassah Thursz and Florence Vigilante for their critical and incisive comments on the manuscript. The errors that will inevitably appear in the final version are those of the editors.

Daniel Thursz
Joseph L. Vigilante
Garden City, New York
June 1976

1

THE CANADIAN WELFARE STATE
AND FEDERALISM

ALBERT ROSE

THE DILEMMAS OF INTERGOVERNMENTAL RESPONSIBILITIES

Canada, a nation of 24 million persons in 1976, is a federal country. An understanding of its constitutional arrangements and the nature of the responsibilities of its three levels of government (or four levels, if regional governments are taken into consideration) is essential if the provision of social welfare services to its people can be analyzed. In its traditional place in history—as intermediary between the British and the American viewpoints on the responsibilities of government as well as in a host of other aspects of interpersonal relationships—Canada has a constitution; but it resembles neither that of the United Kingdom, which is considered to be unwritten, nor that of the United States, which is encompassed within a written document standing alongside the legislative framework enacted by Congress.

The Canadian Constitution is literally the British North America Act of 1867, a statute enacted by the Parliament of Great Britain following a series of constitutional conferences which began within the four provinces existing in British North America in 1864—specifically, Nova Scotia, New Brunswick, Lower Canada (Quebec), and Upper Canada (Ontario). This basic statute could thus be amended only by action of the British Parliament, and such action has occurred less than 15 times during the past 108 years. Moreover, the *interpretation* of the basic constitutional framework under which Canadian governments operate has been a responsibility of the Parliament in Westminster and assigned to the Judicial Committee of the Privy Council, a committee of the Law Lords in the upper house. After 1867 the allocation of responsibilities for the newly emerging services of government was determined by consideration of civil cases referred for interpretation to the Judicial Committee.

Section 92 of the British North America Act assigns responsibility for "property and civil rights" to the governments of the provinces. The four original provinces had grown to nine by 1905, and a 10th province (Newfoundland) joined the Confederation in 1949. The interpretation of "property and civil rights" by the British Law Lords resulted most often in the governments of the provinces being assigned the responsibility for what is usually understood to be "social legislation." By the end of the 19th century the provinces had thus been required to assume responsibility for education, health services, welfare services, and the broad area encompassed within labor relations. In the 20th century "property and civil rights" clearly embraced, in addition, provincial responsibility for housing and urban planning.

It is important to emphasize that, in addition to the jurisdictional disputes between the federal and provincial governments, the constitutional statute makes it entirely clear that the municipalities are "the creatures of the provinces." With rare exceptions (perhaps only two cities, Halifax and Winnipeg, have charters), the emerging areas were not possessed of "home rule" responsibilities. The federal government has always had very substantial and productive sources of revenue by comparison with the provincial governments, at least since the introduction of the income tax in 1917. However, the division of constitutional responsibilities between the government of Canada and the provincial governments made a tremendous difference in the provision and delivery of health and welfare services, as well as related services demanded of local government.

Thus, Canada's situation may be summarized as follows. The federal government, which does not have major responsibility by constitutional interpretation for the delivery of social services, is possessed of the major financial resources; the 10 provincial governments, which by constitutional interpretation do have major responsibility in the areas of service provision, are grievously lacking in financial resources; the municipal governments, where the actual delivery of social services takes place (very often through the assignment of administrative responsibility by the governments of the provinces), constitute the least financially well endowed of all levels of government.

A solution to these dilemmas has been the development of a set of working relationships involving complementary legislation and financial arrangements between the two senior levels of government. For example, in the 1950s the federal government passed an Old Age Assistance Act and invited the provinces to pass "enabling" legislation; this was the way of providing income maintenance on a means-test basis for people aged 65 to 69 who did not meet the criterion for the Old Age Pension payable at age 70. The government of any province which passed the required legislation would thus enable its residents to apply for the appropriate amount of money for which such indigent elderly could qualify. With the passage of this legislation the government of Canada then agreed to pay one-half or more of the administrative costs involved in the delivery of this service. In turn, the provincial governments could request municipal departments of welfare to carry out the necessary administrative responsibilities of determining the eligibility of those who applied for benefits, and the provincial governments might agree to pay all or part of the costs involved.

BENEFITS AND SERVICES

In 1930 Canada was unprepared to meet the impact of a decade of serious economic depression. There was not one province with a department of welfare, by whatever name; and whatever assistance was provided, in cash or in kind, to people in need was undertaken at the local level without the formalities of a full-fledged administration. In the province of Ontario, where more than 40% of the nation's population has resided since the 1920s, the first Department of Public Welfare at the provincial level was created in 1934; the city of Toronto had been forced to create a Department of Welfare within its own administration three years earlier in 1931. Nevertheless, the first significant piece of provincial legislation did not come until the passage of Ontario's Unemployment Relief Act in 1935.

Four decades later Canada has one of the most comprehensive income maintenance programs among Western industrial nations. All three levels of government have engaged in cooperative ventures to meet the income requirements of those who, in Beveridge's words, "suffer the risks of an industrial society" (1942). The most important techniques for meeting the basic tangible requirements of individuals and families have been utilized, and the result is a network of programs which now requires an expenditure of approximately $12 billion per annum—almost one-third of the total federal budget.

Universal Transfer Programs (Demogrants)

The government of Canada has, by virtue of its constitutional shortcomings, utilized as far as possible the universal transfer system to pump back into the economy large sums of money in the form of maintenance. These programs include, first of all, the Family Allowances *(Allocations familles)* legislated in 1944 and in effect since July 1, 1945. In the first decade or so following World War II the federal government paid amounts ranging from $5 to $8 per month, depending upon the age grouping, to the mothers of all children under the age of 16. These sums were later adjusted to two groupings of $6 and $8 per month, the change occurring at the age of 10. The scheme was supplemented in 1964 with the passage of the Youth Allowances Act, which continued these payments for children aged 16 and 17 provided that they remained in full-time school attendance. (The allowance was $10 per month.)

The inauguration of Family Allowances in 1945 was never intended to represent a scheme whereby the full costs of raising children were to be provided by redistribution of income from general federal revenue sources. Many

Canadians, however, believed and continue to believe that these allowances are some inadequate recognition of the costs of child-rearing in a costly urban society. Such allotments were intended from the very beginning to be of some assistance to mothers in improving the standard of living of their children; it was recognized that heads of families were paid according to the nature of their jobs and not by virute of the number of their dependents. Payments have always been made to mothers on the assumption that there is a more likely quarantee that the money will be spent for the benefit of the children.

As the war was drawing to a close in 1944, Canada feared the onset of a depression of the type that afflicted North America in the years 1919-1921. Family Allowances were thus seen to be an important economic element in postwar stabilization; they would pump into the national economy some $250 million per annum at a time when the gross national product was in the neighborhood of about $14 billion but which was expected by some economists to drop sharply when the war ended.

At the close of the 1960s the Family Allowances and Youth Allowances programs were costing the federal government some $650 million per annum, but most Canadians were dissatisfied with the utility of the programs in the light of their understanding of the objectives. The amounts paid out each month for each child were low, and, with a price level three times greater than that of 1945, the individual sums received by most mothers were irrelevant. In December 1970 the federal Minister of Health and Welfare published a white paper, *Income Security for Canadians,* in which he advocated that these payments would be made only to families with gross incomes of less than $10,000 per annum. He recommended a sliding scale of payments, with much higher amounts for families with less than $5,000 per annum and the amount per child to be reduced progressively until it reached zero at $10,000 per annum.

This program was part of the federal government's insistence that universality was no longer a desirable method of providing income maintenance. Rather, selectivity through a simple form of means test (the income tax return was generally favored) would be the preferred mode. The program put forward in 1970 proved, however, to be extremely unpopular with the people of Canada and, in particular, with the provincial governments. The province of Quebec was in the process of demanding responsibility for the payment of demogrants to those residing in that province, provided that the federal government turned over the large sums of money involved for a population of more than six million. Following the election of October 1972, the federal government changed its mind abruptly and completely and advocated a program in which two major changes or concessions were put forward: (1) Family and Youth Allowances were to be continued as universal programs without regard to the total income of the family; the amount per child was raised to $20 per month (or an average of $20, whatever the province decided with respect to the amount paid for one or several children in the family); (2) the province of Quebec received the right to use its resources as it wished, provided that the federal requirement of an average payment of $20 per child per month was set. The financial result was that, commencing January 1, 1974, the cost of the program was expected to be in excess of $1.2 billion per annum.

At the other end of the scale of age distribution Canada has maintained an Old Age Security program on a universal basis since January 1, 1952. In the beginning years all persons over the age of 70 with at least 20 years residence in Canada received $40 per month. This universal benefit increased slowly through the years and reached $65 per month by 1965. At that time the federal government determined to build upon its universal system an additional layer based on the social insurance principle. Accordingly, in 1965 the Canada Pension Plan was legislated whereby, commencing January 1, 1966, all employed Canadians as well as their employers would contribute 1.8% of the employee's annual earnings, subject to an overall income limitation set at approximately $5,000 per annum. The plan was to reach maturity in 1976, at which time those with full benefits would be able to retire at age 65 with approximately $75 per month from the universal scheme plus an additional $104 per month from the pension insurance program.[1]

In the course of the past decade the inflationary process has not only modified but destroyed the twin-pronged approach of the federal government toward Old Age Security. On the one hand, the Liberal government of Pierre Trudeau, which was elected in 1968, first took the view that the universal scheme was irrelevant. *The White Paper on Income Security* attacked strongly the principle of universality and, as already indicated in the case of Family Allowances, came out in favor of selectivity. The Old Age Security Allowance was to be fixed at $80 per month, and the Canada Pension Plan was to be modified with the approval of the provincial governments. As in the case of the Family Allowances program, political considerations and the pace of inflation forced the government to reverse itself within a very short period of time.

By 1976, the Old Age Security portion had been progressively increased to more than $130 per month, and it is now tied to the consumer price index and thus adjusted on a quarterly basis. At the same time, legislation has been introduced to increase substantially the retirement annuity under the Canada Pension Plan. It has been forecast that by 1980 a person who has contributed for at least a decade at the maximum level of earnings will be retired with well over $200 per month from the plan. It is also predicted that the total minimum retirement income from the universal and social insurance programs will amount to more than $350 per month.

Social Insurance Programs

The principles of social insurance were first utilized in Canada during the First World War, when Workmen's Compensation legislation was passed in several provinces. The Canadian system is quite unlike that in the United States in that compensation is determined in each case by a Workmen's Compensation

Board or Commission within the province rather than through the employment of a legal adversary system, as in most American states. Premiums are paid only by employers and are based upon a rating of safety performance within the specific industry and, ultimately, within the particular firm. There is thus a twofold pressure, upon employers and employees alike, to develop programs that work for the successful improvement of the company's safety performance. The premiums are, after all, a charge upon the firm and could result in higher prices, thus affecting the competitive capacity of the company and its employment opportunities.

When the Great Depression struck in the fall of 1929 Canada was less prepared in the field of social insurance than most industrial nations, including the United States. There were no federal or provincial programs to cover such risks as unemployment, sickness, or retirement. In the dying days of a Conservative administration an Unemployment Insurance Bill was passed in 1935 but was soon thereafter declared unconstitutional by the Judicial Committee of the Privy Council in Westminster. A National Employment Commission was created in 1937, and its report became the basis for the first major national social insurance program with the passage of the Unemployment Insurance Act in 1940. This act, as revised and amended from time to time, has formed the basis of a fundamental program during the past 35 years; both employers and employees have paid equal premiums, with the government of Canada assuming the cost of administration estimated at about 20% of total expenditures. By virtue of full employment throughout the war years and high rates of employment (with only slight recessions) during the decade ending 1955, the Unemployment Insurance Fund grew to more than $1.25 billion by the mid-1950s. In the recession of 1958-1962, however, the extension of benefits, the inclusion of groups previously excluded (such as fishermen and agricultural laborers), and generally flexible attitudes toward payments resulted in near bankruptcy of the fund by 1963. During the balance of the 1960s modest supplementation from general federal revenues was required, but the economic recovery of 1963-1969 permitted some breathing space, and the future of the program was studied by special committees and government investigators.

By 1970 the federal government was ready with a new Unemployment Insurance Act on a much more generous basis than ever before. It enunciated the principle that all employed persons must assume responsibility for the fiscal stability of the program. This meant that the maximum level of income governing premiums (the maximum insurable level had been raised a number of times during the previous 30 years to approximately $7,200 in the late 1960s) would be further increased, but more significant was the fact that all employed persons whose incomes exceeded the maximum would pay premiums for the first time in their careers. The legislation and its administration during the 1970s have been a continuous source of controversy, because the potential benefits for a contributor have been far in excess of previous levels. They have been beyond the minimum wage levels on the one hand and the highest possible benefits under public assistance programs on the other. It has been possible in recent years for an employee at the maximum insurable level (now more than $10,000 per annum) to work only 8 weeks and then draw benefits for as long as 20 weeks.[2] There is a considerable argument to justify the view that this program has become "another welfare program," although it is administered under a ministry other than that responsible for the basic social welfare programs.

The principles of social insurance have been utilized in several significant advances in social welfare and health legislation during the past 15 years. By 1959 the federal government had passed enabling legislation in the field of hospital insurance; within a short time all 10 provinces had set up their own programs whereby they levied premiums, with the federal government paying approximately one-half of total expenditures. In more recent years certain provincial governments (Manitoba and Saskatchewan) have assumed the remainder of the cost of such premiums through general revenues.

By 1966 the federal government was in the process of passing similar legislation to cover medical care—in Canada the term "medicare" means a combination of medical and hospital insurance encompassed within one program. In Ontario and other provinces one premium is paid by each individual or family head to cover the cost of standard hospital ward care and other services and to cover basic medical care including visits to or by physicians. Drugs are not usually covered, except within hospitalization. The variety of services differs from province to province, and in some cases the premiums have been assumed by the provincial government. In addition, individuals and families may acquire additional insurance through private plans (such as Blue Cross) for services not provided by the governmental program. It is understandable that the payment of such premiums in all public and voluntary programs has become a matter for negotiation in the fringe benefits portion of collective labor agreements.

It has already been indicated that by 1966 the government of Canada had also legislated an overlay of social insurance in the field of income security for the elderly. The Canada Pension Plan is a classic example, with a clear basis in actuarial principles and premiums closely related to benefits. It is one of the interesting characteristics of social insurance in the welfare field in Canada (although not in the health services field) that the benefits have primarily been wage-related up to the maximum level. Unlike the British system, Canada has had no program of importance in which flat-rate benefits were paid upon the incidence of risk.

Public (Social) Assistance Programs

Canadians of Anglo-Saxon origin who settled in the Maritime Provinces in the 17th and 18th centuries or who came north following the American Revolution brought with them the experience and principles of the British Poor Law system.

These concepts, which dated back to the English experience of the 16th and 17th centuries, included the notions of local (parish) responsibility, residence as a prerequisite for poor relief, transportation to the base municipality if the individual or family were not residents, and, in general, administrative principles which today are considered punitive.

Canada has always had one special circumstance in its substantial population of French origin, now more than six million persons in the province of Quebec, and a further 500,000 to 750,000 persons of Quebecois origin are scattered across the country. The legal system as well as cultural forces surrounding the granting of assistance to needy persons and families in this segment was quite different from that emanating from British Poor Law experience. In brief, the legislation and the administration of welfare assistance in those provinces in which the Anglo-Saxon traditions were paramount involved clear and mandatory means-test application which, in the circumstances of the 1930s, were considered "tough, harsh and primitive." In the province of Quebec, on the other hand, welfare assistance was by tradition and cultural determination left primarily to the Roman Catholic Church, which on a parish basis was in a position to assess and determine need, to assemble resources from its parishioners, and to grant assistance in kind or in cash.

It appears that the farther one proceeded west of Ontario the more generous the public welfare provisions and the more liberal the administration. The basic reasons were similar to those in the United States—a mixture of agrarian radicalism customarily described as "populism," together with the views of those engaged in agriculture with respect to the creditor position of persons and institutions in the urbanized eastern regions—sentiments which were combined in legislation that harked back neither to the British Poor Law nor to the Code Napoleon. The fact that the western provinces, with the exception of British Columbia, were settled to a greater degree by persons who were neither British nor French in origin may also have played an important part in these phenomena.

Public welfare in Canada, as has been noted, is a particularly clear provincial responsibility. In the quarter century commencing in 1930 it seemed impossible to contemplate the entrance of the federal government into the field of welfare assistance, whether in terms of the provision of money or social services. At the same time, in the areas of veterans' benefits the government of Canada had developed an almost comprehensive program of social welfare and health services for those who qualified by virtue of problems of health, disability, or disease ascribed to overseas military service. This was a curious phenomenon but accepted by Canadians because of the special debt they felt was owed to many hundreds of thousands of persons who participated in the two extensive World Wars, in each of which Canada lost in dead alone nearly 50,000 persons. This was a high ratio considering the country's relatively small population.

In 1958 the Conservative government under Prime Minister John Diefenbaker passed an Unemployment Assistance Act in which, for the first time, the federal government entered the field of public assistance using traditional legislative methods. This act was a characteristic piece of enabling legislation whereby standards were laid down which, when met by provinces passing complementary legislation, would mean a transfer of 50% of total expenditures from the federal to the respective provincial governments. This was the forerunner of more extensive legislation passed in 1966 and known as the Canada Assistance Plan. The act of 1958 was primarily concerned with general welfare assistance to persons and families and did not interfere with already established federal-provincial programs such as Old Age Assistance (to those aged 65-69), Disabled Persons' Allowances, and Blind Persons' Allowances; nor did it interfere with a fundamental provincial program (dating back in the case of Ontario to 1916) known as Mothers' Allowances (in the United States, mothers' pensions of pre-World War I and wartime initiation).

By the mid-1960s the need for extension of the federal financial role, particularly in the absence of sufficient provincial financial resources, became most evident. The major objectives of the Canada Assistance Act were to coordinate intergovernmental as well as uniquely provincial public welfare legislation, and to improve the quality of administration at both the provincial and municipal levels of organization. To this end the federal government offered to pay one-half the costs of all federal-provincial and provincial public assistance programs wherein agreement was reached to integrate such programs within the rubric of the Canada Assistance Plan. In addition, on the basis of laid-down standards and principles of administration, the senior level would also pay half the administrative costs.

Through the Canada Public Assistance Plan, the federal government shared the cost of the following assistance programs and related services administered by provincial governments:

Care: medical attention, surgery and hospitalization; dental and sight care (dentures and glasses); pharmaceutical products and protheses, as well as miscellaneous health care;

Assistance to mothers of families with dependent children;

Social welfare institutions: the maintenance of needy persons in social welfare institutions, such as homes for the aged, rest homes, centres for unmarried mothers, and special institutions for children;

Social welfare services: rehabilitation, individual social work, orientation and evaluation, adoption services, home visiting, and day care. [Canada, 1973:11]

At the present time (mid-1970s) income security programs in Canada are based upon all three major approaches to the provision of financial assistance —universal transfer programs, social insurance programs, and public (social) assistance programs. In some of the most significant areas of risk in a Western urban industrial society (as in the area of retirement income) the Old Age

Security provisions ensure a uniformity of benefit across the country, despite the fact that living costs vary from rural to urban areas and from region to region. A most recent development by certain provincial governments has been to add to the retirement income laid down by the federal government so that such benefits are greater in some provinces than in others.

Inflation has increased so dramatically since 1970 that there remains considerable dissatisfaction with the level of benefits throughout Canada. Curiously enough, dissatisfaction works both ways: in the case of Unemployment Insurance there is criticism that the level of benefits is too high and that it actively discourages the will to work; at the same time, the view is that the level of benefits in most other programs is too low to maintain an adequate standard of living. At times the criticism is directed to the total program benefit; sometimes it is leveled at one specific component (shelter) of the budgeting process, as in the case of such programs as the Family Benefits legislation (previously known as Mothers' Allowances). In this nation, where the costs of shelter in proportion to available income are among the highest in the world, there is a great difference of opinion on the question of increasing shelter allowances; very often this could simply mean the transfer of additional funds from public revenue sources to private landlords who provide quite inadequate accommodation.

The major issue in the field of income and social security in recent years has been the question of a guaranteed annual income. There are very different views on this subject, stemming particularly from a report of the Special Senate Committee on Poverty (1970), which recommended the initiation of a guaranteed annual income on a negative income-tax basis. The levels of income proposed, the degree of retention of income above the base poverty line, and the proposals in general were considered by many Canadians to be quite inadequate and, in fact, designed to maintain poverty. One group of the Senate committee broke away in the last days of its work and wrote a second report entitled *The Real Poverty Report* (Adams, et al., 1971), in which higher levels of basic income, higher proportions of retention of income earned above the basic levels, and a generally more liberal approach to the whole question of income were proposed. Within the federal government itself there were and are widely ranging estimates of the total additional cost involved in the provision of a guaranteed annual income system.

THE SERVICE ASPECT OF THE SOCIAL SERVICES

At a meeting of the Canadian Labour Congress in Canada in 1965[3] the distinguished social economist, Professor Eveline Burns, commented, "Services will not fill an empty belly." It has been clear from the exposition of income maintenance and social security provisions in intergovernmental legislation that a great deal of Canada's effort during the past four decades has been directed toward the maintenance of income at times of individual or family crisis. Once adequate income security provisions have been developed, however, the great needs of certain groups within the Canadian community—the elderly, the disabled, sole-support mothers with dependent children, high school dropouts, those vocationally handicapped through physical or emotional incapacity—have come sharply into focus. Such services require personnel, with a variety of levels of training, and often facilities; and it is in the social services that Canada is found wanting.

In the development of the Canadian social services since the 1930s the basic tangible aspects of common human need have been the subject of governmental legislation and programs whereby tax revenues have been transferred, primarily through a progressive income-tax system, and complicated social insurance programs have been administered. It is also true that elected public officials and, until recently, most senior public administrators within the social and health services have assumed and thus have determined that, wherever personal services are offered to Canadians who are disadvantaged, they will be the object of *voluntary* efforts.

It is possible to identify throughout Canada, therefore, a variety of local and sometimes regional voluntary organizations, some of which have a history of fifty to a hundred years, solely dedicated to the provision of counseling services on behalf of children, youth, families, and elderly persons. Some of these organizations are the Family Service Association of Metropolitan Toronto, the Family Service Centres of Greater Vancouver Area, and Family Day Care Services (previously known as the Protestant Childrens' Homes of Toronto, founded in 1854). There are the Children's Aid Societies throughout the various provinces, some of which are now entirely under public auspices, some of which receive voluntary contributions through the United Way as well as public funds, and some of which are voluntary in name only since they are almost entirely funded through the governments of their respective provinces.

It has always been difficult to determine exactly how many positions there are in the Canadian social services and, more particularly, how many of these positions require a social worker whose qualifications are a two-year graduate program leading to the degree of master of social work. In 1954 the Department of National Health and Welfare published a major study that indicated that there were about 3,000 positions, one-third of which were occupied by persons with some degree in social work education, that is, one or two years. It would be difficult to estimate the number of positions now available, but a reasonable guess would be between 6,000 to 7,500 throughout the nation.

In the Maritime Provinces the majority of social services are offered under public auspices, and very few voluntary organizations in the formal sense, over and above the level of service clubs, continue to exist. The level of education in a substantial proportion of the positions has, until recent years, been generally low. It was not uncommon for many persons in the public social services, particularly those who were the public's first contact and played a role in eligibility determination, to be of an educational level well below high school graduation. Certainly the enunciated goal of the American Public Welfare Association, that the great majority of persons in the social services should have at least a first college degree, was and is very far from realization. Nevertheless, there has been substantial improvement within the past 10 to 15 years; there are programs of social work education in Newfoundland, New Brunswick, and Nova Scotia which offer the full range (though not in each program) from an undergraduate degree to a master's degree.

In the province of Quebec the voluntary tradition was encompassed within the Roman Catholic Church. Social change during the past three or four decades has tended to diminish the role of the church substantially, and such forces as industrialization and urbanization, along with powerful secular influences, have pushed the provincial government into far more significant roles than it ever before occupied. The transition from voluntary religious auspices, encompassing some financial aid and the availability of counseling, to a public social service system has been moving very rapidly during the past decade. It was government rather than voluntary action that has superseded the role of the church. This was inevitable, given the cost of federal-provincial income security programs and provincial initiatives, as well as the fact that there was no tradition of voluntary organization for the provision of services outside the Jewish community in Montreal and other cities.

Ontario, on the other hand, was very much a voluntary provider in its social service programs, with reasonably strong and effective United Fund organizations in both small and large urban centers and a variety of social service agencies in the five largest urban centers (Windsor, London, Hamilton, Toronto, and Ottawa). On the other hand, in the more rural portions of the province (particularly in northern Ontario) the Children's Aid Society, with jurisdiction on a county or regional basis, was responsible for almost every aspect of the social services. These included a number of functions carried out on behalf of public agencies—for example, the taking of applications, the forwarding of information, the interpretation of programs, and advocacy on behalf of persons disqualified from benefits. There are, nevertheless, certain well-established and traditional voluntary organizations ranging from settlement houses in the large cities developed on the British and American model of the second half of the 19th century to sophisticated counseling agencies in the fields of family welfare and mental health.

The major problem of such organizations at the present time is financial, and the dilemma is the amount of funding to request or accept from public authorities in the form of grants rather than purchase of services. At a certain point in the financial problem the voluntary organization becomes essentially a quasi-public organization (for example, the John Howard Society, which is the most notable in the field of the rehabilitation of discharged offenders). A number of voluntary associations participate in the United Way, but a great many organizations are supplicant before the municipal, regional, and provincial governments for additional grants or funding, most often for normal operating expenses rather than capital facilities or research programs.

The Prairie Provinces (Manitoba, Saskatchewan, and Alberta) have relatively sparse populations, with the exception of Alberta during the past two decades, and they have tended to be served entirely by governmental programs outside the few major cities, such as Winnipeg, Regina, Saskatoon, Calgary, and Edmonton, where certain voluntary organizations developed early in the 20th century. These provinces were established within the federal federation more than 70 years ago, and the tradition of voluntarism came primarily from newcomers from the United Kingdom and European countries who were the bulk of the first settlers.

Until the 1930s, church groups, ethnic associations, and some nondenominational groups were evident, and such groups did what they could to offer relief; the economic lot of many newcomers, both single persons and family groups, was very difficult until World War II. A few important voluntary organizations on a nondenominational basis did come into existence but for the most part people looked to their provincial governments. Their search was relatively unrewarded because of the scarcity of funds. In the mid-1970s the populations of Manitoba and Saskatchewan continue to be less than one million persons each, while that of Alberta has not yet reached two million. Until the mid-1960s the total budgets of these provinces had not reached $250 million per annum. In the past three years, however, agricultural prosperity and oil and gas revenues have led to greatly expanded budgets.

Nevertheless, there was sufficient challenge, to governmental officials and citizens alike, that substantial effort has developed during the past 15 to 20 years to improve the total situation, in both income maintenance and aspects of service delivery. The Prairie Provinces find it easier than Ontario and the Maritimes to introduce social workers into government agencies that offer personal services.

In the province of British Columbia there has always been an uneasy balance between voluntarism and public administration within the social services.[4] This is not to suggest adequacy, but it is a fact that the provincial government was forced more than a quarter of a century ago to mount and develop a social service program by virtue of the rugged geographical features of the province, the relative inaccessibility of some subregions within its jurisdiction, and the almost total lack of services. For a good many years the major employer of the graduates of the University of British Columbia School of Social Work was, indeed, the provincial government.

Voluntary action and voluntarism in the Canadian social services are by no means dormant, but there is an increasingly critical element among the population which contrasts public and voluntary expenditures and assumes that the latter are so insignificant that all social services should be delivered by governmental agencies. The fact is that all United Fund organizations that are affiliated with the Canadian Council on Social Development raise less than $150 million each year, whereas the various levels of government are now spending on health, welfare and social services upwards of $12 billion per annum. The critics assume that the relative expenditures mean the death knell of voluntary community and social organizations in Canada, but this is far from the truth.

For more than 40 years the scant literature in the field of social work and social welfare in Canada has abounded with articles, debates, and commentaries on relations between governmental and voluntary agencies. The traditional role of the voluntary agency was assumed to be that of a pioneering organization that demonstrated the need for a particular service and the method whereby it could be applied to the solution of human social problems. It was further assumed that, once this demonstration had become evident to the participants and to appointed and elected government officials, the service and its financing could safely be transferred to one or another level of government.

This simple sequence of events did not often prove to be true, however, and there were many occasions when appropriate demonstration projects vanished when their funding was exhausted; nor was there any serious effort by government to take over the service and to expand it to meet the needs of those for whom the program was intended. In short, the traditional theory did not work any better in Canada than it did in the United States, and there are many Canadians today who have grave reservations about the fairly common attacks upon the voluntary agencies. They are not convinced that the personal social services will be or can be left to governmental auspices; they are not convinced that Canadians would gladly pay increased taxes to meet the social service needs of their fellow citizens; but they are convinced that the withdrawal of the services of voluntary agencies would simply leave a huge void within the social service delivery system. This is not to suggest that the voluntary agencies are meeting the totality of personal and familial human needs. They are far from adequately funded and staffed, and there is no question that the totality of need is substantially unserved.

The old questions concerning the appropriate roles for governmental and voluntary agencies have not been answered. Although governments in Canada have greatly expanded their income maintenance programs, they are clearly reluctant to expand their social service delivery systems in the form of personal services. Rather, they prefer to purchase services from voluntary agencies if they are to provide services at all, and, in purchasing, they do very little to expand the overall supply of such services available to meet Canadian needs.

POVERTY IN CANADA IN THE MID-1970s

Poverty is on a modest scale in Canada by comparison with many other countries, and, in relative terms, Canadians are in a fortunate position even within the Western industrial urban society. This is not to suggest that there is not poverty in Canada. There are substantial differences of view, however, both between politicians on the one hand and social scientists and social workers on the other and among the members themselves in these professions. The argument centers around two questions: first, the nature of poverty in the Canadian society and, second, the extent of poverty as defined.

During the past 15 years, and particularly since the classic enunciation of a "war on poverty" by the late President John F. Kennedy, Canadians have utilized every form of measurement to judge the extent of poverty within their nation. Studies by the Canadian Welfare Council (now the Canadian Council on Social Development) in the early 1960s took the familiar criterion of an expenditure of 70% or more of an individual's income on food, clothing, and shelter as evidence of poverty. On the other hand, some studies have accepted a fixed amount of income per person within the family as the dividing line between poverty and nonpoverty—such as $70 per person per month. These measurements are irrelevant in a time of rapid inflation, and they have tended to disappear since 1968. Rather, the Economic Council of Canada, an advisory body appointed by the federal government (akin to the Council of Economic Advisors in the United States), has from time to time published in its *Annual Reviews* total income guides as indications of the poverty line for families of different size. For example, in the late 1960s the Economic Council judged that an income of $4,800 per annum for a family of two adults and two children was the poverty line (1968:103-140); this figure was adjusted accordingly for larger or smaller families. The significance of these estimates rests in the fact that the Special Senate Committee on Poverty, which reported in 1970, accepted these data as the base line upon which it could build its proposals for a guaranteed annual income.

The fact is that detailed studies of the cost of adequate standards of living on a regional basis, and particularly for both rural and urban living, have not been undertaken. Such studies are a sine qua non if Canada is truly to develop more advanced approaches to an attack on poverty, including the device which is mentioned more often than any other—the guaranteed annual income. There is a very serious danger that a guaranteed annual income program might very well follow the path taken by the Old Age Security Allowance, which commenced on January 1, 1952. This latter program has been described previously, but the inexorable facts are these: it was never meant to cover the full cost of an adequate standard of living for an elderly person or an elderly couple; it was not adjusted as living costs rose; and it was in fact altered only when the party in power felt that it was politically desirable to raise the allowance. A guaranteed annual income program might very well take the form of an allowance for a family of two adults and two children (with appropriate adjustments for larger and smaller families) which would change only when the party in power was threatened with electoral defeat or when a new party assuming office felt that it was desirable to adjust the allowance by virtue of a campaign promise. Any relationship between these policies and social adequacy is inconsequential.

Poor people in Canada are not difficult to identify. As a general proposition, most members of the native peoples—the Indians and the Eskimos—are relatively poor. Although some bands live on agricultural reserves or on reserves which contain natural resources (including oil) from which they derive a substantial royalty income, most bands are not so fortunate. During the past 20 years, however, the birth rates among Canadian Indians and Eskimos have been far beyond the general population, and both these native peoples now exceed the estimated native populations at the time of the coming of the white man to North America. Infant mortality is extremely high, the incidence of contagious disease is great, and life expectancy is considerably less than for other Canadians who live in both urban and rural areas.

Among Canadians as a whole the most obvious incidence of poverty rests among the (approximately) 350,000 families in which the head of the household is a female who may be deserted, divorced, or widowed. For nearly 50 years, from the end of the First World War to the mid-1960s, sole-support mothers with dependent children received benefits under their respective provincial Mothers' Allowance programs. Such financial allowance for a mother and one or more dependent children was relatively modest, and the regulations governing the ownership of property and other assets were for the most part restrictive. Although most provincial legislation has been reformed since the passage of the Canada Assistance Act of 1966, whereby the federal government pays half the allowance, the economic situation of most mother-led families is unenviable. In fact, in the province of Ontario in 1973 more than one-half of all the applications for public housing accommodation came from such families.

The number of mother-led families has expanded by approximately 100,000 during the past decade, partly as a consequence of new legislation governing divorce and new social attitudes toward the separation of married couples in Canadian society. The general freeing-up and liberalization of attitudes toward marital breakdown has increased substantially the number of mother-led families. Very few of these heads of families are employed or capable of employment. The Royal Commission on the Status of Women, which submitted its report to the Parliament of Canada in 1970, devoted a substantial chapter (pp. 309-331) to the subject of poverty among women and emphasized the plight of this large group of families.

The commission saw as one solution a rapid expansion of day care services to assist mothers, whether already working or seeking employment. The income tax was amended in 1972 to permit deduction of child welfare expenditures for working mothers. The principal difficulty, however, is the fact that in many cases the mother has no marketable skill in the labor market and almost no capacity to earn an income that would be greater than the allowance under Family Benefits. Moreover, there are additional aspects of this social assistance program in terms of dental care, pharmaceuticals, and other privileges, including nonpayment of income tax. A working mother must earn far more than she would receive under Family Benefits to justify employment rather than full-time housekeeping.

It seem clear, therefore, that the children of such families are another group of Canadians in poverty. They are not the only children in poverty, however, because there is also a substantial group of physically and emotionally neglected children in the care of Children's Aid Societies. Statistical record-keeping is not adequate to enable the presentation of a reasonably accurate figure, but an estimate of about 250,000 children would not be untoward.

The most significant group in poverty is the so-called "working poor." There are hundreds of thousands of Canadian heads of families whose lack of skills, whose particular employment, or whose particular geographic location makes it perfectly clear that even full-time employment will pay substantially less than in other industries or in other parts of the country. As a general rule, full-employed persons in the Maritime Provinces earn much less than those in Ontario, Alberta, and British Columbia. Workers in the province of Quebec earn somewhat less than the national average. Those in the Prairie Provinces in recent years earn about the national average, as indicated in the data for nine leading industries covering approximately half the total employment in Canadian manufacturing. In Alberta and British Columbia, wages and salaries are quite high by comparison with all other provinces with the exception of Ontario. There are thus three or four provinces that are very clearly in a "have" position, while the remaining provinces are in a "have not" economic position. The federal government devotes several hundred million dollars per annum of its general revenues to a form of redistribution termed "Equalization Payments" and designed to transfer funds from the "have" to the "have not" provinces.

Nevertheless, there may be as many as one million heads of families whose incomes are well below the national average for Canadian manufacturing. These persons and their dependents constitute Canada's "working poor" population. In terms of the guidelines of the Economic Council of Canada their total self-support income is perhaps one-sixth to one-quarter below the suggested poverty line for families of their size. The "working poor" are judged to be perhaps two-thirds to three-quarters of Canada's poor people. In an overall estimate of three to four million persons in poverty, about one to one and a half millions are considered to be totally dependent upon public funds for the basic necessities of life. These constitute the dependent poor, but they are outnumbered by the two and a half million Canadians who are the "working poor." The "working poor," however, are not simply residents of the Maritime Provinces or other undeveloped areas within the country, nor are they necessarily members of the native peoples. They are very often native-born Canadians of white Anglo-Saxon or French Canadian origin who work in such low-paid industries as textiles and retail and wholesale trade and in clerical positions in finance, insurance, and real estate. More particularly, however, those employed in the service industries (hotels, restaurants, laundries, dry cleaners, etc.) receive hourly wages and weekly earnings that are among the lowest in the nation. These employment activities are often the second source of income for a great many families of newcomers in which the male head cannot earn sufficiently to provide an adequate standard of living.

THE FUTURE: A GUARANTEED ANNUAL INCOME

Most Canadians are agreed that the solution to this problem, in which perhaps one in seven persons is a member of a family that is categorized as the "working poor," lies in the development of a guaranteed annual income program. Although minimum wage levels have been raised on a number of occasions in recent years, it is perfectly clear that this is not the solution to the problem. The imposition by government of higher minimum wage levels is most desirable if it does not destroy the competitive positions of industries in a nation that has always depended upon its exports for some 25% to 35% of its total income. Canada is fortunate in that it possesses vast quantities of agricultural, mineral, and energy-productive resources that are in great demand throughout the world. These are not, however, the kind of economic activities which for the most part provide employment for low-paid employees who constitute the working poor.

After 25 years of universal transfer programs designed in part to redistribute income within a nation through a progressive system of income taxation—both personal and corporate—it is clear that such redistributive activities are not the solution to poverty in Canada. The vast amounts of money involved in the provision of Family Allowances and Old Age Security allowances do not, it has been found, necessarily constitute a transfer of income from those in the upper quartile of the income distribution of taxpayers to those in the lowest quartile of income recipients. In specific studies it has been shown that the redistributive effects of a program such as Family Allowances may very well be horizontal rather than vertical. Under these circumstances there is not a strong emphasis upon income redistribution within existing income maintenance programs, nor is there any determined drive to create new variations on old themes.

The discovery that poverty in Canada was by no means a matter of indigency or destitution but that about twice as many persons as those in dependent poverty were struggling to provide for themselves and their families was a revelation to a great many Canadians in the early 1960s; it is still a shock for those who come to this realization afresh. It has already been pointed out that two important versions of an examination of poverty in Canada commissioned by the Senate of Canada placed before the public a guaranteed annual income as the probable solution.

These two reports—the official document and the unauthorized version—differed primarily in detail, but otherwise their projected solutions stem from the same root. The base lines differed; the proportion of income to be retained above the base lines differed; the point of cutoff at which individuals who reached a particular income would no longer draw upon the federal Treasury differed; but as far as the Canadian public is concerned the fundamental question is simply whether the nation can afford a guaranteed annual income. In 1970 the people of Canada were assured by the federal Minister of Health and Welfare that they could *not* afford such a program and that the additional cost, over and above all public income maintenance expenditures, would be on the order of $2 billion per annum. In the aftermath of a hard-fought and not favorable election from the point of view of the government in power in 1972, a new federal Minister of Health and Welfare has found vast financial resources to bolster the programs of Family Allowances and Old Age Security—resources which his government had either denied to his predecessor or simply did not have available until the effects of a reform in the federal tax system began to be felt by the fiscal year 1973-1974.

The federal government, according to the minister, endorses the guaranteed annual income concept for people unable to earn their own living, but there are some reservations about its application to those able to work. This statement was part of an announcement in late February 1974 that the government of Canada and the government of Manitoba (population one million) would participate jointly in a pilot project described as "the largest social experiment ever undertaken in Canada." The purpose of the project is to test the impact of income guarantees on the willingness of participants to work. The government of Ontario (population 8,500,000) had planned a similar experiment but scrapped it on the grounds that enough information was already available from tests in the United States, particularly with respect to an experiment carried out in New Jersey.

By the summer of 1974 approximately 2,500 families in Manitoba (1,000 from the major metropolis of Winnipeg and the remainder from a smaller community in the province) were participants in either the experimental group or the control group in this major research project. The scheme is designed to last three years at an estimated cost of $17 million. Basic support has been guaranteed by government at three possible levels to suit the particular families chosen: $3,800, $4,600, and $5,400. There is in addition a set of three "reduction" rates of 35%, 50%, or 75% which will have the effect of reducing government support in relation to other earned income. Finally, there will be a break-even point where government support will be withdrawn. There is little likelihood, in the view of most students of the subject, that the results to be derived from the Manitoba study will differ from experiments carried out in other countries.

Nevertheless, it appears essential that a Canadian pilot project be carried out before implementation of a guaranteed income program. Moreover, there is no question that one objective of this undertaking is to forestall the pressure which has been built up during the years 1970-1973 for intergovernmental action in this significant income maintenance and/or antipoverty program. It was estimated that by 1976-1977 the increased gross national product, as well as price inflation, would so increase the revenues of the two senior levels of government that an entirely new social security system, namely, a guaranteed annual income, would be introduced.

The pace of inflation has proceeded so rapidly during the past two years and the budgetary problems of all levels of government have become so difficult that the original time schedule is no longer relevant. In the fiscal year ending March

31, 1976, the federal government will spend in excess of $36 billion, all provincial governments will have reached record levels of expenditure, and local and regional governments will tax their residents more highly than ever before. The result is that there is a significant pressure in Canada toward reduced or, at least, stable levels of government expenditure and a demand for a consolidated attack upon the problem of inflation. The Minister of National Health and Welfare has been forced to move back, at least to 1978 or 1979, the introduction of a guaranteed annual income to which his government has been committed since 1973. Federal and provincial ministers of welfare have been conducting with their senior officials a federal-provincial social security review. The formal press releases indicate that this review is more complicated and must be more prolonged by virtue of inflation and the problem of high unemployment than was originally contemplated.

SOME CONCLUDING OBSERVATIONS

The conclusion that Canada is among the most affluent nations in the world is backed by various statistical indicators—dollar income per capita, the availability of natural resources, the place of the nation among the top five trading entities in the world, the production of steel, the number of automobiles sold each year, the ratio of physicians to population (which is now approximately 1 to 640 persons compared with the 1 to 940 persons 15 years ago), and the relatively high standard of living compared with other nations. Canadians are for the most part very well housed, very well fed, very well clothed, and very well served in terms of health and welfare provisions for which almost every person in the population is eligible. Intergovernmental relationships have developed apace during the past two decades and have reached the level of negotiation which the late Lester Pearson termed "cooperative federalism." Be that as it may, there are gaps, significant problems, and serious social maladjustments in the midst of widespread affluence.

Despite its wealth and its trilevel arrangements in the health and welfare services, Canada's record in terms of such criteria as infant mortality is not distinguished. Moreover, during the past decade the rate of unemployment has consistently exceeded that in the United States and has far outpaced the extent of this socioeconomic problem in West Germany, Japan, the United Kingdom, France, the Scandinavian countries, and the Netherlands. The seasonally adjusted unemployment rate passed 5% of the labor force in 1969 and during the years 1969-1972 it showed between 6% and 7%. At the same time, the Consumer Price Index (which, in the mid-1960s, increased at a rate of 2.5% to 3.5% per annum, exceeded 4% in 1970, exceeded 5% in 1972) showed an increase of more than 9% in 1973. On a year-to-year basis the monthly statistical data for the increase in consumer prices in 1974 was in excess of 11%.

There can be no doubt that there is a good deal of suffering in view of these twin socioeconomic "disasters"—the coincidence of high rates of unemployment and high rates of inflation. Although it can be argued that the latter is not excessive by comparison with a great many nations in the world, the same argument cannot be made with respect to unemployment. The facts are that Canada, by virtue of its extremely high birth rate during the years 1944-1959 in particular, has one of the most rapidly expanding labor forces. The total labor force, which was approximately 4.5 million at the end of World War II, passed 10 million in 1975 and is expanding at the rate of about half a million persons per annum. Although much of this expansion can be traced to the aforementioned birth rate, there is no question that high living costs have brought into the market a tremendous number of housewives and other persons who might not normally have entered or reentered the labor force. The problem for the nation as a whole is to create as many as half a million new jobs per annum while, at the same time, providing additional employment opportunities to cut into the backlog of unemployment.

The problem is not even that simple. The bulk of the unemployment in the nation is concentrated among young Canadians in the age bracket 15 to 24. In this age group the rate of unemployment is consistently twice that of the national average; it may even be higher, depending on the statistical interpretation of part-time employment. Married men and women over the age of 25 have relatively little unemployment by comparison—about 3.5%. Unemployment among older persons who remain in the labor market is, of course, relatively high. The proportion of women in the labor force has increased considerably since the end of World War II, when it was judged to be somewhat less than 25% of the total. It is now estimated that women constitute more than 40% of the labor force in Canada; in total numbers they have expanded from perhaps one to one and a half million in 1946 to 3.5 million in the 1970s. These social trends constitute significant implications for the social and health services.

At the 25th annual meeting of the Industrial Relations Research Association the author stated (Rose, 1973:436-446):

There has been much criticism in Canada with respect to the social welfare system. It has been viewed as a patchwork quilt in which the several levels of government, uniquely or in cooperation, have either added programmes in response to public pressures or where there appeared to be gaps in the provisions. Nevertheless, Canada has developed a social welfare system in which there seems to be considerable degree of logic. The universal transfer system, for example, is clearly within the constitutional prerogatives of the federal government and makes sense in view of that government's power in the fields of taxation and fiscal policy. This approach to income security—income requirements of retired persons and in a programme such as Family Allowances—is uniquely suited to mass need.

The field of social insurance is also far better suited to federal rather than provincial control and administration, because it involves a substantial proportion of the total population. Almost 100% of the Canadian population is covered by hospital insurance and medicare, both in cooperation with the provincial governments. In unemployment insurance and the provision of an additional layer of income security for the elderly the federal administration is far better suited if only by virtue of the basic requirement for portability across the nation.

In the field of public assistance, where the administrative responsibilities should be localized, the provinces have exercised their constitutional responsibilities as far as possible. Nevertheless, they are very short of financial resources and the Canada Assistance Plan of 1966 was designed to provide them with 50% of the required funds to maintain more adequate programmes without regard to patterns of categorization. Provincial-municipal cooperation in the actual administration of public assistance programmes is clearly a further logical necessity.

There are, therefore, many students of the subject who believe that we have in fact created a logical social welfare system that is not merely a patchwork quilt. However, a great many Canadians are agreed that a great deal of improvement could be made: administration could be improved, eligibility requirements and benefits could be updated, and social planning is indeed conspicuous by its absence.

These comments were made with particular reference to social security and income maintenance programs. In the broad area described loosely as "the social services" there is increasing concern in Canada that a great deal remains to be accomplished. The Canadian Council on Social Development recently completed a major study of the social services, which without question uncovered enormous gaps.[5] At the same time, the whole question of voluntary services and voluntarism remains clouded, not only by virtue of lack of funds but by the consequences of such deficiencies as increasing reliance upon public authorities and tax funds for financial support. The major consequence is an irrational demand by many groups, very often persons with radical perspectives, who continue to insist that all social services should be provided by governmental authorities. All students of these problems are agreed that there can be no guarantee that even the modest services now existing would be continued or strengthened by the public authority. The alternatives, however, are inadequacies, not so much in quality but in quantity of services available under voluntary auspices—inadequacies by virtue of the slow and deliberate approaches taken by government in its absorption of social programs under voluntary auspices. It is characteristic of modern urban society that, once government has indicated it will provide certain services, a quantitative explosion of unmet need is the immediate result. Governments in Canada are therefore hesitant; they continue to call for more study and more exploration of certain programs until available financial resources through tax reform and inflation "catch up" with the costs of meeting social needs.

In the meantime, the native peoples of Canada suffer from a gross inadequacy in terms of the availability of services—a problem that is compounded by ill health, poor education, and unemployment. There remains also the problem of the "working poor," who constitute the great majority of Canada's poverty population. Recent estimates indicate that not more than one in eight Canadians in receipt of social assistance could possibly be employed, other than in sheltered workshops, toward self-support. In one of the most affluent nations of the world these problems appear significant. By comparison with the countries of Asia, Africa, and South America, Canada is in a most fortunate position, whether its social and health services constitute a system or not, by whatever definition.

NOTES

1. Annual contributory earnings for the Canada Pension Plan have increased from $5,000 in 1966 to $8,300 in 1976. Those retiring on full pension in 1976 will thus receive substantially more than the benefit originally contemplated.

2. Amendments to the legislation to come into effect in 1976 have increased the number of weeks of employment to be recorded for maximum benefit.

3. At this meeting, held in Niagara Falls, Ontario, the author presented a paper, "The Unfinished Business in Social Security" (Rose, 1965).

4. On January 1, 1974, the Vancouver City Department of Welfare and Rehabilitation was formally taken over by the provincial Department of Human Resources. Other voluntary agencies will also be absorbed in the near future.

5. In the course of the federal-provincial social security review, which began early in 1974, there has emerged a draft "Social Services Act" designed, in the view of the federal minister, to replace the Canada Assistance Act and to provide Canadians with a more satisfactory level of cost-shared social services to meet a variety of needs, some of which have not previously been funded by the government of Canada.

REFERENCES

ADAMS, I., CAMERON, W., HILL, B., and BENZ, P. (1971). The real poverty report. Edmonton: Hurtig.

BEVERIDGE, W. (1942). Social insurance and allied services: The Beveridge report. New York: Macmillan.

Canada (1970). "Report of the Royal Commission on the Status of Women in Canada." Ottawa: Information Canada.

——— (1973). "Health and Social Security." Ottawa: Information Canada.

Canada, Department of National Health and Welfare (1970). Income security for Canadians. Ottawa: The Queen's Printer.

Canada, Special Senate Committee on Poverty (1970). "Poverty in Canada: The Croll report." Ottawa: Information Canada.

Economic Council of Canada (1968). "The problem of poverty" (Fifth annual review). Ottawa: Author.

ROSE, A. (1965). "The unfinished business in social security." Paper presented at the Canadian Labour Congress on Social Security Conference, Niagara Falls, Ontario, March 15.

——— (1973). "The work ethic and welfare reform: A Canadian point of view." Pp. 346-446 in Proceedings of the 25th annual meeting of the Industrial Relations Research Association, 1972. Madison: University of Wisconsin Press.

2

SCOTTISH GOVERNMENTAL REORGANIZATION AND HUMAN SERVICE DELIVERY BY TEAMS

JOHN M. GANDY

The estimated population of Scotland was 5,211,700 as of June 1973 with approximately 80% of the population concentrated in central Scotland, which includes the cities of Edinburgh and Glasgow with a combined population of almost a million and a half persons. With the discovery of oil and gas resources in the North Sea in 1971, there has been an increase in industry that has resulted in some movement of population into the north and northeast areas of the country. Scotland, however, has a long history of high unemployment, seasonal employment, and poverty. Lack of job opportunities and the depressed shipbuilding and mining industries have been among the important factors contributing to the emigration of young persons to England and overseas (British Information Services, 1974). A recent report (Wedge and Prosser, 1973) on disadvantaged children in Britain indicated that one of every 10 children in Scotland is socially disadvantaged as compared with one child in 16 for all of Britain. Poverty and the increasing proportion of older persons in the population are indicative of the formidable task facing the social services in Scotland.

Although Scotland has shared one sovereignty with England and Wales since 1603, it has retained its national identity, some of its institutions, and enjoys special arrangements for the conduct of many of its affairs. Since World War II, there has been a marked increase in the devolution of power in the administration of Scottish affairs (British Information Service, 1974). This devolution of administrative power has made it possible for Scotland to administer its social services in a distinctive fashion within the system of government of the United Kingdom.

In the last 30 years Scotland, like most other Western countries, has experienced a sharp increase in the expectations of its citizens with respect to the quantity and quality of social services. The initial response to these rising expectations was the expansion of existing services and the addition of new services, which resulted in a patchwork of social services that did not meet the needs of the consumers and was less than satisfactory from the perspective of those responsible for providing services. One report described the services developed in the post-World War II period as inefficient, inaccessible, wasteful of human and fiscal resources, and unable to respond to the needs of the community (Edinburgh University, 1969). In 1969, Scotland replaced its fragmented pattern of social services with a decentralized and comprehensive structure designed to increase the efficiency and effectiveness of its social services through greater integration of services and an improved system for service delivery. The restructuring of the social services provided an opportunity to operationalize, through new approaches to organization and staffing, some of the recommendations made in reports and studies of social services in England and other countries with similar traditions and values concerning the provision of social services.

The social services were reorganized with the passage of the Social Work (Scotland) Act, 1968. The provisions of this act were designed to implement a number of ideas and positions that had been advanced by committees and working parties (Scottish Home and Health Department and Scottish Education Department, 1966) in the period 1961-1968. The major objectives of this legislation were (1) to integrate separate social services into single local authority social work departments, (2) to replace the juvenile courts with a system of "children's hearings," (3) to make each local authority responsible for the promotion of social welfare in its area, (4) to create a structure within which the social work departments in the local authorities would be able to play an "important part in co-operation with other public and voluntary services in community planning and the prevention of social difficulties" (Scottish Education Department, 1970). The act thus provided the framework and authority for the reorganization. As one observer noted shortly after the passage of the act:

> The Social Work (Scotland) Act, 1968, established comprehensive departments of social work in place of a number of small, separate and specialized services which had preceded them and gave them very broad terms of reference. The new departments were to be concerned with "the promotion of social welfare" and not merely the amelioration of specific problems. They were enjoined also to place the greatest possible emphasis on the family and community as objects of concern, and not merely on the individual with a problem. [Young et al., 1973:11]

The legislation did not, however, deal with the specifics of implementation at the local level. Nevertheless, the general mandate for local social work departments is relevant to the issues of service delivery and is thought by many persons to be the most important section of the legislation in that it sets forth what is expected of local social work departments. As this mandate is very relevant to the question of service delivery, it may be quoted in full:

It shall be the duty of every local authority to promote social welfare by making available advice, guidance and assistance on such a scale as may be appropriate for their area, and in that behalf to make arrangements and to provide or secure the provision of such facilities (including the provision or arranging of or the provision of residential and other establishments) as they may consider suitable and adequate, and such assistance may be given to, or in respect of, . . . in kind or in cash. [United Kingdom, 1973b:8]

The implications of this mandate for the delivery of services at the local level are threefold. First, the mandate indicated that each local social work department is expected to respond to the needs of the area that it is serving and to promote services to meet these needs. Second, it makes provision for dispensing financial assistance under certain conditions. Third, it is made clear that government is not expected to provide all the required services.

The legislation made specific provisions for transferring probation, after-care, and certain services formerly provided by the health department to the new social work department. It also resulted in the social work department being given the responsibility for the following groups which had been served previously through other departments: the aged, the handicapped (physically and mentally), children in need of care or support, probationers, ex-prisoners, prisoners, and patients in hospitals and clinics. In addition, the social work departments were given the responsibility for persons in need of some form of guidance or assistance in dealing with personal difficulties. Thus, all government programs that employed trained social workers were made the responsibility of local social work departments. Although it was anticipated that most direct service and administrative positions in social work departments would be filled by social workers, the staff complement was expected to include such supportive staff as social work assistants, home-helps, occupational therapists, a variety of institutional staff, nurses, and psychologists.

At the time of reorganization, there was a shortage of trained social workers in Scotland, with the result that most of the senior positions in the new departments were filled either by persons who held senior posts prior to reorganization but were not trained social workers or by trained social workers from England and elsewhere in the United Kingdom. To help meet the shortage of trained staff, the government provided financial assistance for the expansion of social work courses, which resulted in an increase in the number of graduates from social work courses in Scottish universities and colleges from 112 in 1970 to 298 in 1974 (Scottish Education Department, 1971, 1975).

Scotland has a large and intricate network of voluntary agencies, many of which date back to the 19th century. An important dimension of social work services in Scotland is the support of voluntary organizations by both the local authorities and the central government. Both levels of government make grants to voluntary agencies for special projects, staff training, and capital expenditures. The voluntary agencies that received substantial financial support from one or both levels of government include: marriage guidance councils, citizens' advice bureaus, children's institutions, homes for the aged, community centers, organizations and services working with the physically handicapped, and organizations working for penal reform. The reorganization of social services coincided with the publication of the Aves Report on voluntary social work (Aves, 1969), and the effect was to encourage government and voluntary agencies to examine the range of services provided by voluntary agencies and look for ways of improving communication and coordination between social work departments and the voluntary sector. The following section on benefits and services will indicate the nature and scope of services provided by voluntary agencies with the encouragement and support of government.

BENEFITS AND SERVICES

Financial Assistance

The social work departments in Scotland do not have the primary responsibility for meeting the financial needs of persons without resources or of persons whose resources are insufficient for their needs. The various social security programs that are designed to provide cash payments for old-age pensioners and for people experiencing ill health, industrial injury, and unemployment are administered by the Department of Health and Social Security of the British government. Means-tested programs administered by the Supplementary Benefits Commission, an administrative unit within the Department of Health and Social Security, provide supplementary pensions for those over the pension age (men 65 years and women 60), supplementary allowances for those 16 years of age and older whose resources are less than their income requirements, and exceptional-needs payments for emergencies.

The responsibility for casework and other social services is seen as distinct from income maintenance and these services are not available through the Department of Health and Social Security. Although the Supplementary Benefits Commission is the major resource for persons in need of financial assistance, Sections 12 and 24 of the Social Work (Scotland) Act, 1968, make it possible for social work departments to make cash grants or loans under special conditions, related to a casework assessment of the situation. These special conditions include situations in which a cash grant or loan would, for example, diminish the need for taking into care a child under the age of 18, avoid causing the local authority greater expense in giving assistance in another form, reduce the probability that the aggravation of the person's need would cause greater expense on a later occasion, or enable persons under 21 years of age to meet expenses connected with education or training (United Kingdom, 1973b:9, 17). Social work departments have made extensive use of cash grants and loans to pay persons' rent (in order to prevent their being evicted), to pay their overdue utilities bills, and to pay their overdue hire-purchase charges to forestall the repossession of furniture. The difficulty encountered by persons trying to get exceptional-needs grants (from the Supplementary Benefits Commission) for emergencies such as those noted above has been a major factor in the greater use of cash grants and loans under Section 12 of the act than had been expected. The exercise of discretion by the social work departments and the Supplementary Benefits Commission in the granting of funds for emergencies has been a matter of major concern for the welfare rights groups and social workers.

Home-Help

One of the most significant supportive services provided by social work departments in Scotland is the home-help service. The 1968 act placed a duty on local authorities to provide this service which had been the responsibility of the National Health Service and administered by the local medical officer of health. Social work departments are required to provide home-help for "households where such help is required owing to the presence, or the proposed presence, of a person in need or a person who is an expectant mother or lying/in, and . . . provide or arrange for the provision of laundry facilities for households for which home-help is provided" (United Kingdom, 1973b).

The priority that this service received from local governments is indicated by the increase in the number of home-helps in Scotland from 5,700 in 1970 to 7,800 in 1973. Most of the home-helps have worked with the elderly, but other eligible groups in receipt of this service include households with one of the following situations: long term illness or severe handicaps; the absence of one parent because of illness or social reasons; and the presence of parents who are not competent to run the household or provide an acceptable standard of child care. Home-help services may be provided for an extended period if it is determined that the provision of this service will sustain the family as a unit or prevent the breakup of the household.

Child Care and Protection

The social work departments have responsibility for (1) the provision of care for children who have no parent or guardian or whose parents or guardians are unable to provide proper care and (2) the care or supervision of children found to be in need of compulsory supervision in an institution or the community. In a recent study it was reported that in 1973 approximately one-fourth of all children in care or under supervision were placed in foster homes and approximately one-third in institutions (Newman and Mackintosh, 1975). The majority of the children who are placed in institutions are in institutions under voluntary auspices, which is a reflection of the significant role that voluntary organizations have in the provision of residential accommodation in Scotland.

Social work departments are expected to provide residential and day nurseries for preschool children requiring this type of care on social grounds. In addition, local health departments operate a few residential and day nurseries for children needing this type of accommodation for health reasons. To supplement the day nurseries, some departments provide care in private homes with a paid "day carer." The departments also have the responsibility for the registration of voluntary day nurseries and child-minders.

Although the responsibility for adoption services rests with the social work departments, this responsibility is shared with voluntary agencies. About an equal number of children are placed for adoption by the social work departments and the voluntary agencies. The central government of Scotland is financing several joint endeavors of voluntary agencies and social work departments that have as their objective the increasing number of adoptions of children with special handicaps.

The Social Work (Scotland) Act, 1968, replaced or amended existing legislation that dealt with bringing children before the courts, and it established a system of "children's hearings." The procedures developed for implementing this new approach to handling children who are considered in need of compulsory measures of care were very important in influencing the demand for social work services from 1970 onward.

Space permits only a brief discussion of the operation of the children's hearings, an important and new approach in the handling of juveniles in conflict with the law or in need of care and protection. However, many readers will find it useful and rewarding to examine some of the descriptive and evaluative reports on their operation (Social Work Services Group and Scottish Education Department, 1970; Morris, 1972; Bruce and Spencer, 1974).

Children who are considered to be in need of compulsory care because of violation of the law, cruelty, neglect, lack of control, truancy, or moral danger are referred to the "reporter"—an official of the local government—who decides whether a child should be referred to the children's hearings or disposed of informally. Children may be referred to the reporter by social workers, educational authorities, police, neighbors, physicians, or parents. In the event that the child and his parents challenge the facts on which the allegation is based, the child is referred to the adult court for a ruling on the accuracy of the facts in the allegation. If the facts are found to support the allegation, the child is referred to the children's hearing for disposition.

Alternative dispositions available to the hearing are (1) to discharge the child if he is found not to be in need of compulsory supervision, (2) to continue the hearing, for not more than 21 days, pending further investigation that may require the child to be examined in a clinic, assessment center, or hospital, (3) to have the child supervised in the community by the social service department or a voluntary agency, (4) to place the child in a residential establishment, (5) to refer the child to an educational authority for assessment of his need for special education, and (6) to refer the child to a mental health officer to consider an application for his admission to a hospital or to guardianship.

Children's hearings are not the responsibility of the local social work departments, but a substantial proportion of their work is generated by the "reporter" and the hearings. The reporter may ask the social work department to conduct a preliminary inquiry to assist him in determining whether a child should be dealt with informally or referred to the hearing. If the reporter decides that the case will be dealt with informally he may ask the department to take responsibility for making arrangements to provide advice, guidance, and assistance to the child and his family on a voluntary basis. If the reporter decides to refer the child to the hearing for disposition, the social work department is asked to prepare a background report to be considered by the hearing, and the social worker who prepares the background report is expected to attend the hearing in which the report is considered. In the event that the hearing decides that the child is in need of compulsory care, either the social work department or a voluntary agency is expected to provide supervision in the community, secure the recommended residential care, or arrange for further assessment. Thus the social work departments and the voluntary agencies are responsible for the supporting infrastructure of assessment and services for the hearings. A major criticism has been that the social work departments lack the resources to implement the recommendations made by the hearings. The lack of resources is particularly acute with respect to residential facilities, both diagnostic and custodial, and intermediate treatment (i.e., programs between residential treatment and supervision in the community). The social work departments have a statutory responsibility to provide services to the reporter and the hearings, and the volume of work that is required by both is an important factor in determining the amount of staff time and resources that are available for other social service programs.

Services to Families

One of the most influential and pervasive ideas underlying the reorganization of social services in Scotland was that the family should be the target for social work services rather than the individual (Smith and Harris, 1972). The strength of this idea may be seen in the services that are designed to prevent the breakup of families or the separation of children from their parents. However, the services available to families are, for the most part, designed to assist the family in meeting instrumental problems such as homelessness or poor financial management. With respect to the latter it is assumed that the income maintenance programs will provide a source of income which, if managed properly, will be adequate to meet ongoing expenses, an assumption that is challenged by many welfare rights groups in Scotland.

Despite the large amount of public housing that has been built in Scotland since World War II, Scotland still has a severe shortage of housing for low-income families. One result is that families who are evicted from public or private housing find it very difficult to secure new housing accommodations, and often it is necessary to place children in foster homes or institutions until new accommodations can be found. Although a high percentage of the housing in most communities in Scotland is owned by the local government, social work departments have not worked closely with housing departments except on problems of recent arrears or nonpayment of rent. This problem has been examined in some depth by the Morris Committee (Scottish Development Department, 1975), which has recommended changes in the formal and informal administrative arrangements designed to produce closer cooperation between housing and social work departments.

Most social work departments that work with families who are threatened with eviction because of rent arrears or nonpayment of rent (Gandy, 1975) do so in an effort to reduce the disruption of family life resulting from homelessness. Some local governments refer all cases of rent arrears to the social work department, which is expected to work out a plan with the family for repayment over an extended period and supervise the repayment. In emergencies the social work department will make loans or grants to the family under Section 12 of the act if it appears that a long-term repayment plan is not feasible. In the event that the family has a history of nonpayment, some departments will collect the rent directly from the families in some fashion—by having the families deliver the rent money to the social work office, by arranging to have a housing officer available in the office on the days that pension checks are received, or by having a social worker pick up the rent money. Similar methods are used to deal with clients whose furniture is in danger of repossession or who are threatened with suspension of utilities because of nonpayment.

Persons who have demonstrated an inability to manage their funds—usually persons receiving pensions or supplementary benefits—are assisted with budgeting and, if necessary, given continuing supervision in the use of their income. The control that the social work departments exercise in the instances described above goes well beyond what would be regarded as appropriate or desirable by social workers in Canada or the United States. The Scottish social work departments would defend the methods used on the basis of the financial and human costs that would result from a more permissive approach to the management of income.

Prior to the reorganization of the social services, family casework services were provided in many Scottish communities by the City Councils of Social Service. Consequently, the reorganized departments were expected to provide casework and counseling services to families with marital or other relationship problems. These services are generally available in social service departments throughout Scotland, but there is considerable variation in the quality and quantity of the service due to the shortage of trained staff and the statutory responsibilities of the departments to provide a variety of other services to children's hearings, institutions, and the adult courts. Many social work departments refer families with marital problems to the Marriage Guidance Councils that have offices throughout the country. These councils are nongovernmental agencies that use volunteers as counselors; however, they have an excellent reputation among social workers and are regarded by many departments as a major resource for those families needing casework or counseling services because of marital problems.

Services for the Elderly

Approximately one of every eight persons in Scotland is 65 years of age or older (Scottish Education Department, 1971). A substantial proportion of the social work resources are used to provide services for this group of almost 650,000 persons. The wide range of programs and services for the elderly are designed to assist and encourage older persons to live in their own homes as long as possible or to provide them with domiciliary care when necessary. However, the programs and services designed to assist elderly persons to remain in their own homes have a high priority.

Social work departments work closely with, and make grants to, voluntary organizations in providing services to the elderly. The nonresidential services provided by departments include home-helps, assistance in getting reestablished in the community on discharge from a hospital, supportive casework services, structural adaptations to living units, occupational therapy, financial assistance to relatives to enable them to visit, and neighborhood aides. The neighborhood aides are persons who are paid a small honorarium to undertake supportive tasks for their neighborhood elderly—such tasks as shopping, preparing meals or tea, cleaning, checking on heating, and checking periodically to determine whether there are health or other problems. This service is provided for those persons who are not viewed as requiring the level of assistance provided by home-help.

Residential services for the elderly are administered by the local social welfare departments, and all applications for these services are investigated and processed by the social work staff in the area where the applicant lives. Social work departments in some communities have worked with housing departments to provide shelter for the elderly within public housing. The departments are authorized to financially assist the housing department in the provision of special housing accommodations for the elderly and infirm.

Services for the elderly are an area in which voluntary agencies are very active, with the financial support and encouragement of the social work departments. Meals-on-wheels is a joint effort of the departments and voluntary agencies in most communities in Scotland. Day centers, luncheon clubs, and friendly visiting are provided under voluntary auspices, with financial support from social work departments. Holidays and outings are also provided by voluntary agencies. Age Concern Scotland, the national voluntary organization concerned with the problems of the elderly, gives leadership in the development of community services.

Services for the Physically and Mentally Handicapped

With the passage of the Chronically Sick and Disabled Persons (Scotland) Act, 1972, local governments were required to conduct periodic household surveys of the number and condition of chronically ill and disabled persons living in their area and maintain a roster of such persons. These surveys, undertaken by social work departments, have as their objective the creation of a body of data on the physically handicapped to be used in the planning and delivery of services.

Services for the physically handicapped, as with the elderly, are designed primarily to permit the handicapped to remain in their own homes. However, it should be noted that an estimated 7 out of 10 physically handicapped persons are also elderly, which means that elderly disabled persons benefit from services for both the elderly and the physically handicapped. Social work departments provide personal aids and appliances, make structural adaptations in the living quarters, furnish telephones, and give casework support as needed.

Voluntary agencies in Scotland have the major responsibility for the entire range of services for the blind and deaf, with financial support from the local and central governments. Although a few local social work departments provide services for the blind and deaf, the general pattern is that voluntary agencies act as agents of the social work departments in the administration of these services. In recent years this arrangement has been questioned on the grounds that it separates the disabled from other community services (Anderson, 1975).

Services and programs developed by social work departments for persons handicapped by mental illness or deficiency include the following: senior training centers, day care centers, sheltered workshops, after-care for persons released from mental hospitals, supportive casework services, and group homes. Sheltered workshops, group homes, and training centers have been developed and administered by both local social work departments and voluntary agencies. Much of the leadership for the development of group homes has come from the Scottish Society for Mental Handicaps, a voluntary agency, which has assisted local governments by making interest-free loans to local governments for the capital costs. The cooperation of voluntary agencies and the government in the development and delivery of services for the mentally handicapped continues to be an important factor in the quality and quantity of services available to this group.

Other Services and Programs

With the passage of the 1968 act, persons on probation or parole and those for whom a supervision order has been made become the responsibility of the social work departments. In 1973 the prison welfare service, responsible for social work in institutions, was transferred from the Scottish Prison Service to the social work departments in the communities where the prisons and other correctional institutions are located. This has meant that the social work departments are involved at every stage of the correctional process from the preparation of background reports prior to sentencing to after-care services for released prisoners. Hostel and other accommodations for ex-offenders are most often provided by voluntary agencies.

The transfer of social work services in hospitals and clinics from the National Health Service to social work departments was carried out in 1974-1975. This transfer represented the end of the consolidation of all governmental social work programs in the local social work departments.

The central government of Scotland makes grants to local governments to improve social service programs and facilities in urban areas. These urban aid grants cover 75% of the cost of small building schemes and the salaries of staff on special projects. Among the types of projects financed through these grants are preschool playgrounds, community centers, nursery schools, family service units, and community development programs.

Eligibility for Programs and Services

As was pointed out earlier in this section, the Supplementary Benefits Commission is responsible for the administration of the major program designed to provide financial assistance to persons and families whose income is insufficient to meet their needs. Eligibility for financial assistance is established by a means-test which is not unlike that used by local welfare departments in the United States and Canada. Means-tests are also used in determining eligibility for a number of other programs such as rent rebates, assistance with dental and prescription charges, free school meals, and legal aid, which are not administered by the social work departments.

Few programs and services administered by social work departments have eligibility requirements other than the applicant's need for services. Of those programs that are means-tested, the purpose of the means-test is to determine whether there should be payment for the service rather than to determine entitlement or eligibility. Thus an applicant for certain services is assessed to determine how much he will pay for a service if he has income from sources other than pensions or supplementary benefits. Although local governments use the means-test for different sets of programs and services, there are some programs in which there is a statutory requirement that the user contribute to the cost of the service if he is able, and there are other programs in which a decision has been made by local authorities that a contribution is expected if the applicant has resources in excess of his needs (Adler and du Feu, 1973).

The Social Work (Scotland) Act, 1968, specifies that in the child-care and home-help services the local government shall attempt to collect full or partial payment for child-care and home-help services. Parents, whose income exceeds their needs, are required to contribute to the care of a child under 16 years of age who has been placed in a foster home or institution. With respect to home-help services, the local social work department is empowered to recover the costs of providing service if the client is financially able to pay part or all of the costs. For home-help service, social work departments have established a fee scale based on income, and it is used by the supervisor in setting fees for individual recipients of the service. Another service in which a fee scale has been established is day nursery care.

Eligibility for grants by the social work department under Sections 12 and 24 of the 1968 act are also means-tested. However, the assistance under these sections is also based on a casework assessment and is usually a one-time grant for a specific purpose, which distinguishes it from the other programs. The government of Scotland has succeeded in eliminating the means-test as a measure of entitlement for most of its social work services, but it has retained the requirement that clients contribute to the cost of some services, and it uses a means-test to determine the level of payment of the contribution. There are no eligibility requirements with respect to residence or citizenship.

ORGANIZATION OF SOCIAL SERVICES

In 1975 local government in Scotland was reorganized under the Local Government (Scotland) Act, 1973. This legislation created 9 regional and 53 district councils to replace the 52 local government units, counties (and districts within them), cities and large and small burghs that had been allocated the responsibility for providing social work services in the Social Work (Scotland) Act, 1968. The regional councils were given the responsibility for providing social services, and the former social work departments that were the responsibility of local councils became district social work departments administered by the regional social work departments. The major impact of this change on the organization of social services has been to make the social work departments, created by the 1968 act, accountable to the regional councils, with the necessary administrative and support services. We will examine the organization of regional and district social services after looking at the responsibilities of the Scottish Office—the central government—for social services.

The responsibility of the regional councils, an elected body, for providing social services is carried out in consultation with, and under the general supervision of, the Secretary of State for Scotland. The Secretary of State is an elected member of the British Parliament and the member of cabinet who is responsible for the operation of all the departments making up the Scottish Office. With respect to the social services, the Secretary of State has the power to make regulations in relation to the performance of the functions assigned to regional councils by the 1973 act and those activities of voluntary organizations undertaken to provide services covered in the 1968 act. For example, empowered he sees to it that persons are boarded out by regional councils and voluntary organizations; he assesses the state for the management of residential establishments, foster homes, or voluntary organizations; and he inspects the records of local social work departments with respect to persons receiving advice, guidance, or assistance under the act (United Kingdom, 1973b).

The Secretary of State is required to appoint an Advisory Council on Social Work to advise him on the performance of his functions and those of local authorities with respect to social welfare and the activities of local social work departments and voluntary organizations connected with those functions. The Advisory Council is composed of 24 persons selected on the basis of their experience in various aspects of social work or in other fields of public life.

The Social Work Services Group, a part of the Scottish Education Department, has the responsibility for discharging the Secretary of State's functions with respect to the social services. It is an administrative unit composed of trained social workers and administrators with the following responsibilities: to advise and guide social work departments in the implementation of the Social Work (Scotland) Act, 1968, to act as liaison with voluntary organizations in the social work field, to plan and conduct training programs for staff in local social work departments, to draft regulations and procedures for implementing the act; to conduct and support research in social welfare, and to implement the Urban Aid program.

The central government does not appropriate funds earmarked for the day-to-day operation of social service departments. Through grants and purchase of service, however, it does assume financial responsibility for supporting national voluntary organizations, providing training courses for staffs of local social work departments, supporting special projects of national interest, paying half the cost of institutional care for children under compulsory supervision, and providing consultative services to local social work departments.

The expenditures for the social work departments are the responsibility of the regional councils. The source of funds is the "rates" (a form of local property tax). The expenditures cover all day-to-day operating costs of the social work departments. An expected result of this financing arrangement is that there are considerable differences between regions in the per capita amounts spent on social services.

The regional social work departments are staffed by administrators and specialists in social work and related services. The staff are expected to assess the need for social services in the region, formulate policy, and monitor programs and services. More specifically, this administrative unit is charged with developing organizational and operational guidelines for field services provided through the district social work departments; managing a range of residential and nonresidential institutional programs; recruiting, training, and deploying professionals and other staffers; providing specialist services, including research; and fostering links with voluntary organizations. An important change, and one that should strengthen the social work services in Scotland, was the acceptance of the continuing assessment and evaluation of programs and services as a responsibility at the regional level and the addition of research staff to carry out this function. Prior to regionalization, a minimum amount of research was undertaken by social work departments.

It is hoped that regionalization will result in a closer working relationship with officials in education and housing. However, it should be noted that the health services continue to be administered separately and have different regional boundaries, which can only be considered a weakness in the overall plan to bring together all the personal services within one administrative structure at the regional level.

The nine regional social work departments serve populations ranging in size from the two and one-half million persons in the Strathclyde region, which includes Glasgow and is highly industrialized, to the 100,000 rural persons in the border region. A related statistic is the density of population per square mile, which ranges from 1,100 persons in the Lothian region, which includes Edinburgh, to 18 persons in the Highland region. The differences in the regions are also indicated by the number of district social work departments for which the regional offices have responsibility, ranging from 3 in the Central region to 15 in the Strathclyde region (United Kingdom, 1973a). The above differences are indicative of the enormity of the problems related to the delivery of different types of services and programs.

The 53 district social work departments operated as local social work departments for towns, cities and counties prior to reorganization and developed their own patterns of service and staffing. With the new administrative structure these departments lost their autonomy in the areas of policy formulation and administration. Each of the district departments has a director of social work who is responsible for the organization and administration of social services in the district within the policies and operating guidelines established by the regional departments. The district departments are expected to: serve as liaison with the "reporter" at the children's hearings and provide reports for the hearings; to organize and administer the home-help and emergency services; to provide casework services as needed; to operate administrative systems and procedures; to deal with inquiries from the public; and to maintain close working relations with the public.

DELIVERY OF SOCIAL SERVICES

The reorganization of social work . . . which followed the publication of the Kilbrandon Report, relating to Scotland, . . . marked the firm establishment of the area team as the primary organizational unit for the provisions of fieldwork services by local authority social work . . . departments. [Ames and Smith, 1975:2656]

On the basis of the recommendations of the Kilbrandon Committee (Scottish Home and Health Department, and Scottish Education Department, 1964) and the response of a variety of bodies to its recommendations, the government of Scotland prepared a white paper, *Social Work and The Community* (Scottish Home and Health Department and Scottish Education Department, 1966), which included proposals designed to improve the efficiency and effectiveness of the delivery of social services. This document recommended that social work departments administer all programs that utilize the "insights and skills of the profession of social work" in order to "provide a single door on which anyone might knock to ask for help with confidence of getting it." An equally important proposal was that in large areas the social work departments "should work through area offices easily accessible to the community and staffed by trained workers able and empowered to provide an effective social service at the local level" (Scottish Home and Health Department and Scottish Education Department, 1966:14).

When the Social Work (Scotland) Act, 1968, was passed, the Social Work Services Group appointed a Working Party on the Organization of Social Work Departments in Local Authorities, which was charged with the responsibility for developing policies and procedures for the implementation of the act. In its report the Working Party emphasized the need for strong local operational units and the importance of these for the delivery of services:

The social work department must ensure that the services it provides are readily accessible and known to all members of the community. Accessibility can be ensured only through a system of local operational units serving cohesive population groups and each offering a comprehensive range of services to enable the great majority of day to day social work needs to be dealt with at first hand. [Social Work Services Group, n.d.]

More specifically they recommended that these local operational units be area offices staffed by a team of 10 to 12 social workers and supporting staff responsible for catchment areas of about 50,000 persons. Within each area social work team, there would be two subteams supervised by a senior social worker responsible to the team leader. The area social work team would include both trained social workers (graduates of social work programs in either universities or colleges) and welfare assistants, the latter to undertake "routine duties which need not take up the time of trained social workers" (Social Work Services Group, n.d.). It should be noted, however, that, since this report, the size of many area social work teams has increased to 20 or more social workers.

Initially, the area social work teams were staffed with persons whose work experience had been limited to specialized services. Many of these staff members resented the elimination of the specialized services and were apprehensive over the prospect of functioning as "generalists" in the area social work teams. In the area teams very limited use is made of specialists to deliver services, because this would have countered the basic philosophy underlying the "team" approach, that only one worker should be assigned to work with a family. As we will note later, the problem of implementing the generic approach is still largely unresolved.

In the remainder of this section we will draw on the experience of four area social work teams studied in 1973-1974 in order to highlight some of the issues that are central to the delivery of services in Scotland (Gandy, 1975).

Decentralization and Accessibility of Area Offices

As noted earlier, a major objective of the reorganization of social services in Scotland was to improve the delivery of services by providing convenient and attractive access to services through decentralized offices staffed by social work teams. It was also intended that the area social work teams in the decentralized offices would develop programs to meet the needs of persons living in the catchment area of the team. In order to accomplish this, area social work teams had to have autonomy at the operational level. The British Association of Social Workers has emphasized the importance of this aspect, as indicated in the following comment (1973:5):

> Physical decentralization implies clear delegation of operational decisions to the local teams, with authority to take responsible action and to spend money within specified limits without the delay of reference to head-quarters.

Gandy (1975) found that the autonomy of area social work teams is uneven, with considerable variation between and within local social work departments. In the four social work teams studied, he found that most of the staff felt that the teams had considerable autonomy in the development of programs to meet local needs as long as these programs did not involve capital expenditures or the employment of additional staff. At the same time there were few instances in which the area teams had developed new or innovative programs related to the special needs of their catchment areas.

Most commonly in Scotland, the monitoring and supervision of the area social work teams is done by senior staffers from the headquarters of the local social work department, who hold individual and group conferences and consultations with the senior staff of the teams. The headquarters staff, through these meetings and conferences, exert considerable influence, with the result that within local departments there tends to be a high degree of conformity in program, service delivery, and use of staff. Most of the social work teams, therefore, are operating as branch operations of the local social work departments rather than as autonomous decentralized units as was envisioned at the time of reorganization. It is clear, however, that the full potential of the area social work teams to meet local needs will not be realized until they have and use authority to make operational decisions in their catchment areas. Some social work departments have developed projects to meet the needs of special groups, but in the main these have operated as separate administrative units in the catchment areas of the teams.

Accessibility is often seen as a concomitant of physical decentralization. However, the experience in Scotland has been that decentralization frequently does not result in increased accessibility. We will examine two dimensions of the accessibility: convenience of access and access to knowledge of the services.

The question of where area social work teams should be located to maximize clients use of services has not been researched in Scotland. The lack of attention to this question is probably one of the factors accounting for the unsatisfactory accessibility that exists in many area offices. The physical location of area offices was determined, in many instances, by the availability of space in public buildings rather than by the needs of the clients. Gandy (1975) reported that the staffs in 3 of the 4 area offices studied considered the convenience of access to their offices to be less than satisfactory. The reasons given were poor and/or expensive transportation and the location of the office at the edge of catchment areas. Another factor that reduced accessibility was the almost universal practice of not providing for office visits, except by appointment, in the evenings or on Saturdays.

The size of the catchment areas and population density were also factors that contributed to poor accessibility. The formula of providing one area social work team for about 50,000 persons has not been found to be viable for rural areas with low population densities. Experience would suggest that uniformity in the population of catchment areas is neither desirable nor functional and that consideration should be given to a more flexible approach to the size of population that is the responsibility of an area office. Little attention has been given to the establishment of outposts or other schemes to increase convenience of access.

When we look at the other dimension of accessibility—knowledge of services available through the area office—the area social work teams have found themselves in a dilemma that is familiar to most social welfare agencies. A committee of the Social Work Services Group identified the nature of this dilemma as follows (1974:2):

> The creation of the new social work departments increased the expectations of members of the public who need help. It also increased the awareness of the public of their entitlement to help. But there is evidence that even the resulting increased demand is much less than the total need. Social work departments, though overburdened, must continue to seek out persons with needs, although such identification requires staff time and immediately raises problems of determining priorities for operation.

No effort has been made to estimate the size of the group of potential clients who need, but are not using, the services available through the social work teams. However, the failure of the teams to seek out potential clients despite the mandate in the Social Work (Scotland) Act, 1968, that they do so is explained by pointing out that an increase in the number of clients would only exacerbate a situation in which staffs are finding it difficult to cope with the existing level of demand for services. One critic of this position points out that the failure to publicize services and promote their use is a type of indirect rationing that adversely affects those who are most in need of service (Association of Social Workers, 1969:47).

The decentralization of services has brought the services closer physically to the users and potential users of service. However, it is obvious that research and experimentation will be needed to achieve the level of accessibility that was intended at the time of reorganization. It is believed that, with the regionalization of social work departments and the establishment of research departments in regional offices, more attention will be given to ways of making the area offices more accessible. Ames and Smith (1975:2657) have suggested that research departments should also seek an answer to the more fundamental question of whether accessibility is a significant variable in the use of services.

Organization and Staffing of Area Offices

In the area offices, the staff who provide casework and other social services are responsible to the leader of the area team, and the clerical staff are responsible to an administrative officer. This organizational structure follows the traditional division in the British civil service of separate professional and administrative lines of responsibility. Thus in each area office there is an administrative officer who is responsible to a senior staff member of the social work department, usually an assistant director. The division of the service and administrative responsibilities in the area offices has meant that the clerical staff do not participate as full members of the area social work team. Although there is a close, and sometimes productive, relationship between the administrative and service staff, the nature of the relationship depends on the individuals in the positions of area team leader and administrative officer.

The staff complement of area offices varies according to the size of the catchment area, the characteristics of the population, and the demands of the courts and children's hearings. With respect to the types of staff that provide direct service there is considerable uniformity, with staff complements that include senior social workers, basic grade social workers, social work assistants, trainee social workers, home-help organizers, and occupational therapists. Some teams have community development officers and unqualified social workers in their staff complement. The unqualified social workers are staff with experience in social work but no formal training.

The area social work teams are divided into subteams, with senior social workers as leaders of the subteams. The membership of the subteams includes basic grade social workers, social work assistants, and trainee social workers. If there is a community development officer assigned to the area office, he or she usually is not assigned to a subteam. The staff most central to the delivery of services are the basic grade (trained) social workers. They provide casework services for the range of persons seeking help from the office and services for the courts and the children's hearings, and they may be responsible for such specialized services as adoption. The original plans for the establishment of area teams included provision for one or more social work assistants for each subteam in the area office. It was anticipated that social work assistants would undertake duties that do not require the knowledge and skill of a trained social worker, and these duties were to be undertaken in respect to cases for which a trained social worker carried the major responsibility. The shortage of staff and the difficulty of implementing the proposal for a sharing of responsibility for cases have meant that the original proposal for the use of social work assistants has not been realized. The most common practice with respect to the use of social work assistants is to assign them caseloads which are heavily weighted with clients whose major problems are rent arrears, overdue utility bills, or problems with hire-purchase agreements. Trainee social workers are staff who are serving an apprenticeship with an area team before entering a social work course at a college or university. This scheme has succeeded in greatly increasing the number of trained social workers in Scotland since 1970.

A home-help organizer often shares office space with the area social work teams but is not administratively responsible to the area team leader. Gandy (1975) found that the home-help organizers do not consider themselves members of the area social work team nor were they considered such by the social work staff. He suggested two reasons for this: (1) less than 5% of the cases active with the home-help service were also active with the social work team, and (2) home-helps work more closely with general practitioners than they do with social workers. The home-helps represent a supporting service available to the teams, but there is little coordination in the delivery or provision of service. A similar situation exists with respect to occupational therapists, the major difference being that few occupational therapists share office space with the area teams. The work of the occupational therapists consists of assessing the need for aids and adaptations and providing advice and consultation to the physically handicapped.

Area social work teams have experimented with a variety of ways of using the subteams to deliver services. The method most widely used is to divide the catchment area into small areas and assign a subteam to each area or "patch." The "patch" approach has widespread support because it is believed that, as members of a subteam become familiar with the resources and the population of their area, they will make more efficient use of their time in the field. However, many area teams have been forced to abandon this approach because of the high turnover in staff and the limited flexibility in adjusting workloads for a small unit. Some area teams have established subteams as training groups, placing inexperienced workers with an experienced senior social workers as subteam leader. Area social work teams that have borstals, prisons, and/or hospitals in their catchment areas have established special subteams assigned to work with persons in the institutions. However, the preferred model is still the "patch" method, which is regarded as the most compatible with the philosophy underlying the decentralization of services.

The reorganization of social services in Scotland has as one of its objectives the development of a generic approach to the delivery of services. It was not clear at the outset if the term "generic" was intended to describe the range of services available through one office or if it also included generic or mixed caseloads. The mixed or general caseload has become the norm in Scotland, but social work departments have become aware of the need for specialists in such areas as adoption, child care, the courts, community development, and mental health services. It was recognized that specialists-practitioners could not be placed in all area teams, and most social work departments appointed a group of specialists at the central office who are available for consultation and handle a limited number of cases requiring special attention. The result has been less than satisfactory from the point of view of the area teams because of the limited accessibility of the specialists and their lack of knowledge of the situation in the catchment areas of the teams. Area social work teams are now encouraging some staff to develop knowledge about a limited area of service and permitting them to have caseloads that are weighted with certain types of cases. The staffers who do develop special knowledge and skills are considered team specialists who are available for certain areas of service or certain types of clients. The limited movement toward specialization at the team level is designed to meet the requests of team members that they have an opportunity to develop expertise in single areas.

SUMMARY

The reorganization of the social services in Scotland which began in 1969 has not been completed. The Social Work (Scotland) Act, 1968, provided the legal basis and framework for initiating the reorganization, but, before this was completed, regional social work departments had been created. At present the administrative structure and the service delivery system are continually being changed to meet new demands both within the system and from clients. In the early stages of reorganization, many decisions were taken with limited data and no experience in providing service using the team approach; thus many changes were subsequently inevitable. Space has not permitted a discussion of many of the administrative problems, most of them procedural. However, many of the weaknesses in the organization of services in Scotland are the result of the imbalance between consumer demands and resources—an imbalance resulting from the rising expectations of the public concerning the quality and quantity of services that would be available through the new departments, together with the rising requirements of the courts and children's hearings. A recent development that should have an impact on the planning and delivery of services is the establishment of a formal structure to link the social services with housing and educational services at the local level. These linkages are being established through a corporate structure which utilizes a management team approach at the regional level.

Scotland's reorganized social service system has been described by Webber (1974:303) as a model that embodies "an adaptive learning process and represents a fundamentally sound approach to the development of social service delivery systems." We agree with this assessment but would qualify it by observing that it will be some time before the potential of this effort to develop a decentralized comprehensive social service system is realized. Among the positive factors that should contribute to the realization of the potential are the professional and financial support that regional and local social work departments receive from the central government, which is committed to a decentralized comprehensive social service system for Scotland, and the increasing number of trained staff at the local level.

REFERENCES

ADLER, M., and Du FEU, D. (1973). Welfare Benefits Project: Final report. Edinburgh: Department of Social Administration, University of Edinburgh.

AMES, J., and SMITH, G. (1975). "Social work area teams: Numbers and locations." Health and Social Service Journal, (November 29):2656-2657.

ANDERSON, D. (1975). "Time for statutory control." Focus, 43(October):7-8.

Association of Social Workers (1969). New thinking about welfare: Values and priorities. London: Author.

AVES, G.M. (1969). The voluntary worker in the social services. London: Allen and Unwin.

British Association of Social Workers (1973). Living with change: Papers delivered at annual study conference, 25th and 26th October, Blackpool. Birmingham: Author.

——— (1974). Conference papers: Reorganization of local government: A second coming for social work. London: Author.

British Information Service (1974). Scotland. London: Central Office of Information.

BRUCE, N., and SPENCER, J. (1974). "Children's hearings and the Scottish courts; Some lessons from the case of Mary Cairns." Pp. 221-231 in K. Jones (ed.), The year book of social policy in Britain, 1973. London: Routledge and Kegan Paul.

GANDY, J. (1975). Social service delivery in Scotland: A study of four social work teams. Toronto: Faculty of Social Work, University of Toronto.

Edinburgh University, Department of Social Administration (1969). Social work in Scotland: Report by a working party on the Social Work (Scotland) Act, 1968. Edinburgh: Author.

JOHNSTON, J. (1974). "Five years on: The first five years—Success or failure?" Focus, 33(November):16-20.

KAHN, A. (1973). Social policy and social services. New York: Random House.

MORRIS, A. (1972). "Children's hearings in Scotland." Criminal Law Review, (November): 693-701.

NEWMAN, N., and MACKINTOSH, H. (1975). A roof over their heads: Residential provision for children in south east Scotland. Edinburgh: Department of Social Administration, University of Edinburgh.

Royal Institute of Public Administration (1971). Supportive staff in Scottish social work departments. London: Author.

Scottish Development Department (1975). Housing and social work: A joint approach. Edinburgh: Her Majesty's Stationery Office.

Scottish Education Department (1970). Social work in Scotland in 1969. Edinburgh: Her Majesty's Stationery Office.

——— (1971). Social work in Scotland in 1970. Edinburgh: Her Majesty's Stationery Office.
——— (1972). Social work in Scotland in 1971. Edinburgh: Her Majesty's Stationery Office.
——— (1973). Social work in Scotland in 1972. Edinburgh: Her Majesty's Stationery Office.
——— (1974). Social work in Scotland in 1973. Edinburgh: Her Majesty's Stationery Office.
——— (1975). Social work in Scotland in 1974. Edinburgh: Her Majesty's Stationery Office.
Scottish Home and Health Department and Scottish Education Department (1964). Children and young persons: Scotland. Edinburgh: Her Majesty's Stationery Office.
——— (1966). Social work and the community: Proposals for reorganizing local authority services in Scotland. Edinburgh: Her Majesty's Stationery Office.
Scottish Information Office (1974). The Scottish office. Edinburgh: Her Majesty's Stationery Office.
SMITH, G., and HARRIS, R. (1972). "Ideologies of need and the organization of social work departments." British Journal of Social Work, 2(spring):28-45.
Social Work Advisory Service (1972). Social work in Scotland today. Edinburgh: Author.
Social Work Services Group (1974). Fieldwork staffing (Scotland): Summary of a report by the Advisory Councils Committee on Social Work Staffing. Edinburgh: Her Majesty's Stationery Office.
——— (n.d.). "Report of a working party on the organization of social work departments in local authorities." Unpublished paper.
Social Work Services Group and Scottish Education Department (1970). Children's hearings. Edinburgh: Her Majesty's Stationery Office.
SPENCER, J. (1970). "Social service changes in the U.K.: Their implications for Canada." Canadian Welfare, 46(October):10-13.
United Kingdom, Her Majesty's Stationery Office (1973a). The new Scottish local authorities: Organization and management structures. Edinburgh: Author.
——— (1973b). Social Work (Scotland) Act 1968 (Chap. 49). London: Author.
WEBBER, S. (1974). "Social work in Scotland: Lessons for America." Journal of Social Work, 19(May):298-304.
WEDGE, P., and PROSSER, H. (1973). Born to fail. London: Arrow Books.

3

EVOLVING SOCIAL WELFARE
IN AFRICAN RHODESIA

MTSHENA SIDILE

Rhodesia, a self-governing country in southern Africa, declared unilateral independence from British colonial rule on November 11, 1965. Its government is in the hands of the few whites as compared with the original inhabitants, the black people. Its total population as of June 1969 was estimated at 5,093,700, comprising 4,840,000 Africans, 230,000 Europeans, 15,000 Coloureds, and 8,700 Asians. According to racial and political recognition, Africans are regarded as third-rate citizens.

The parliamentary form of government in the country was inherited from the British. The most developed public service is education, while other public social services are still evolving. The Ministry of Education serves all races; however, this ministry has separate divisions for Europeans, Coloureds, and Asians. European, Coloureds, and Asian education is compulsory and free at the primary level, while African education is not compulsory and not free at any level. In this paper, a description of education will be followed by a description of the development of welfare services in one African municipality, Bulawayo.

EDUCATION

Historical Development of African Education

Missionary societies from overseas were responsible for starting the first schools for Africans in about 1859. Since then they have played a dominant role in the African educational system. The first mission station for African education was established by the London Missionary Society in 1859 in the Matebeleland province of Rhodesia. This was followed by other stations established about 1870, 1879, and 1893 by the Jesuits, the Dutch Reformed Church, and the American Board of Foreign Mission. During this time the country was governed or administered by the British South African Company; it made grants of lands to missionaries totaling 325,730 acres. In 1899 the first education ordinance was enacted. It was mainly concerned with Europeans, Coloureds, and Asians, but it also provided financial assistance, though inadequate, to missionary societies responsible for African schools. In this way the system of grant-aided schools for Africans was born and still forms the backbone of the whole educational system for Africans.

A committee formed in 1910 to investigate the question of African development and education came to recommend that the type of education offered should be a combination of religious, industrial, and academic training. Nevertheless, crafts and skills, which were thought might lead the Africans to improve their life in the rural environment, continued to be emphasized, while academic work received attention only as it was required for a proper understanding of the industrial and religious subject matter of the curriculum. Between 1920 and 1921 the government opened two industrial and agricultural training schools which provided basic knowledge of elementary building, carpentry, and farm practices. By 1923 a newly elected legislature was paying considerable attention to African education, and the government had begun expressing dissatisfaction with the quality of the missionary schools. For their part, the missionaries complained about the insufficient grants in aid from the government and viewed government criticisms as a threat to take away education from them or to control African education. Thus, yet another commission to investigate African education was appointed in 1924. The result of this body's recommendations in 1925 led in 1927 to the establishment of a separate Department of Native [African] Education, which in 1929 was absorbed into the new Department of Native [African] Development, an agency that became responsible for all aspects of African development, particularly education, agriculture, industrial training, and community welfare. The period from 1927 forward was one of consolidation rather than expansion, though new efforts were made, particularly in the field of community development, to improve low standards of teaching.

About 1935 the social impact of urbanization began to be felt. There was an increase of Africans flowing into the towns to look for employment. This gave rise to calls for academic and character training to help Africans cope with new conditions and to provide educational facilities for the growing urban population. In particular, the government began thinking about establishing its own schools in towns to meet the growing African urban population, but, for lack of funds and staff, it was unable to establish its own school until 1944. The wars of 1939-1945 imposed severe restrictions on all progressive efforts, at a time when Africans were awakening to the benefits of education. Before the wars, the problem had been to get African parents, headmen, and chiefs to allow children even to attend school; they ordinarily preferred that their children help in performing household tasks, herding cattle, or hoeing lands. However, in the postwar years, Africans assumed the opposite position, desiring free formal education and demanding it. Such voluntary organizations as the Federation of African Welfare Societies (renamed the Rhodesia Institute of African Affairs in 1956) were criticizing missionary control of schools and were pressing for increased government support of African education. Their demands led to the appointment of the Kerr Commission under the chairmanship of Dr. Alexander Kerr, who had formerly been principal of the University College of Fort Hare (South Africa). This commission recommended, among other things, however, that the partnership of government and missionaries in running African education should continue.

In 1956 the Department of African Education was freed of its subordination to general "native affairs" and given independent status as a full-fledged government department headed by a Minister of African Education. It was in this year that the government introduced the following:

(a) A five-year-plan of development aimed at producing more teachers;

(b) A proposal for providing for at least five years of school attendance in rural districts and at least eight years in urban areas;

(c) A proposal for expanding secondary school facilities and providing more opportunities for technical, vocational, and commercial training.

In 1953 a Federation of Rhodesia (Southern and Northern) and Nyasaland had been created. The federal government assumed responsibility for European, Coloured, and Asian education as well as for the higher education of all races, yet African primary and secondary education remained the responsibility of individual territorial governments. According to the Rhodesia government, this division of education for Africans, between territorial governments and the federal government, provided the opportunity to devote more attention to and increase the amount of resources toward improving the African educational system. In 1952-1953, before federation, the total amount voted by the Southern Rhodesian government for African education had been $1,644,548; for the financial year 1963-1964, when the federation was dissolved, the total amount was $11,351,546. During the same period, pupil enrollment in primary schools increased from 241,300 to 590,795 and in secondary schools from 867 to 7,055. The number of teachers employed increased from 7,768 to 15,079. In 1959 a new education act created a unified teaching service, providing uniform salary scales, uniform conditions of service, and uniform disciplinary codes for teachers in mission and government schools.

The Judge Commission, which presented its recommendations in 1963, was appointed with the following charge:

To consider the present position of education now falling within the responsibility of the Government of Rhodesia and the future development of the people of Rhodesia, having regard to the cultural, social and economic needs of its individual citizens, and in particular, to examine and reassess the relationship between state and aided schools, the allocation of resources to the various variations of primary and post primary education, the distribution of responsibility and the work of governing advisory bodies. To make such recommendations on these matters as the commission may deem desirable.

A new plan for African education, announced by the minister in 1966 and scheduled to be implemented over a period of 10 years, provided for the following:

(a) A full course of primary education;

(b) Advances in the provision of secondary education. Three hundred new junior secondary schools were to be opened in a 10-year period, which would accommodate 37.5% pupils completing the primary course. The plan would also accommodate a further 12.5%, comprising the more gifted pupils, in full, formal four-year secondary courses;

(c) Rationalization, coordination, and modernization of teacher-training institutions;

(d) Government financing with the aid of self-help and voluntary agencies.

During the past several years, the Rhodesian government has been working on the concept of local government stemming from the framework of community development. For African education, this has involved community boards, rural councils, or others taking over the responsibility of primary education from missionaries. The process is just beginning, but there are a number of community boards and councils already running primary education, especially in the tribal trust lands or rural areas. The government of Rhodesia maintains that African education is the highest single item in the Rhodesian budget. For example, it states that in 1968-1969, 9.7% or $16,500 million of the national budget was devoted to African education.

The Economics of African Education

Over the years the Africans' desire for education has grown by leaps and bounds. The demand for government support of schools has also become increasingly great. This is in part due to changes in the African population, which has multiplied rapidly since the disappearance of wars and raids between tribes and between tribes and settlers. In 1947 there were 205,511 pupils attending primary schools and 252 attending secondary schools, at a cost of $803,268 to the government. Five years later attendance had increased to 241,300 primary and 867 secondary, and the annual expenditure (1952-1953) had risen to $1,764,542. The Rhodesia government stated, however, that funds were not available to permit full universal education.

What then was to be done? Was education to be sectioned so that one small group should enjoy the full range of education from Sub A (beginner) through Form VI while the majority were left illiterate? Or should the policy be to construct the educational system on a broad base and slowly build to a state where a reasonable standard of education would be available to the majority of children of school age? The government under Garfield Todd elected for the broad base system with an initial target of providing five years lower primary education (Sub A to Standard 3) for all as soon as possible and gradually extending the upper primary (Standards 4, 5, and 6) so that a full eight years of primary education would be available for all children by 1974. At the same time, provision was made for secondary education to be offered to all students who had proven their ability to benefit from it. In determining the requirements for secondary education, it has been found that only those who have graduated from Standard 6 or Grade 7 with the high marks of Division I have the ability to hold their own in a secondary school. The number of those passing Standard 6 at this level is roughly 20% to 25% of those who sit for the examination. The overall enrollment in secondary schools in 1966 was 13,587, of which 10,937 were in Forms I and II, the balance in the remaining Forms III, IV-VI.

The African educational system in Rhodesia is one of partnership between missions, parents, and government. In the rural areas, the missions have contributed to the supervision and management of the primary system and have established part of the secondary system, while the parents of children have built schools and teacher's houses, and bought books and equipment necessary for the classrooms. The government's share in the partnership has been to determine the teaching standards for schools, to pay salary grants for all approved teachers, to control the syllabuses and provide an inspectorate, and to assume responsibility for full primary schooling facilities in the urban areas, together with secondary facilities as its resources allowed. In 1947-1948 only 3.1% of the national budget was spent on education for Africans. Ten years later (1957-1958) the amount had risen to 12%. Since then the annual increase has varied until 1968-1969, when it reached the figure of $16,500,000, or 9.7% of the budget. The estimated figure for 1969-1970 was $17,570,000.

The New Plan

The Rhodesian government maintains that no country can have a better education than its economy can afford, and it therefore feels that the maximum that it can afford for African education is 2% of the gross national product. However, the system has been redesigned, rising by 4% per annum to something in the region of $22,000,000 in 1974. There were two steps planned to reduce the cost of primary education in order to release funds for expansion in other sections of the educational system. In January 1967, instead of one teacher in the primary class up to Grade 5, the school timetables were so arranged that only four teachers were required to teach five classes (Grades 1 to 5). As of

January 1, 1970, the full primary course became a seven-year course instead of an eight-year course as previously.

WELFARE SERVICES IN BULAWAYO

In Bulawayo, as in other urban centers in Rhodesia, the earliest social amenities were provided or operated by a local African Welfare Society with the cooperation of the local government or authority. In 1931-1932 areas were set aside for sports fields, and in 1936 a communal hall was opened and named Stanley Hall after the then governor of the British colony of Southern Rhodesia. This was the only venue for concerts, dances, and meetings of every description. In 1937 the African Welfare Society employed a trained African social worker as its welfare officer. He was trained at the then Jan Hofmer School of Social Work in Johannesburg, South Africa, which offered a diploma in social work. His salary was met by the Bulawayo city council and the central government on equal shares, and he operated from Stanley Hall. He ran a public library for the African public. He helped to establish a sporting body known as the Bulawayo African Football Association, which became one of the first organizations for competitive football of various clubs (initially administered by an elected representative of Africans, with a European treasurer, this organization still exists today, run solely by Africans). This African social worker's main task lay in the personal services that he provided for those in any kind of need. For 20 years he was the only professionally qualified social worker in the country, not only in Bulawayo. The African Welfare Society relied upon his close contact with the people to keep in touch with township (residential area) conditions and dispense through him such relief in kind as it was able to provide. He acted also as an information center for newcomers to Bulawayo, locating friends or relatives for the newcomers and finding them sleeping accommodations. The African population grew during this period from under 10,000 to over 100,000.

Welfare Service in Bulawayo: A Responsibility of the Municipality

The Bulawayo Municipality resumed the responsibility of social services for Africans in 1946, taking over such services from the African Welfare Society. The municipality's earliest employees or staff for welfare services were designated social organizers. They were merely concerned with encouraging Africans to engage in sports and entertainments. The need to occupy the leisure time of the wage earner was paramount.

Many Africans in Bulawayo worked in industrial commerce and as domestic servants. They had eight to nine hours of work per day and had free weekends and public holidays. A population of many young adults left to their own devices were likely to employ their leisure in socially unacceptable ways. Before the first welfare facilities were provided, the people amused themselves as best they could, and one of the favored "sports" among young bloods was gang fighting or individual fistfighting. A leisure time pursuit which surpassed all was beer drinking.

In the initial stages, the Bulawayo municipal welfare services tried to organize boxing matches in order to try to displace the factional fights. For years, the main emphasis was on mass recreation and public entertainment. It was very common in those days to hear Europeans, such as district officers and secretaries of native affairs, say "What shall we do with hundreds of Africans who wander up and down the streets of our cities talking too loudly or whistling and in fact just loafing." It was not altogether the African's fault and had to be expected until amusements both indoor and outdoor were provided for them while they were off duty.

In 1949, the Bulawayo Municipality established a department called the African Affairs Department (later called the African Administration Department), whose welfare staff consisted of two male social organizers and a bandmaster for the Bantu Brass Band, which was transported from area to area to provide mass entertainment. The welfare service activities consisted of mass recreation, boxing, football, athletic sports, and communal hall dances of the traditional western pattern. The Progress Report of 1950-1951 stated that the Bulawayo City Council had broken new ground by appointing a female welfare officer, who was to teach domestic science and housewifery to African housewives and domestic servants, male and female; in the following year the first women's club was started, representing the beginning of a group-work program among African women. In the African Administration Department's annual report of 1953, the director reported:

The usual activities, i.e., boxing, cinema shows and sports meetings, continue to flourish. Boxing remaining the most popular form of entertainment among Africans and crowds ranging from 8,000 to 10,000 attend the more important events. A new field for football has been leveled and others fenced. An enclosure for boxing and cinema shows was nearing completion and asbestos recreation hall has been built.

The report concluded:

Cookery classes for women domestic servants and the African Women's club remain popular. Eight women coached by the female welfare officer assistant passed the St. John Ambulance preliminary examination in June.

The Bulawayo Municipality's First Four-Year Plan for Social Services for Africans

In 1955, the Bulawayo Municipality employed both a Senior Welfare Officer with a doctorate degree and an experienced social welfare service worker. This was the beginning of an organized approach and deliberate social planning of services for the African community in Bulawayo. In his first report to the city council in 1955, the Senior Welfare Officer summarized the welfare services available to the Bulawayo African population (now numbering far above 100,000): the open-air cinema showing mostly western films; the boxing matches (very popular); the football games (second most popular); dancing (tribal, jiving, and ballroom); the women's club, which was then doing little more than knitting and sewing; the youth work, consisting of some physical training, boxing instruction, and supervision of indoor and outdoor games; the brass band and a choral society. At the top of popularity were the beer gardens, the pastime that occupied people's leisure time more than any other.

The report went on to spell out new proposals that marked a turning point in the approach to social needs. The policy was defined in positive terms "to create a stable, active, contented, healthy community," which would be achieved through a program that would concentrate on activities promotive of social health and would render remedial or rehabilitative schemes unnecessary. The report further recommended encouraging Africans toward self-reliance, initiative, and civic pride. From among the masses that had completely lacked initiative and responsibility—everything was to be done for them—there would emerge groups who could do something for themselves and an elite who could provide guidance and encouragement. There were proposals suggesting how the plan could be implemented, such as proposals for improved facilities and an augmented staff (to include trained European welfare workers to carry family casework). To implement the staff proposals, advertisements were issued in England in 1956 seeking qualified and experienced workers; and to guide the new staff, notes were prepared that contained such advice as "The Social Organizer's job is to cheer up the African Township—to prevent and arrest disintegrative forces of town life; to provide decent, gay, attractive and constructive recreation as an alternative to beer swilling and fornication." At the end of 1956 five new European staff members, two women and three men, were appointed, bringing the staff total to nine. The European staff were expected to function through Africans. This applied particularly to group activities, which were now possible on a greatly increased scale and for which leaders were needed. Trained African social workers were not available, and to remedy the deficiency, the new European staff in 1957 launched a six-month training course for 60 African men and women. Forty were successful and offered permanent appointments as club leaders and sports organizers. (The first Rhodesian African to obtain a diploma in social work came from Oppenheimer College in Lusaka, Zambia, in 1964. Others would train for the diploma at the Jan Hofmer School of Social Work in Johannesburg, South Africa.)

When the six-month training course ended, a building program provided halls and clubrooms for the workers. In 1957 there had been four clubrooms, and by the end of 1958 there were 32, primarily for boys. There was little interest among the girls.

The 1959 Second Four-Year Plan

The second four-year plan was designed by the present Senior Welfare Officer to transform preventative social work services into promotive services. The development was envisaged under four headings: public recreation, social group work, social casework, and community organization and development. Fundamentally, and ultimately the plan was to move toward a view defined by community needs and awareness rather than by the social conscience of the Bulawayo city council as an agency.

Community Organization and Development. The plan defined community organization and community work in terms of their particular locality and community sentiments and interests. The interests of Africans at this stage centered on work, leisure, and religion, and the plan aimed at encouraging, educating, influencing, or helping them to become actively involved in meeting some of their own needs. They were to be encouraged to improve the conditions of community life and the capacity for community integration and self-direction. The result was the emergence of rent-payer's associations, community guilds, civic associations, burial societies, women's church groups, and several cultural entertainment groups. The rent and lease holders association became an action group, pressuring for better housing and accommodations and street lighting. Today, township advisory boards are elected, and they are the representatives of the African population to the white city council of Bulawayo (the local authority).

Each African Township Advisory Board advises the local authority about all affairs in the township—e.g., housing, trading, liquor, social services, and health. In the spirit of community organization, Africans have formed a number of voluntary groups that deal with such welfare services as aid to the physically handicapped and disabled (e.g., the Jairos Jiri Association, the Old People's Home, the Entembeni Homes Society). Burial societies care of the dead, offer aid to dependents, and provide opportunities for social get-togethers. Different denominational religious churches run youth programs and family counseling programs. There are also drama societies in most African townships.

Casework Services. Casework services cover more than family counseling and are handled by professional personnel who hold university degrees and college diplomas.

In the early days, municipal housing administrators (superintendents) were on the receiving end of all residents'complaints and problems. The pioneer casework service (family counseling and relief of the destitute) started before 1958 at an African township residential area in Mpopoma under the management of a caseworker who was a graduate from the United Kingdom. Later, another casework service office was opened at Njube township in a residential area occupied by married couples and families. By 1960 every superintendent's area had a caseworker. The principle adopted in Bulawayo was that the client rather than the agency should determine the fields of work; the caseworker's responsibility was to respond meaningfully to anyone who sought help. In the early sixties in Bulawayo, there were no other agencies in the field, so that a refusal was final so far as the client was concerned.

A caseworker's annual report in Mpopoma township in 1963 gives some idea of the variety of problems handled in the 848 cases during the year. More than half the cases concerned unemployment, poverty, and destitution; the rest consisted of matrimonial problems, child neglect or child misbehavior, and help to the sick and imprisoned. Another 500-odd investigations and inquiries involved such matters as school placements, student scholarships, lost persons, food vendors, and applications for vegetable garden allotments. The number of new cases (families visiting the casework office) doubled that of the previous year. The problem was reduced during the following year because the central government introduced a relief scheme called "Public Assistance," which provided funds to families of the unemployed, widows, divorcées, and other persons in distress. Aid generally consisted of rations and a portion of house rent.

Another new relief scheme, called the African Welfare Society, was administered (and is still administered) by voluntary citizens with the help of Bulawayo municipal caseworkers. Funds are raised by means of appeal to the Bulawayo public, black and white, and the Bulawayo city council gives an annual grant of $4,000. Monthly, an average of $700 is used to distribute "mealie meal" (maize) and meat and to pay for house rents and electricity and water bills. Some 600 family breadwinners receive rations at some time or other, and, when one considers that some families contain seven to 10 children, these rations are grievously inadequate. In addition to its other funds, the African Welfare Society receives about $5,000 from the Bulawayo Mayor Christmas Cheer Fund, which is an annual event of appeal to the people of commerce and industry and the public. Through the casework offices the society then buys various foodstuffs and clothing for all family age groups. The society also appeals to voluntary agencies for other services for poor people, such as meals for preschool children.

Christmas parties are another avenue of aid. Over 1,000 children from poor families are annually entertained with cool drinks, buns, sweets, toys, and music and dancing. Old people among the poor are also feted with a meal, beer, and traditional dances and modern music. Many of the old, female and male, perform traditional dances to entertain their comrades. Funds for these Christmas events come from such voluntary organizations as the Round Table, Rotary, and Toc H.

Welfare Services in Bulawayo Today

Organization. The municipal African welfare services have been designed, first, to assist in the adjustment to urban living and, second, to stimulate the potential for self-fulfillment. For their strength and direction they look to the social initiatives of the people. There are more than 70 centers and offices providing welfare services in the municipal African townships. (For an organizational perspective, see Figures 1 and 2.) Outdoor facilities include two major parks and 25 children's playgrounds, numerous football fields, tennis courts, athletic and cycling tracks, basketball courts, and three swimming baths. Eight offices provide family casework services, handling over 1,000 new cases a year, as well as nearly 2,500 investigations and inquiries, including more than 18,000 interviews. In conjunction with the African Welfare Society, municipal caseworkers operate a scheme for the relief of distress among families who do not qualify for other aid. Some 200 indigent families are provided maize meal every month, and preschool children receive meals at least part of the year. An annual clothing appeal is also held. Twenty municipally sponsored African women's groups attracted over 2,000 participants to their programs in 1974, organizing their own management committees, raising their own funds, and engaging in community service. Nine of the clubs ran winter soup kitchens for needy children.

Youth Services. About 5,000 young Africans participate in the municipal youth services. Most are paid-up members of clubs and plan their own programs through elected committees. Club members take an active part in community service, helping in fund-raising fetes and street collections. Members of the Sixteen Plus clubs are entirely self-supporting and have formed their own youth councils to coordinate their affairs. During 1973, 94 special events were organized in the African townships for (and often by) youth. Fifteen clubs took part in the annual drama festival, writing as well as producing their own plays. The Sixth Annual African Youth Festival attracted 39 clubs and lasted eight days and included displays of every aspect of youth club life.

A new youth venture camp on the Hyde Park Estate will provide a range of courses for youngsters of both sexes and all ages. Vigorous activities of the "Outward Bound" type will predominate, but cultural activities, nature study, agricultural and craft skills will also be developed. Work parties from the youth clubs built two 30-bed dormitories and two leaders' huts at the Venture Camp, fabricating their own bricks.

Eighteen municipally sponsored preschool centers have maximum enrollments of 30 pupils each. Parents' committees raise funds and assist with management; some are sponsoring extre preschool units.

A fund to help school-leavers has been set up by the Township Advisory Board. It is supported by an annual fete at Barbour Fields. Last year, the fund awarded scholarships totalling $550 to 33 students in typing, welding, and metalcraft. Three placement centers for African school-leavers seeking employment offer programs designed to maintain physical fitness and morale and to develop skills. Only about one-quarter of the African school-leavers who register for employment find jobs each year through the Employment Exchange; others find their own jobs, but a great number remain frustrated: the problem of unattached and unoccupied youth is a major challenge to the welfare services.

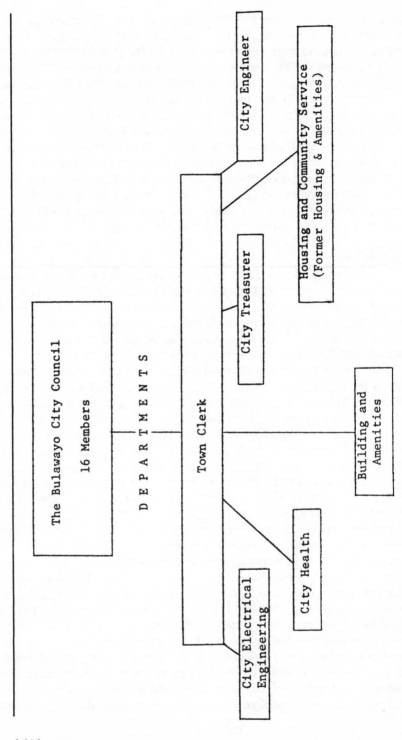

The Bulawayo City Council
16 Members

DEPARTMENTS

Town Clerk

City Engineer

City Treasurer

Housing and Community Service
(Former Housing & Amenities)

Building and
Amenities

City Health

City Electrical
Engineering

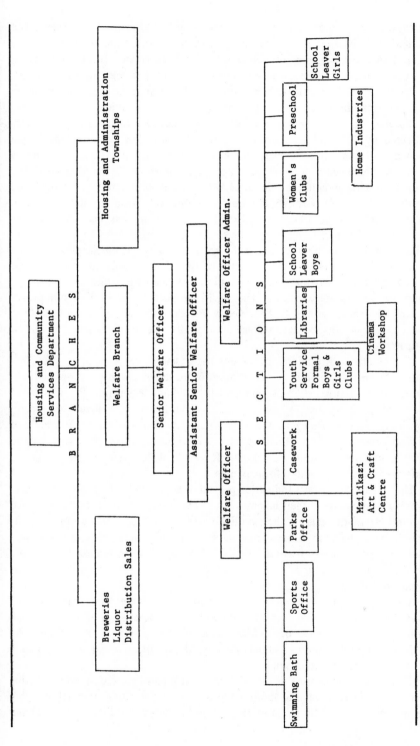

Figure 2: THE HOUSING AND COMMUNITY SERVICES DEPARTMENT

Three workshops provide prevocational training for African school-leavers. The curriculum is based on income-earning projects, varying from traditional crafts to modern enterprise. Boat-building has been very successful. Girl school-leavers, many of whom are now work-seekers or have little chance of employment, engage regularly in income-earning schemes. There are nine groups engaging in such crafts as embroidery, beadwork, basketry, and mat-making.

Libraries. In the three municipal African libraries last year, book issues increased by 37% and membership by 50%. A fourth library has recently been opened. On the average, every book in the municipal African libraries is borrowed six times a year. The average reader borrows 27 books a year. The municipal African children's libraries often stand with empty shelves. Some 3,500 children borrowed 76,000 books in one year from a stock of 4,500 volumes. African children attend Ndebele story-telling sessions in one of the libraries every Saturday morning. The stories are taped and played back to more children in the other libraries and in the children's wards of the hospital.

Art and Craft Center. The activities of the Mzilikazi Art and Craft Center include painting, clay modeling, ceramics, woodcarving, stone and soapstone sculpture, and pottery-making. The Mzilikazi pottery works is a non-profit-making enterprise set up to help needy African families to supplement their incomes. Some 100 workers average about $10 a month each from the sale of their products.

The Mzilikazi Art and Craft Center has a school-leaver program providing courses from one to three years in duration in drawing and painting, pictorial composition, figure study, commercial art and lettering, slip and glaze decoration, pottery-making, modeling, and carving. The participants are mainly boys between the ages of 12 and 15 who are too young to seek work. Sales of African ceramics and wood and soapstone sculpture from the Mzilikazi Art and Craft Center in 1974 totalled $3,000. The bulk of this went to the artists and craftsmen, after a deduction for expenses.

The Bulawayo Home Industries project was set up to help needy African families to supplement their incomes. Last year about 100 workers averaged $10 a month from the sale of their products. Bulawayo Home Industries products include batik, ilala crafts, decorator and boutique products, raffia, sisal bags and mats, and small items of wood. The undertaking operates from capital provided by the municipality and is run by a municipal staff under an independent committee of management.

Recreation and Entertainment. Attendances at the two main African swimming baths in 1974 were 217,000 and 123,000 respectively. A third, small bath had an attendance of 70,000. Most of the swimmers are children. An African school Swimming Association awards certificates and holds regional galas and annual championships.

There are three centers in the African townships where regular weight-lifting sessions are held under the sponsorship of the Weight-lifting Association. Nine competitions were held there in 1974, and African weight-lifters have attained national standards. Africans participating in the National Fitness scheme have been rewarded with numerous gold, silver, and bronze medals. Regular training sessions are held at the gymnasium and interest is stimulated by public displays.

Sixteen cinema shows are presented in the African townships each week for public entertainment, and there are also showings of educational films for youth clubs and adult groups. In 1974 the 650 shows for which there was an admission charge attracted 141,000 patrons. The African townships are served by eight communal halls. Apart from cinema shows, these were engaged last year for 3,189 functions, ranging from concerts and dances to tribal courts, church meetings, wedding receptions, a mini-trade fair, and various other cultural and social activities.

Financing. Extensive welfare services in the municipal African townships are funded from liquor profits. This does not mean that liquor is sold in order to pay for welfare, but that the profits of the trade are used for social improvement rather than private benefit. It also means that in African welfare as in African housing the entire cost is met from African sources. Over $700,000 a year is spent on welfare and recreation services and on the upkeep of parks and sports grounds in the municipal African townships. This is about $4 per person a year for the population served. More than 400 workers are employed in these services, of whom some 250 are laborers, groundsmen, or semiskilled workers. There are 175 social and community workers, youth and other group leaders. About 7% of the municipal African welfare budget is allocated for grants-in-aid to voluntary organizations. Welfare funds have also been used to build four secondary schools and to provide other assistance to educational institutions.

4

SOUTH AFRICA:
RACIAL DIVISIONS IN
SOCIAL SERVICES

ISADORA HARE
BRIAN McKENDRICK

Because of factors in South Africa's historical and political past, South African society attaches great significance to racial differences between people. The present National Party government came to power in 1948 on the basis of its policy of apartheid, "a formula for political and social 'separateness' . . . for the different population groups, to ensure the maintenance, protection and consolidation of the White race as the bearer of Christian civilization in South Africa, and to enable it to fulfill its function of responsible trusteeship to guide the other groups towards eventual freedom in a peaceful manner" (de Kock, 1971:43). The use of the Afrikaans term "apartheid" to describe this policy is now officially regarded as a "cardinal error" (de Kock, 1971:46), and other terms such as "separate development," "parallel development," and "multi-national development" are encouraged. However, the average South African still prefers to call it "apartheid" (Lever, 1975:32). Proponents of the policy describe it as a system of political independence coupled with economic interdependence, while its opponents consider it "a symbol of repression and discrimination and White domination" (De Villiers, 1971:406).

The *Official Yearbook of the Republic of South Africa* states that "in terms of historicity, ethnical or racial descent and life-style" the national population of South Africa comprises "four distinctive demographic units, namely, the Whites, Coloureds, Asians and Bantu (Blacks)" (South Africa, 1974:73). Demographic data for the country is therefore presented in terms of these categories. The

AUTHORS' NOTE: *The writers wish to acknowledge the assistance of Mr. Smuts of the South African Embassy in Washington, D.C., and of Professor C. Muller of the School of Social Work, University of the Witwatersrand, Johannesburg, in the acquisition of data used in the writing of this chapter.*

Asian group is mainly Indian but also comprises a smaller number of Chinese. Japanese temporarily resident in the country, usually for business reasons, are afforded White status. Parliament has from time to time defined the different population groups in legislation. In 1950, race classification for the entire adult population was introduced by the Population Registration Act. This act defined a "native person" as one who is "in fact or is generally accepted as a member of any aboriginal race or tribe of Africa," that is, a black person. A Coloured person (one of mixed descent) is defined as a "person who is not a white person or a native," and a White person is one "who in appearance obviously is or who is generally accepted as a white person, but does not include a person who, although in appearance obviously a white person, is generally accepted as a Coloured person." This legislation, along with the Group Areas Act of 1949, which crystallized patterns of residential segregation, has cardinal significance for the delivery of social welfare services in South Africa, which are divided along racial lines. Sexual relations across the color bar are punishable by imprisonment, and interracial adoptions are prohibited in terms of the Children's Act.

The policy of separate development has been designed by the National Party government to provide for the political aspirations of those South Africans who are not classified as White. The focal points of this policy are those areas of the country which were not appropriated by White settlers and were set aside for the Blacks during the course of history. These, formerly called reserves, have now been designated homelands, and in terms of the policy of multinational separate development it is envisaged that "eventually a number of self-governing politically independent Bantu nations" will develop (South Africa, Department of Information, 1971:16). At present, there are nine such homelands: the Transkei, Ciskei, KwaZulu, Lebowa, Venda, Gazankulu, Bophutatswana, BasothoQwaqwa, and Swazi Territory. The Transkei was granted self-government in 1963 and is scheduled to become independent on October 26, 1976. Negotiations about land allocations and consolidation are still under way. For example, in 1972, KwaZulu consisted of 40 fragmented areas widely distributed (Wilson, 1972:90). However, the upper limit is defined by legislation passed in 1910 and 1936. When the final transfers of land are made and all the homelands consolidated, the total area allocated to the Blacks will be about 38 million acres. This represents approximately 13% of the total land in the republic, the total land area being 472,359 square miles or 302 million acres.

In furtherance of the policy of separate development, groups of African people have been relocated in order to eliminate so-called "Black spots," that is, areas of black settlement in places predominantly occupied by Whites. In many cases, the required social and other services were not provided in the resettlement areas prior to the arrival of the resettled populations, and this resulted in hardship.

The governments of most homelands now administer their own welfare and social benefit schemes, as well as grants or allowances to aged, blind, indigent or

mentally and physically disabled Black people (South Africa, 1974:711). The
Department of the Interior in the Transkei deals with social pension applications
and the registration of voluntary welfare organizations. In the other homelands,
there are social welfare sections or Departments of Community Affairs with
trained staff to handle applications for pensions. Maqashalala (1975:154) has
commented that these Black social workers often have to work under White
senior officials who are not social workers and that this situation is incongruous.

In terms of government policy, the Coloured Persons Representative Council,
consisting of 40 elected and 20 nominated members of the Coloured
community, is the avenue of political expression for this group, while the South
African Indian Council is an advisory body and serves as "a contact body
between the Government and the Indian population" (South Africa, 1974:148).
While these councils have certain social welfare responsibilities, the government
Departments of Coloured Relations and Indian Affairs and the Administration
of Coloured Affairs have major powers in relation to social welfare matters for
their respective population groups. Neither of these groups has its own
homeland.

DEMOGRAPHIC DATA

A realistic assessment of social welfare needs and of the services required to
meet those needs demands an appreciation of demographic data. South Africa is
in an interesting position demographically, because it represents in microcosm a
model of the world population position. The White group has the demographic
and economic characteristics of the rich West, while the other groups show those
features exhibited by the economically less affluent peoples of the globe.

According to the last census taken in 1970, the population of South Africa
was 21,739,000, but by June 1974 the estimated population was close to
25,000,000, made up as shown in Table 1.

The White birthrate has been continuously decreasing this century while the
Coloured and Asian rates have declined only recently. According to indirect
estimates, the birthrate for Africans is 43 per thousand and has remained
constant at this high level for a long time. The question of family planning has

Table 1.

	Number	Percentage
Africans	17,745,000	71.2
Whites	4,160,000	16.7
Coloureds	2,306,000	9.3
Asians	709,000	2.8
Total	24,920,000	100.0

SOURCE: Horrell, Horner, and Hudson, 1975:52.

received a great deal of attention in the country recently. The State Department of Health both runs and subsidizes clinics throughout the country where contraceptives are provided free to members of all population groups. Population projects by the Human Sciences Research Council estimate that the South African population will reach 46,000,000 by the year 2000. The present population is expected to double in less than 30 years, with Blacks showing the largest growth, from 15 million in 1970 to 33 million in A.D. 2000.

In terms of age distribution, the Whites are the oldest group, while all three of the other groups have a high ratio of children to adults. "With this high ratio of dependents the non-White population groups will find it rather difficult substantially to raise their standard of living and socio-economic status in the near future" (South Africa, 1974:73).

This problem is aggravated by the economic facts of life in South Africa. Since industrialization, the South African economy has prospered, and increasing urbanization has been the major consequence. Per capita real incomes for all races more than doubled in less than 50 years. At 1948 prices, real income per head of population (all races) averaged R68 in 1919 and R174 ($234) in 1962. However, there are large discrepancies in the distribution of wealth. Studies have indicated that the average per capita income of Whites is over 13 times higher than the average income of Africans and almost 7 times higher than that of Coloureds (Sprocas Economics Commission, 1972:19-20). The Bureau of Market Research estimated that minimum living costs nationally for an African family of six persons was R56.77 in 1971 and indicated that 77% of all African families had incomes of less than R60 per month.

One of the most important demographic trends during the last century has been the development of large-scale urbanization. David Welsh (1971:173) has commented as follows on this process:

A legacy of conflict between the different sections of the population gave urbanization in South Africa a peculiar configuration. . . . Tensions that arose in other conditions, in the frontier wars between white colonists and African peoples, or from Afrikaners' attempts to free themselves from British domination, were carried over and compounded in the new urban setting . . . and partially obscured the truth that the towns were co-operative enterprises that reflected the ever-closer intertwining of all groups in a common society.

Welsh proceeds to say that the "drift of rural people to the towns was the combined effect of the push of rural poverty and the pull of rapidly expanding industries, thirsty for labour" (1971:75).

The agrarian crisis of the twenties led to the development of a "Poor White" problem, involving mainly Afrikaners, that was to become the major impetus for the development of state welfare services and professional social work in South Africa. Black poverty, on the other hand, was viewed somewhat differently. According to Welsh, African reserves were regarded as reservoirs of labor for the

SOUTH AFRICA

SOUTH AFRICA   [75]

white-owned farms and industries; and congestion, landlessness, and crop failure were welcomed as stimulants to the labor supply (Report of the Native Affairs Commission for 1939-1940, paragraph 14). However, public policy denied Blacks permanent residence in the towns and cities and from early times the conception of the urban African as a "temporary sojourner" developed. The policy of migrant labor was encouraged in order to preserve segregation. Up to the present, 99% of the Black labor force in the gold mines are migrant laborers and are housed in all-male compounds (Wilson, 1972:10). (The majority of these people come from outside South Africa.) Many migrant workers outside the mining sector, both men and women, are housed in large single-sex hostels.

By 1946, certain groups in the society recognized that the presence of a settled permanent black population in the cities was an incontrovertible fact, but for the white population in general this was unacceptable and in 1948 the slogan "apartheid" brought the National Party to power. Black mobility continues to be restricted by influx control, a pass system whereby all Africans over 16 years of age must carry reference books, and violations incur criminal penalties which swell the prison population in the country. According to official policy, "Black workers in White South Africa can be used for certain categories of employment only" (South Africa, 1974:143). Practical economic realities are altering these determinations at present, but the basic policy remains unchanged.

The increasing urbanization of Blacks in South Africa, as in other regions of the world, has resulted in housing problems. The huge influx of Africans into the towns after 1939 aggravated the already existing housing shortage and led to the growth of squatter settlements. Emergency camps were established by municipalities in the large cities, and many people lived in slum conditions. After 1948, the Nationalist government vigorously tackled the urban housing problem, and by 1960 the situation was much improved. Today the incidence of urban slums has been greatly reduced, although urban Blacks and Coloureds still face a critical housing shortage, and, according to experts, the country as a whole will be confronted by "staggering housing problems" before the turn of the century. Black people are not permitted freehold title or home ownership in the areas where they reside alongside the "White" cities, and single women particularly are subject to stringent limitations on their ability to rent homes. "A woman newly widowed who has dependents, already in a house, may retain it if the Chief Bantu Affairs Commissioner gives his consent" (Hellmann, 1973:19).

According to Welsh (1971:219), "the tensions, upheavals, and dislocation accompanying the urbanization of any people were exacerbated for Africans by official policies directed against the stabilization of urban African communities." These concomitants of Black urbanization in South Africa have produced certain deleterious effects on family life and social interaction both in the cities and the rural areas. The migrant labor policy has dislocated the family system and contributed to prostitution, illegitimacy, alcoholism, juvenile delinquency, and other indices of social disorganization. To quote Welsh once more: "Although the urban African townships are often gay and vibrant places, insecurity of life and property are ever-present. . . . Violence and fear have become woven into the very fabric of life" (1971:219).

In terms of apartheid policy, African hospitals not essential in "White areas" and institutions such as those for the blind and the deaf, as well as old-age homes, must be transferred to the homelands, and no new ones may be established in "White" areas (Botha, 1964:17). Of necessity, some hospitals do exist, and here patients are entitled to virtually free treatment. The largest hospital on the African continent, Baragwanath Hospital, is situated in Soweto, the Black city of almost a million inhabitants on the outskirts of Johannesburg. However, a survey of health and social services in the Johannesburg area in 1974 revealed that there were no aged homes for Africans at that time and only two institutions for African children (Schreier, 1974:22, 54). According to the Report of the Department of Bantu Administration and Development for 1973-1974, these two homes accommodated 150 children, and in the rest of the "White areas" there were an additional four homes subsidized by the department. The same report stated that the department itself controlled two places of safety and detention for Blacks in major urban areas—that is, institutions for delinquent children and children in need of care—and added that two more such institutions were planned at Kimberley and Bloemfontein (South Africa, Department of Bantu Administration and Development, 1974:7).

Stabilizing influences in the Black urban areas are the development of a middle class and of a large number and variety of associations based on a similarity of interest. Women's associations, sports clubs, church groups, welfare organizations, and professional associations of teachers, social workers, and others are examples of such associations. These are important forces in community development in the Black cities and are inevitably growing in spite of official policy. The African Self-Help Association is an example of such an organization, and it runs about 35 day nurseries in the Soweto area.

A BRIEF HISTORY OF SOCIAL WELFARE SERVICES

Prior to the 19th century, there were no organized social welfare services as such. For the Blacks, the extended family system provided for the human needs of all people in accordance with tribal custom. During the first two centuries of colonial rule, White pioneer families or groups of families also provided for their own needs. In the 19th century the Dutch Reformed Church, to which most Afrikaners belonged, was very active in early efforts to establish a variety of social welfare services, and other religious denominations, Protestant, Catholic, and Jewish, followed suit. Gradually, voluntary welfare organizations, some with international affiliations, such as the Red Cross and the Salvation Army, appeared in the Cape Colony. Afrikaans women's organizations and child welfare societies were formed in the early years of the 20th century. Union in 1910 made national planning possible, and the first separate legislation for the protection of children nationwide was passed in 1913.

The industrialization and urbanization in the wake of the discovery of diamonds and gold led to many social problems. The rising incidence of poverty among Whites caused major concern. In 1928, the Carnegie Corporation of New York financed a Commission of Investigation into the Poor White Problem, and a comprehensive national survey was undertaken. Its report, published in 1932, made a major impact on the development of social welfare in the country. A National Conference on the Poor White Problem took place at Kimberley in 1934 and resulted in 1937 in the creation of a State Department of Social Welfare, which employed social workers in its own right and subsidized similar posts in voluntary welfare organizations in the community.

In 1958, a new state Department of Social Welfare and Pensions was formed which united "the rehabilitation services of the Department of Social Welfare and the social security measures administered by the Department of Pensions, including the provisions of old-age pensions which dated back to 1928" (Brümmer, 1968:4).

With the advent of the apartheid policy after World War II, this "Department has largely limited its practical activities to promoting the social welfare of the White population" (South Africa, 1974:705). The Official Yearbook states further (1974:705):

> As regards the non-White groups, these responsibilities have been assigned as an interim measure to the Departments most closely concerned with the administration of Bantu, Coloured and Indian Affairs, respectively, with the ultimate intention of transferring such responsibilities to the governing authorities of these groups themselves as they acquire increased political status, practical experience and economic resources.

An Interdepartmental Consultative Committee on Professional Welfare Matters has existed for several years with representatives from all departments mentioned above, all of whose senior officials are White. The present government holds the view that:

> Among the Black nations . . . the traditional social system and family structure are such that a considerable amount of what is usually regarded as public welfare assistance and poor relief in Western societies is carried out on a customary basis by relatives and associates. . . . For this reason, inter alia, it has been found necessary and advisable to differentiate between these groups and others as regards the nature and scope of the assistance provided. [South Africa, 1974:705]

However, this position has to be viewed against the background of family disorganization, poor living conditions, "a disquieting collapse of those ethnic values basic to the maintenance of social stability [and] considerable artificial deculturisation" (South Africa, 1974:143) acknowledged by the government and emphasized by critics of the present policy. (See Wilson and Thompson, 1971, vol. 2.)

THE SOUTH AFRICAN SOCIAL WELFARE SYSTEM

The South African social welfare system is based upon the concept that both the state (at national, provincial, and local levels) and the community share responsibility for the provision of human welfare services.

State Social Welfare Services

As the senior partner in a joint enterprise, the state assumes responsibility on a national basis for the country-wide planning and coordination of social welfare programs and for the formulation and administration of social legislation. Although organized at the national level, state-sponsored social welfare services are delivered regionally and locally. State welfare provision is not centered in any single government department, and major welfare functions are shared by four different departments each of which serves the needs of different groups in the population. Thus, in the case of most statutory social services, White persons would receive service from the Department of Social Welfare and Pensions, Coloured (i.e., mixed-race) persons from the Department of Coloured Affairs, and Black persons from the Department of Bantu Administration and Development. The nature of the services offered by these four departments is generally similar and falls into the two categories of social welfare: security provision and the delivery of service programs.

State Social Security Provision. In the Republic of South Africa, social pensions are noncontributory and are paid out of state revenue. With minor exceptions the pensions are granted subject to a means-test; that is, income levels are laid down which fix the maximum allowable income including pensions. If the total income exceeds this amount, the applicant will not be awarded a pension. When these totals are being calculated, a certain sum is permitted, called "free income" which does not affect the amount of pension that may be granted. Free income can be made up of earnings, interest from investments, profits from agriculture, and so forth (Barratt, 1975). The principal social pensions are old-age and blind pensions and disability grants. The pensions, and the maximum free income allowed for the payment of the pensions in full, are shown in Table 2.

In addition to the major social security provisions shown in Table 2, provision is also made for war veterans' pensions; maintenance grants to enable children to be cared for in the community, rather than in institutions; family allowances for families with a low income and three or more dependent children (Whites and Coloured only); social relief; and grants to certain leprosy sufferers and their dependents.

War veterans' pensions for Africans were authorized for the first time in February 1975. The provision states that "any [Bantu] war veteran granted a social pension shall be paid, in addition to such pension, an amount of R30 per annum." Africans served as noncombatants during the two World Wars but do not carry arms in the South African Army.

Table 2: A. Old-Age and Blind Pensions and Disability Grants, 1974*

	Whites	Coloureds & Indians	Blacks
Maximum Pension	64.00	34.00	15.00
Free Income Allowed	42.00	21.00	6.66
Total	106.00	55.00	21.66

B. Persons in Receipt of Old-Age and Blind Pensions and Disability Grants, 1974

Pension	Whites	Coloureds & Chinese	Indians	Blacks
Old Age	128,645	71,573	12,075	168,514
Blind	853	1,623	193	4,638
Disability	24,416	31,819	10,378	54,410

*Amounts in South African Rand; R1 equals $1.14 as of 1976.
SOURCE: Horrell and Hodgson, 1976.

The South African parliament has often discussed contributory pension schemes and universal social security measures, but these proposals have not been accepted by the government. Although the means-test has been progressively liberalized in recent years, the policy of the state remains that

the responsibility for every citizen's social security rests in the first place with the citizen himself. Only if his own efforts prove inadequate is the state prepared to step in with help and guidance. The independence of the individual, the family and the community must be maintained and encouraged. This principle is in keeping with the traditions of South Africa. [Brümmer, 1964]

State Social Welfare Programs. The Department of Social Welfare and Pensions, which has responsibility for the White population group, has as one of its purposes "to prevent and combat social maladjustment and indigency in the family and the community" (Brümmer, 1964), and to this end it offers professional social work services at its regional and local offices. As well as carrying out statutory social work (for example, probation services) the more than 250 social workers employed by the department work with such issues as family problems, poverty and indigence, child neglect, unemployment, alcoholism, crime and delinquency, ill health, illness and temporary physical disability, permanent physical handicaps, epilepsy, mental disorders and mental retardation, old age, blindness, and deafness (South Africa, Department of Social Welfare and Pensions, 1970).

Mental hospitals are administered by the Department of Health, but social service departments in these institutions are staffed by social workers employed by the Department of Social Welfare and Pensions. In December 1972 there were 27,414 beds available in state mental hospitals. Only the more serious cases are accommodated here, because in general the policy is to treat mentally ill patients in psychiatric wards in general hospitals whenever possible. General hospitals are controlled by the provincial administrations.

During the year 1971-1972, 69% of the "new contacts" made by social workers in the employ of the Department of Social Welfare and Pensions had to do with preventive services, and 31% concerned activities which are assigned as the result of court orders. The department analyzed its workers' participation in various areas of preventive activity as shown in Table 3. The department's activities in relation to court orders included probation and supervision services (23%), reconstruction services (57%), and aftercare services (20%) (South Africa, Department of Social Welfare and Pensions, 1973).

The three departments dealing with the needs of Coloured, Indian, and Black persons offer social welfare programs similar to those of the Department of Social Welfare and Pensions and, in some instances, offer additional programs unique to their departments, such as the Department of Coloured Affairs' six-month voluntary youth camps for adolescents who are disaffiliated from their communities or who have behavior problems.

Beyond the welfare programs offered by the Departments of Social Welfare and Pensions, Coloured Affairs, Indian Affairs, and Bantu Administration and Development, there are a number of specialized social welfare services rendered by other state agencies. Vocational rehabilitation, for example, is provided by the Department of Labour; social work services to persons in the defense force are provided by the Department of Defence; the rehabilitation of adult offenders in prison is carried out by the Department of Prisons; and the Department of the South African Police employs social workers to cater to the needs of members of the police force. The fragmentation of welfare responsibility among state agencies is increasing with the creation of independent Black states within the Republic of South Africa. The first of these, the Transkei, has established its own Department of Health and Social Services, and it seems probable that other evolving Black states will follow this lead.

Table 3: Social Work Contacts by Activity Areas

Area of Activity	Percentage
Uncontrollability of children	12
Child neglect	18
Divorce	2
Juvenile delinquents	6
Adult offenders	4
Workshyness	4
Alcoholism and drug dependence	22
Aged and handicapped persons	5
Marriage guidance	2
Other family and child welfare services	25
Total	100%

At the provincial level, the four provinces of the Cape, Natal, Orange Free State, and Transvaal each offer social work services in general hospitals. Local authorities play a minor role in the delivery of welfare services because their activities are restricted to the provision of recreational and leisure-time programs.

The major pieces of social legislation affecting service delivery to individuals and families and implemented either partially or fully by the state departments concerned with social welfare are the following:

The Children's Act, No. 33 of 1960 as amended, provides for the care and protection of children, the prevention of abuse and neglect, children's courts, institutions for children, adoptions and other related matters.

The Aged Persons Act, No. 81 of 1967, provides for a wide range of measures for the protection of the aged.

The Blind Persons Act, No. 26 of 1968, provides for the registration of blind people, workshops for the blind and other related matters.

The Abuse of Dependence-Producing Substances and Rehabilitation Centers Act, No. 41 of 1971, as amended, provides for the establishment of rehabilitation centers and other measures to serve individuals addicted to alcohol or drugs and individuals who lead "idle, dissolute or disorderly" lives.

The Mental Health Act, No. 18 of 1973, provides for the treatment of various types of mentally disordered persons.

The Social Pensions Act, No. 37 of 1973, and other pension legislation provides various pensions.

The Mentally Retarded Children's Training Act, No. 63 of 1974, provides for the training of mentally retarded white children in the age group 6-18 years and control over such training by the Department of Vocational Education. Special education for black children is controlled by separate legislation.

The Department of Labour administers legislation providing for unemployment insurance and workmen's compensation. The former applies to the majority of workers, but persons earning more than R4,264 per annum and Africans earning less than R546 a year are excluded (South Africa, 1974:530).

Community-Sponsored Social Welfare Services

Community-sponsored social welfare programs are undertaken by autonomous sectarian and nonsectarian agencies registered as welfare organizations in terms of the National Welfare Act, No. 79 of 1965. In accordance with the existing state-community welfare partnership, community-sponsored agencies are allocated responsibility for the initiation and maintenance of social welfare services in areas that are not covered by state-sponsored programs. Community-sponsored welfare organizations generally, but not always, operate in fields that do not have statutory dimensions, and it is accepted that welfare organizations in the private sector have a particular responsibility to pioneer new fields of social welfare activity.

As of February 1976, 1,908 community-sponsored welfare organizations were registered in terms of the National Welfare Act. The principal fields of service in which these agencies operate are care of the aged, alcoholism and drug dependency, child and family welfare, corrections, mental health, and physical disability. There were in addition 2,034 organizations operating in terms of letters of delegated authority from these registered welfare organizations. This latter group consists of branches of the first group and will possibly become independent agencies at some time in the future. A wide range of services is offered by these agencies, including material assistance, institutional accommodation, day-care facilities, community care, rehabilitation services, referral services, and counseling in relation to all these functions as well as other situations of human need. As with state agencies, there is a division of welfare responsibility within the private sector, principally on account of specialization or the delivery of services exclusively to one or another population group.

The predominant eligibility criterion that is applicable in community-sponsored welfare organizations is that of race. During 1966, the Department of Social Welfare and Pensions notified registered welfare organizations that it was opposed to multiracial bodies and that separate welfare agencies should be established for Black, Coloured, Indian, and White persons. As White-dominated organizations tended to be the longest-established and most powerful, it was suggested that White organizations should initially sponsor and guide "Black" organizations toward independence. Most, but not all, welfare organizations complied with the suggested policy, and the effect can be illustrated by the example of the South African National Council for the Blind. Previously, members of any racial group were entitled to be members of the council's executive committee. Now, the executive committee is an all-White body; separate committees and divisions have been set up for each racial group, and in time it is planned that all office-bearers will be members of the group concerned. White members of the executive committee attend meetings of the divisional committees serving the other racial groups in an advisory capacity, and representatives of the "Black" committees may be invited to attend meetings of the central executive committee and express their views when matters affecting their particular groups are under discussion.

In addition to racial criteria for the receipt of community-sponsored welfare services, some agencies restrict their services to members of particular religious or language groups. Thus, for example, the Transvaal Jewish Welfare Council delivers services mainly to persons of the Jewish faith, while the Armsorgraad organizations generally serve members of the Afrikaans-speaking community.

Central Trends in the Organization and Delivery of Welfare Services

Fragmentation of Responsibility. It would seem that the distribution of welfare functions among a large number of state and community-sponsored agencies on the basis of specialization, race, and, to a lesser extent, linguistic and religious groupings, leads to a fragmentation of welfare services and programs. The process in turn may inhibit the concerted, unified application of available welfare resources to individuals and families in need, and multiplies the cost of welfare services. For example, an elderly white woman living in a large South African city could be receiving social services from state, provincial, and community-sponsored sources, without any organized coordination between them. She could receive her old-age pension from the state Department of Social Welfare and Pensions and her health care (perhaps with a concurrent social work service) from a provincial hospital, and she might make use of services such as a home aide, meals on wheels, and attendance at a social club, with each of these latter facilities being organized by different autonomous community-sponsored welfare agencies.

Coordinating Structures. The fragmentation of welfare responsibility in South Africa has resulted in a proliferation of bodies, each of which has been allocated, or which has assumed, coordinating functions. As might be expected in a welfare system where the central government plays a major role in the planning and provision of welfare facilities through a number of state agencies, coordination of welfare activity is largely along a series of hierarchical or vertical lines from national or central bodies down to the local level. Each of the four state departments with major social welfare responsibility (Social Welfare and Pensions, Coloured Affairs, Indian Affairs, and Bantu Administration and Development) has a coordinating function, as does the National Welfare Board.

The National Welfare Board is a statutory body that is advisory to the Minister of Social Welfare and Pensions, who appoints the majority of its members from persons nominated by registered welfare organizations, professional associations of social workers, and institutions of higher education which train social workers. The functions of the board as laid down in the National Welfare Act, No. 79 of 1965, are as follows:

(a) to advise the Minister [of Social Welfare and Pensions] in regard to matters affecting social care or arising out of the operation of the National Welfare Act;

(b) to keep in touch and consult with the Department of Social Welfare and Pensions in regard to welfare matters arising out of the operation of the National Welfare Act or affecting the interests of registered welfare organizations;

(c) to afford guidance and exercise control over the activities of commissions and regional welfare boards;

(d) to regulate the registration of welfare organizations;

(e) to regulate the registration of social workers;

(f) to promote and encourage coordination of the activities of registered welfare organizations;

(g) to provide information and guidance in connection with matters relating to social care.

The commissions referred to in section (c) above are four statutory commissions responsible to the National Welfare Board, commissions which deal with the specified areas of welfare organizations, social work, family life, and welfare planning. The regional welfare boards referred to in the same section are established in each region of the republic in which the Department of Social Welfare and Pensions has a regional office. Regional welfare boards carry out the work of the National Welfare Board in their areas of operation and are concerned with planning and promoting the coordination of social welfare services in their regions. Regional welfare boards have difficulty in fully meeting their responsibilities for many reasons, including a lack of enforcement powers, the heterogeneity and geographical vastness of some regions, a limited number of board meetings per annum, insufficient staff to service boards, and the competitive welfare environment that is engendered by fragmentation. The structure and functioning of regional welfare boards is currently under examination, and changes are expected in the near future.

Although individually autonomous, community-sponsored welfare organizations operating in specific fields have shown a pattern of affiliating together at the national or provincial level. Thus, for example, most community agencies in the field of alcoholism and drug dependency are affiliated with the South African National Council on Alcoholism and Drug Dependency, itself a nationally registered welfare organization with coordinating functions within its specialized area of operation. There are 23 such nationally or provincially registered welfare organizations in existence in the republic, their creation stimulated by the government practice of subsidizing only those community-sponsored organizations which are affiliated with a national or provincial body.

At the local level, nonstatutory coordinating bodies exist in some cities. One example is the Johannesburg Coordinating Council of Registered Welfare Organizations, with which less than half of the registered welfare organizations in the city are affiliated. In such other cities as Cape Town, Durban, Port Elizabeth, and Pietermaritzburg, a measure of indirect coordination is achieved through the activities of local community chests.

Overlapping and Overlooking. In addition to the erosion of social welfare resources through duplication of services for various groups with its concomitant extra expenditure, fragmentation of welfare responsibility may have resulted in the "overlooking" of human needs and the overlooking of gaps in existing services. Two examples may serve to substantiate this statement.

In the case of public housing schemes (which are the joint responsibility of the state Department of Community Development and local authorities and in

SOUTH AFRICA [85]

which the Department of Social Welfare and Pensions is not directly involved), professional social work and social welfare services are not routinely included in the resettling of large communities in new townships. Bearing in mind that 117,869 Coloured, Indian, and White *families* have been, or have to be, compulsorily relocated in terms of Group Areas legislation (Horrell and Hodgson, 1976), the absence of social workers and systematically planned social welfare programs in resettlement projects can be considered a serious lack. Another instance of overlooking concerns the educational system. Taking the White group as an example, the school system for White children is organized by the provincial authorities, whereas the delivery of social welfare services to children and families is the function of the state and community-sponsored agencies. There are thus no school social workers employed in public schools for Whites. Education for Whites is free and compulsory from the age of 6 or 7 until age 16 years. Education for Black children is neither compulsory nor free. "When central State control of Bantu education was introduced in 1955 . . . the first priority of the department was . . . to ensure that every child was placed within reach of a school so that he or she could benefit from at least four years' schooling . . . [but] the target has not yet been attained" (South Africa, 1974:765).

In 1970, 1,013 Black senior secondary pupils qualified to go to university. This represented about 0.007% of the total Black population of approximately 15 million at that time. By 1972, the number had increased to 1,800 (South Africa, 1974:765).

Planning. In all fields of social welfare activity, and particularly in those fields where the private sector has special responsibility, there is a shortage of comprehensive middle-and-long-term planning based upon objective research findings. In part, this may be due to gaps in data-collecting machinery (for example, for establishing the extent of physical disability in the republic) or to available data not being shared with nongovernmental agencies, as occurred, for example, in February 1976, when the Minister of Bantu Administration and Development told Parliament that he refused to publish the findings of a government inquiry into the migratory labor system on the grounds that the report was considered to be a confidential departmental working document for official consumption only. In part, the shortage of comprehensive middle-and -long-term planning may also be due to South Africa's position as a partly developed and partly underdeveloped country, facing the challenges of urbanization, industrialization, and westernization and facing a consequent demand for organized social welfare services that cannot be fully met by existing welfare programs. An illustration from the field of child and family welfare is the statement by the South African National Council for Child and Family Welfare that community-sponsored organizations associated with it can cope with only one-third of those persons requiring services (*Rand Daily Mail,* July 19, 1971). The emphasis in the organization of social welfare services is therefore upon programs to meet immediate need.

Control of Social Welfare Enterprises. As a result of historical and traditional factors, the control of both state and community-sponsored welfare agencies tends to be mainly in the hands of middle-class White people. A large proportion of clients, however, tend to be persons from the lower socioeconomic groups or from the Black groups, and there thus exists a dichotomy between the controllers of services and the consumers. Such a situation is conducive to developing a lag between services that are required and those that are available, as well as to restricting the potential power of consumers as instigators of change in welfare organizations and programs.

Nature of Services Delivered. Within South Africa's social welfare system there is, for historical and practical reasons, a consistent emphasis upon therapeutic services to ameliorate problems already in existence (such as child neglect, disability, alcoholism, and so forth). Thus, for example, child and family welfare programs concentrate upon the rehabilitation of families already in distress, rather than upon family life education and programs to enhance the quality of family living; mental health organizations focus upon care and recovery of those people who are mentally ill, rather than upon promoting sound mental health in the community; and agencies concerned with the well-being of the aged channel most of their resources into therapeutic and supportive services for those who are already old, rather than into retirement preparation programs and other facilities to equip people to make the most of their later years.

Perhaps because of the predominant therapeutic orientation of the republic's welfare system, the major helping method used is that of social casework. Social group work has only recently emerged as a common means of rendering service, and community organization is relatively neglected. In recent years, however, a number of welfare and allied organizations which do not follow an exclusively therapeutic orientation have come into being in urban areas. Some of these agencies have been sponsored by universities or university-based groups, and examples include SHAWCO (of the University of Cape Town), WITSCO (of the University of the Witwatersrand, Johannesburg) and the Chatsworth Community and Research Project (of the University of Durban-Westville, in Natal). In rural areas, there has been a growth of community development projects, often with state support.

Location of Services. On a national basis, the majority of social welfare services, especially those of a sophisticated and specialized nature catering to a White clientele, are located in or near towns and cities. Most welfare services are office-based, without priority programs to reach out toward individuals and groups at risk. Office-based services in urban settings are frequently located in central city areas that are inconvenient to consumers, particularly to Black groups who have often been compulsorily relocated in outlying areas of cities, but a trend can be observed in some agencies where offices are being decentralized to outlying townships.

As stated earlier, an unusual feature of the South African welfare system is that institutional services for Black people are discouraged in the large urban centers because these are located in areas officially designated as "White." Those services which do exist are generally sited in the rural Black homelands. Grek reported in 1975 that there were four homes for aged Africans accommodating a total of approximately 197 persons situation in "White" areas but that these were gradually to disappear. A total of 2,566 persons were accommodated in 22 institutions in the homelands according to the latest information at that time (Grek, 1975:7). Statistics published in 1976 indicated that one small home for aged Black people has been established in Soweto, Johannesburg's Black satellite city of an estimated one million inhabitants, but that only 15 homes for old people are available in the homelands (Horrell and Hodgson, 1976).

Differential Services. In South Africa's fragmented welfare system, where access to particular services is often determined by the potential client's population group, imbalances exist in the quantity and quality of welfare resources available to members of the country's different racial communities. In terms of quantity of service, members of the White group generally have access to a more comprehensive and sophisticated range of services. To take mental health care in Johannesburg as an example, Black outpatients have access to two mental health facilities, while White outpatients have access to four. In a 1972 analysis of the activities of the major community-sponsored mental health agency in Johannesburg, it was found that although Black clients outnumbered Whites, Whites accounted for 86% of all attendances at the agency for service and for 75% of all home visits by agency personnel. A clear example of differential quality of service exists in the republic's social security provisions, where the pensions paid to Whites, Coloureds and Indians, and Blacks are in the approximate ratio of 4 : 2 : 1.

Financing of Welfare Programs

Following the republic's declared policy of joint state and community responsibility for the provision of social welfare programs, the funding for welfare enterprises comes from both government and community sources. The state is the major source of finance. According to figures published by the Receiver of Revenue in 1976, 28.5% of each tax rand is spent on social services, which includes expenditures on health, pensions, food subsidies, and welfare and community services. This expenditure compares with expenditure on security services of 23.87%, education 18.62%, economic services 14.6%, general administration 6.8%, and public debt 7.1%. In the most recent comprehensive study of social care services in South Africa, Potgieter (1973) reported that annual state expenditure by the 12 state departments concerned with health, welfare, and educational services totaled R190,864,846. This represents about 5% of the country's budget, which in 1973 was R3,461 million. During the same year welfare organizations in the private sector raised R15,657,089 from community sources, and in addition received state subsidies totaling

R11,276,995. The latter sum included subsidization in respect of social workers salaries in approved posts; the erection and furnishing of institutions, clubs, and service centers; the running costs of some services; and making per capita grants to organizations such as homes for the chronically ill, the aged, and children. Over the last decade there has been a steady increase in state subsidy to the private sector, although state subsidization in the social welfare field remains less than in other comparable fields of human welfare. Thus, for example, there is an increase of 3.5% per annum in state subsidization for new social workers posts, while teachers posts increase at the rate of 4.8% per annum (Winckler, 1969).

Despite state assistance to the private sector, community-sponsored welfare agencies in all fields experience difficulty in raising adequate funds for their operating expenses, and the issue of fund raising from community sources is currently under investigation by a government-appointed commission of enquiry.

SOCIAL WELFARE RESEARCH

Social research in South Africa is still on a fairly limited scale relative to Britain and the United States (Lever, 1975:41). The major emphasis in South African research has traditionally been in the physical and natural sciences. In 1971, a total of approximately R45 million was spent on research, of which about R29 million was spent by the state and the remainder by industry. Of this, a little over 1% was allocated to the social sciences (Welsh, 1975:19).

The Human Sciences Research Council was established in 1968 as a statutory body and in 1969 took over the functions of the National Bureau of Educational and Social Research (established 40 years earlier) and of the National Council for Social Research. The HSRC is governed by a council appointed by the Minister of National Education and consisting of individuals "who have distinguished themselves in the field of the human sciences and who have special qualifications in relation to some aspect of the functions of the Council" (South Africa, 1974:781). The functions of the council are as follows: to undertake, promote and coordinate research in the human sciences, to advise the government and other bodies on the utilization of research findings, and to disseminate information on the human sciences. As a body it contains 10 research institutes which actually conduct or promote research, and in addition it makes research and publication grants to individual scholars or to academic departments in universities. In 1970-1971, a total of R325,000 was disbursed on research grants which contributed to the financing of research on social welfare conducted by students in departments of social work in the various universities throughout the republic. The results of this research are to be found in published and unpublished dissertations and theses presented for master's degrees and doctorates. Some of these projects are summarized for publication in *Humanitas,* a journal published by the Human Sciences Research Council itself.

In an analysis of 75 social work research projects conducted in South Africa between 1941 and 1963, Potgieter (1967) found that the vast majority centered on applied research or, to use Greenwood's term, operational social work research. Only eight studies could be classified as basic social work research, and of these only one appeared to contribute to measurement theory in social work.

From the time that the state assumed responsibility for aspects of social welfare in 1937, research has formed part of its activities (Winckler, 1965). In 1962, the Department of Social Welfare and Pensions established a special research division which publishes research material in its Research and Information Series. More than 65 titles were issued in this series in the first 10 years of its existence. Most of the research conducted relates to services available or required. Research on social welfare topics is also conducted by national councils of welfare organizations and by autonomous bodies with a research interest. In 1972, for example, the South African National Council for Child Welfare established the Andries Stulting Research Division as part of its Research and Information Service. Institutions such as the South African Institute of Race Relations, the African Institute of South Africa, and the Abe Bailey Institute of Interracial Studies at the University of Cape Town are active in research on more general topics relating to social welfare in South Africa.

Social research in South Africa can be complicated by legal issues. For example, White persons cannot enter Black areas without government permits whether for research or other purposes, and one scholar, Dr. B. van Niekerk, has been prosecuted for publishing his research into the possible relationship between judicial behavior and racial attitudes in the republic.

Information on a variety of aspects of social work and social welfare is to be found in two journals published in South Africa: *Social Work—Maatskaplike Werk* is a bilingual professional journal for social workers published quarterly in close association with the University of Stellenbosch, and *Social Welfare and Pensions—Volkswelsyn and Pensione* is published biannually by the Department of Social Welfare and Pensions.

SOCIAL WELFARE MANPOWER: THE SOCIAL WORK PROFESSION

Although volunteers are important in the social welfare system in South Africa, they operate mainly in an administrative capacity, and it is the social work profession which plays the major role in the delivery of service to consumers. The recognition of the desirability of this situation originated with the Carnegie Commission of Inquiry into the Poor White Problem in the early thirties and has continued to grow since that time.

Education for Social Work

The first formal social work training in South Africa was a diploma course offered by the University of Cape Town in 1924, and since then the development of social work education has occurred in three distinct stages (Muller, 1968). The initial stage was from 1924 to 1939, during which time seven universities established undergraduate social work courses of either three or four years in duration. This growth was stimulated by such factors as approaches from Women's Organizations, the Carnegie Commission of Enquiry into the Poor White Problem of 1932, and the scheme introduced by the newly formed Department of Social Welfare in 1938, whereby subsidies were paid from state funds to community and church-sponsored welfare organizations that employed trained social workers. By the end of the period, a liaison body, the South African Inter-University Committee on Social Studies, had been formed, comprising representatives from training institutions offering courses in "social studies." The second stage, from 1940 to 1960, has been termed a period of consolidation. Significant events during this time include the 1944 National Conference on the postwar planning of social work, where it was suggested that social workers should have a generic, undergraduate training encompassing both theory and practical work. During the third stage, which consists of the 1960s and early 1970s, five new university colleges were created by state initiative, all of them offering social work training to Black people. In 1965, the new National Welfare Act was promulgated which made provision for a Social Work Commission.

The latter period is significant for three developments which affected social work education in South Africa. First, there was state intervention in establishing separate training institutions for Black higher education, accompanied by legislation which imposed racial criteria for admission into those universities that had previously offered education to students of all races. Thus "open" universities, such as the Universities of Cape Town, Natal, and the Witwatersrand, which had formerly admitted social work students without regard to race, were restricted to accepting White students only. Second, regulations made in terms of the National Welfare ACt, No. 79 of 1965, stipulated the exact nature of courses which students must complete in order to become eligible for registration as social workers, and some degree of national uniformity in the education of social workers was thus ensured. In terms of the act, registration as social workers may be permitted to those persons who have

> satisfied all requirements for a Bachelor's Degree or for a diploma of any University or College in the Republic after pursuing a course of study for that degree or diploma of not less than three years, which included not less than 3 courses in social work and either not less than 3 courses in sociology and not less than 2 courses in psychology, or not less than 3 courses in psychology and not less than 2 courses in sociology. [The courses referred to are each of one year's duration.] [*Government Gazette*, Notice R1249, 1970]

Third, the establishment of a statutory Social Work Commission, charged among other things with responsibility for the development of standards for academic social work qualifications, may have considerable implications for social work education in the future, particularly if the commission should move in the direction of "accrediting" individual social work courses.

At the present time, 16 residential training centers in South Africa offer 25 different undergraduate programs that are recognized for the purpose of statutory registration as a social worker: 15 are first degree courses, while 10 are at the undergraduate diploma level; 20 are three years in length, and 5 are of four years duration. In addition, the University of South Africa (a nonresidential institution operating through the medium of correspondence studies) also offers courses leading to recognized social work qualifications. All undergraduate social work courses in the republic include a study of social work theory and associated field instruction.

At the commencement of the 1975 academic year, an estimated 3,000 persons were registered for undergraduate social work courses at South African training centers. Research studies have shown a regular increase in the number of persons who register for courses of social work study, although the bulk of students remain White. For example, of the 1,237 persons who registered for first-year social work courses at residential training centers in 1975, 75% were White, 17% African, and 8% were either of mixed blood or Indian extraction (McKendrick, 1975). South African universities also provide postgraduate social work qualifications, but entry into such programs of study is limited to those persons who have already completed the basic undergraduate training in social work. Those universities with three-year undergraduate degrees normally offer an honors course (or sometimes a graduate diploma course), the content of which may be either advanced studies in generic social work theory and practice or concentrated studies in a particular field of practice (for example, medical social work). All universities provide facilities for postgraduate study and research in social work at the master's degree and doctoral levels.

The Professionalization of Social Work:
Subsidization, Registration, and Conditions of Practice

In recent years, a number of developments have contributed to the increasing professionalization of social work in South Africa. As well as subsidizing posts of social workers in voluntary welfare organizations from the time of its inception in 1937, the Department of Social Welfare granted professional status to social workers in its own employ in 1955, thereby enhancing the professional status of social work in the country as a whole. The department's subsidy scheme has continually grown in scope. In 1971, the number of subsidized posts was 685, and the total amount of subsidy increased almost 200% from R580,000 in 1964-1965 to R1,700,000 in 1971-1972. The scheme has also been extended to include certain senior posts, thereby enabling agencies to enhance the quality of their professional work (Winckler, 1972:237).

A major breakthrough in the professionalization of social work occurred in

1965 with the passing of the National Welfare Act, which replaced the Welfare Organization Act of 1947. As stated above, this act provides for a National Welfare Board with nine regional boards and four commissions. The Social Work Commission was empowered to register social workers, and the title "registered social worker" is protected.

In 1969, there were about 1,200 practicing social workers, with only a small percentage of them non-White (Theron, 1972:184). Up to February 1972, a total of 1,581 social workers had been registered. Of the 466 registered between July 1972 and June 1973, 394 were White, 34 Coloured, 13 Indian, and 25 African (Social Work-Maatskaplike Werk, 1974:96). Latest figures issued in February 1976 revealed there were 3,690 registered social workers of all races in the republic.

At the present time, the private practice of social work is not widespread although there are a few private practitioners in the larger cities. White social workers continue to render service to Black clients in certain settings, but Black social workers are not permitted to engage in service delivery to White clients.

Government policy in the republic decrees differential salary scales for professional people based on racial identity. This applies to doctors, nurses, and teachers, as well as social workers. In August 1974, the salary scales for social workers were as follows (Ratoff and Ratoff, 1975:82):

White Social Workers	R3,840 to R5,460 (4-year degree)
	R3,480 to R5,100 (3-year degree)
Coloured and Indian	R2,700 to R3,600
Black Social Workers	R2,400 to R3,600

In January 1975, the Department of Social Welfare appointed a committee of inquiry into separate legislation for the social work profession under the chairmanship of Dr. A.J. Auret, chairman of the Social Work Commission. This committee will report on matters such as the registration of social workers, disciplinary action against social workers, the accreditation of training institutions, and the financial implications of its recommendations.

Professional Organizations

In considering the professional status of social work, the question of the professional organization of social workers is of importance. In this connection too the heterogeneity of South African society is a major factor, and the situation is a complex one. Until recently, there were three professional associations in the country: the White Social Workers Association of South Africa, the South African Black Social Workers Association, and an organization for Coloured social workers, formerly called the Social Workers League of the Western Cape and now known as the Africa South Social Workers Association. Indian social workers have not formed a separate association.

The first organization was formed in 1951 as a national body uniting a number of independent professional organizations. Some of these might have had nonracial membership provisions, but the national organization restricted its memberships to White persons only and consequently in 1970 changed its name from the Social Workers Association of South Africa by adding the adjective "White" to its title. In 1972, the present writers initiated a proposal to open membership of this association to all social workers irrespective of race, but this was defeated in a national vote (Hare, 1972:205).

The second body listed above was first formed in 1946 and entitled the South African Non-European Social Workers' Association. In 1968, it became the South African Black Social Workers' Association (SABSWA). In a personal communication to the writers, the national president, Mr. Michael Rantho, stated in 1976 that he hoped that his organization would not be viewed as supporting separation and division among people but rather as aiming at enabling Black social workers to raise their level of consciousness of their own identity and increase their sense of solidarity. Both Black and White associations have adopted codes of ethics affirming social work values.

To meet the requirements of membership of the International Federation of Social Workers (IFSW), the three associations in South Africa in 1973 formed a Coordinating Council for the Professional Associations of Social Workers in South Africa. This council, which succeeded an earlier Liaison Committee and Coordinating Agency, consisted of about three representatives from each organization and met once or twice a year. In September 1974, the South African Black Social Workers' Association withdrew from the Coordinating Council. Its motion noted that SABSWA had been formed so that Black social workers could close their ranks and that its membership in the council was a contradiction in terms; further, that "black social workers can never and will never have the same opportunities, luxuries and powers like the white social workers" and "it is sheer pretense and artificiality to form such a Coordinating Council as it is clearly calculated at using S.A.B.S.W.A. as a stepping stone by white social workers to escalate into the international arena." The association therefore resolved to notify IFSW of its action, pointing out that the SABSWA "represents the majority of the racial population groups in South Africa" and requesting observer status at IFSW meetings. In terms of the IFSW constitution, South Africa would have to withdraw its membership from the international organization should there fail to be a coordinating council representing all social workers' associations in the country. Possibly in order to forestall this, the Africa South Association, formerly for Coloured social workers only, has recently altered its constitution to make social workers of all population groups eligible for membership, and one or two branches of the White association have disbanded with the intention of reconstituting themselves as multiracial organizations.

CONCLUSION

What of the years ahead? Will the policy of multinational development prove to be a viable solution to meeting South Africa's human needs in the broadest sense? Or is it a mere facade for inequality which under the impact of massive social change in neighboring states will bring turmoil and strife to the republic? The complexities of South African society make it difficult to fathom the future.

In spite of the twin ills of inflation and recession, which South African presently shares with other industrialized countries of the West, she also faces the challenges of growth which are found in Third World countries. Economic and social development is a fact of the present in South Africa. On the welfare scene there are forces promoting cooperation and collaboration as well as divisive forces. The University of the Witwatersrand in Johannesburg, for example, has ambitious plans for the postgraduate education of social workers of all population groups and for services to the "Black" universities to enable them to enrich the curricula that they offer social work students. Yet, South Africa's position in international social work organizations is uncertain because of her racial preoccupations.

The future of South African social welfare is inextricably bound up with the socio-political future of the country as a whole, and *that* only time can divine. One can but hope that growth and change can continue unimpeded by major civil disorder, which aggravates human need and disrupts the delivery of service, and can be facilitated by flexibility in social attitudes on the part of those who wield political power.

REFERENCES

ARONSTAM, S.M. (1969). "Jewish welfare work in South Africa." Social Work-Maatskaplike Werk, 5(1):3-6.

BARRATT, I. (1975). A guide to social pensions. Johannesburg: South African Institute of Race Relations.

BOPAPE, M. (1967). "Training of social work students to serve the needs of a changing South African Bantu society." Social Work-Maatskaplike Werk, 3(1):24-27.

BOTHA, M.C. (1964). "Ons Stedelike Bantoebeleid Teen die Agtergrond van ons Landbeleid." Journal of Racial Affairs, 15:17.

BRUMMER, F. (1964). The structure and policy of welfare services in South Africa with particular reference to the role of the state. Pretoria: Government Printer.

——— (1968). "Milestones in the development of social welfare policy in South Africa." Unpublished paper, Johannesburg Coordinating Council of Registered Social Welfare Organizations.

——— (1972). A changing face of social welfare. Johannesburg: Witwatersrand University Press.

CARE (1968). "Welfare services for South Africa's peoples." Pretoria: Department of Information.

De KIEWIET, C.W. (1941). A history of South Africa: Social and economic. London: Oxford University Press.

De KOCK, W.J. (1971). History of South Africa. Pretoria: Department of Information.

De VILLIERS, R. (1971). "Afrikaner nationalism." Pp. 365-423 in M. Wilson and L. Thompson (eds.), The Oxford history of South Africa (vol. 2). London: Oxford University Press.

De VOS, A.S. (1972). "Maatskaplikewerk–Navorsing in Suid-Afrika–'n Beknopte Oorsig." Social Work-Maatskaplike Werk 8(4):255-262.

GREK, E. (1975). "Homes for the aged." Race Relations News, 37(5):7.

HARE, I.R. (1972). "Face to face communication needed." Social Work-Maatskaplike Werk, 8(3):205.

HELLMANN, E. (1973). "Soweto." Optima, 23(1):14-21.

HORRELL, M., and HODGSON, T. (1976). A survey of race relations in South Africa, 1975. Johannesburg: South African Institute of Race Relations.

HORRELL, M., HORNER, D., and HUDSON, J. (1975). A survey of race relations in South Africa, 1974. Johannesburg: South African Institute of Race Relations.

Income Tax Information Brochure (1976). Pretoria: Government Printer (IT/38/5).

LEVER, H. (1975). "Some problems in race relations research in South Africa." Social Dynamics, 1(1):31-44.

MAQASHALALA, T.N.V. (1975). "The changing role of social workers in a changing society." Social Work-Maatskaplike Werk, 11(3):151-157.

McKENDRICK, B.W. (1975). "The first year as basis for social work training." Social Work-Maatskaplike Werk, 11(3):129-134.

MULLER, A. (1968). "An historical review of university education for social work in South Africa." Social Work-Maatskaplike Werk, 4(1):3-10.

POTGIETER, M.C. (1967). "Die Taak van die Maatskaplike Werker ten Opsigte van Navorsing." Social Work-Maatskaplike Werk, 3(4):163-171.

––– (1973). "Maatskaplike Sorg in Suid Afrika." Stellenbosch: Universiteituitgewers-en-Boekhandelaars.

RATOFF, P., and RATOFF, L. (1975). "Social work in South Africa." Social Work Today, 6(3):80-82.

SCHREIER, A. (1974). A guide to health and social services in the Johannesburg area. Johannesburg: University of the Witwatersrand.

Social Work-Maatskaplike Werk (1973). "South Africa moves into staggering housing problems." 9(1):20-21.

––– (1974). "Die Registrasie van maatskaplike Werkers." 2(2):96-98.

South Africa (1974). Official yearbook of the Republic of South Africa, 1974. Pretoria: Department of Information.

South Africa, Department of Bantu Administration and Development (1975). Report for the period 1 April 1973 to 31 March 1974. Pretoria: Government Printer.

South Africa, Department of Information (1971). This is South Africa. Pretoria: Government Printer.

South Africa, Department of Social Welfare and Pensions (1970). Report for the period 1966-1970. Pretoria: Government Printer.

––– (1973). Report for the period 1971-1972. Pretoria: Government Printer.

SPROCAS Economics Commission (1972). "Report: Power, privilege and poverty." Johannesburg: SPROCAS 1972.

THERON, E.T. (1972). "The changing welfare scene in southern Africa and the contribution of social workers." Social Work-Maatskaplike Werk, 8(3):184-188.

WELSH, D. (1971). "The growth of towns." Pp. 172-243 in M. Wilson and L. Thompson (eds.), The Oxford history of South Africa (vol. 2). London: Oxford University Press.

––– (1975). "Social research in a divided society: The case of South Africa." Social Dynamics, 1(1):19-30.

WILSON, F. (1972). Migrant labour in South Africa. Johannesburg: South African Council of Churches and Sprocas.

WILSON, M., and THOMPSON, L. (eds., 1969, 1971). The Oxford history of South Africa (2 vols.). London: Oxford University Press.
WINCKLER, A.T. (1965). "Social work research as a state activity." Social Work-Maatskaplike Werk, 1(2):35-41.
——— (1969). "Recruiting social workers." Journal of the Department of Social Welfare and Pensions, June, pp. 2-7.
——— (1972). "Social work policy today." Social Work-Maatskaplike Werk, 8(4):233-237.

5

THE AUSTRALIAN WELFARE STATE: GENERAL PROGRAMS AND PROGRAMS FOR MIGRANTS AND ABORIGINES

THOMAS BRENNAN

A HISTORICAL REVIEW[1]

Social welfare services began soon after settlement in each of the six states, which originally started as separate colonies and remained separate until federation in 1901. By the time of federation, state and voluntary services had developed in the fields of health, the aged, children's services, correctional services, relief of the poor, and education. State and voluntary agencies worked in cooperation, and there was a ready exchange of information and of personnel on boards and committees.

For the first 40 years of its existence, activities of the commonwealth (i.e., federal) government[2] were restricted in the welfare field to the provision of old-age and invalid pensions and maternity allowances, which, incidentally, like New Zealand's, were financed out of general revenue rather than out of insurance or through subsidies to Friendly Societies. Up to the period of the Second World War this pattern of services remained unchanged. From 1941, however, commonwealth responsibility for cash benefits was extended into the fields of child endowment, widows' pensions, unemployment insurance, and pharmaceutical and medical benefits. During this period, the commonwealth was responsible for financial support, while the states and voluntary agencies were responsible for personal services.

A very limited involvement of the commonwealth in providing personal services was established in 1941 with a scheme for vocational training of invalid pensioners. At the same time the first social worker was employed in the commonwealth service. Since the late 1940s and 1950s, however, social work services to individuals and families have developed in the commonwealth departments of social services, which carry out these services within the boundaries of the states as well as within the commonwealth territories, which it governs directly. The earlier clear-cut division between the functions of commonwealth and state no longer exist.

Until 1954, it was mainly the state governments which subsidized voluntary agencies directly. The earliest aid went toward building homes for the aged. Later, direct subsidies, usually on a matching basis, were extended for welfare services to migrants and to the aged and for agencies providing marriage counseling, etc.

During the early period of settlement, local government paid little attention to matters of welfare. This has been explained partly by the pattern of settlement, which concentrated populations in the capital cities of each state, a pattern which still holds. The other part of the explanation probably is the absence of any traditional magisterial class caring for the needy, which might have led localizing communities to take responsibility (Davies and Encel, 1965). Over the last decade, however, local authorities, supported by grants from both state and commonwealth governments, have become increasingly involved in providing welfare services to youth, the aged, and migrants.

Since the end of World War II, workers have garnered many so-called "fringe benefits," many of which are a part of social welfare and are in fact financed partly out of public funds via tax concessions. Private enterprise has provided welfare services directly, rather than incidentally, in the form of such fringe benefits as the provision of nursing homes for the aged, and these have been subsidized by public funds.

More generally, although most individuals who draw cash benefits draw them directly from an agency of the federal government, many of these people, along with others not receiving cash benefits, will also be receiving personal services from voluntary agencies, local or state government, or private enterprise. These bodies might be operating and deliverying services directly from their own funds, or they may be operating on funds and delegated authority passed from one level of government to another or from the public to the private sector.

In August 1972, an independent Commission of Inquiry into Poverty was appointed to investigate the extent of poverty in Australia and the special categories of persons or localities affected and to make recommendations for improvements. The newly elected Labour government in February 1973 extended both the terms of the Commission and its membership. Since then the Commission has sponsored or commissioned a number of research projects covering a wide range of subject areas, including the organization and effectiveness of welfare services, community studies, fatherless families, intact families on low means, homeless men, the aged, the disabled, aborigines, migrants, the rural poor, housing, legal aspects of poverty, education and poverty, health services and poverty, and the poor as consumers. Hundreds of reports will eventually be made, and these, when considered along with the results of the commission's own studies, will make the overall report the most comprehensive study of poverty ever undertaken in Australia. Publication of the main reports began toward the end of 1975.

So far, the chief recommendations of the commission include the standardization of benefits and pensions for many kinds of recipients who currently are dealt with by piecemeal schemes and the substitution of cash for many fringe benefits. The main idea behind these recommendations is obviously that of the guaranteed income. The same general principle appears to be behind its recommendations on housing; i.e., it rejects schemes for comprehensive rent control in favor of information and financial measures to allow more people to buy their own homes. On welfare services they recommend generous subsidies to a wide variety of self-help groups to enable formal structures to build on the existing informal networks of help. This in turn would favor a community-based and family-oriented service such as the Seebohm Report recommended for Britain. But even here they argue for poor people it "is more efficient to provide them with money rather than with a complex range of means-tested services. Our aim is to get right away from the notion that home help, for instance, is a charity to be doled out sparingly to poor and needy people. We also want to avoid the provision of separate services for low income people, as this leads to services that are stigmatized and often inferior." Many will see the sentence just quoted as the most significant in all the thousands of pages which the commission will produce and judge that their recommendations will be very much more about redistribution of income than about welfare services.

In addition to reviewing these recommendations, the government has set in operation a number of steps to complete the development of the welfare state in Australia. At the beginning of 1973 it announced its intention of carrying through developments in four particular areas: (1) national health insurance and health services, (2) a national compensation and rehabilitation scheme, (3) a national superannuation scheme, and (4) the Australian Assistance Plan. Although none of these schemes is yet fully in operation, they comprise the important units in what is likely to be the pattern for the future. They are discussed in more detail in the final section on "Prospects and Plans."

METHODS OF PROVISION

One important descriptive category often used in discussing welfare provision in different countries is the method (sometimes referred to as the strategy) of provision, whether the main provision is by universal benefit, by self-insurance, by grants of assistance to those in need, or by some mixture of the three. All these methods are employed in the Australian System in providing benefits for different populations. Below is a description of the most important items in the whole list of welfare services.

Child Endowment and Maternity Allowance

These two benefits, which constitute a large proportion of commonwealth government's spending, are provided universally and without regard to the means of the applicant. The maternity allowance is payable as a single payment ($30-$35 in 1974), depending on the number of children, to help meet birth expenses over and above those payable under the health scheme, i.e., the subsidized benefits and medical benefits scheme.

The child endowment (which, next to old-age and invalid pensions, represents the largest single item of expenditure out of the National Welfare Fund) is also provided universally at rates which range from 50 cents per week for a single child to $11.00 per week for six children, with higher rates for seven or more children. In addition, a student allowance is payable for children attending school full-time up to 21 years of age.

Old-Age, Invalid, and Widows Pensions;
Unemployment and Sickness Benefits

All the above benefits are paid after a means test. For unemployment and sickness benefits, the test centers on income, but in the case of pensions it takes account also of the applicant's property. Australia is one of the few countries to retain a means test restricting availability of pensions and other cash benefits. One reason for this is that Australia has had no experience with the poor law or of the connotations associated elsewhere with the "means test." The other reason is that the standards are fairly generous. A couple on old-age pensions, for example, can own a car and a house worth about $20,000, have an income more than three-quarters of the pension rate, and still receive the full amount of the pension. They can have assets or an income about three times the pension rate before they lose the right altogether to some part of the pension. Eligibility for some part of the pension also makes an applicant eligible for a number of fringe benefits, such as the pensioner medical service, travel concessions, and reduction in telephone charges. The main argument for the means test is, of course, that assistance should be given where it is most needed. Acceptance of the opposite argument, that people should not be penalized for being thrifty, has resulted in the "test" becoming more lenient. Present opinion seems to be in favor of further relaxation. Up until recently, the means test applied to pensioners under 75 years old. The age has now been reduced to 70. Total abolition of the means test, if it takes place, will likely be done by progressively lowering the age of application.

National Health Service

The national health service has three main parts: a general system of subsidizing the contributions of citizens enrolled in voluntary health organizations, which insure them against the major costs of medical and hospital treatment; a system which provides a wide variety of medicines and drugs at a nominal cost ($1.00 per item in 1975); and a pensioner service which provides free general practitioner service to pensioners and their dependents. The doctors are paid on a fee-for-service basis directly by the Australian government.

Under the medical benefits scheme, the government subsidy amounts to roughly a third of each bill; the private insurance fund pays another third; and the contributor has to pay the remaining third in cash. This latter expenditure and the cost of taking out the insurance are tax deductible. In recent years there have been big changes in medical charges, followed by necessary increases in contribution and benefit rates. The subsidies have not kept pace, however, and the three-way formula is a description more of how the scheme should work than of how it does work.

Under the hospital benefits scheme, the Australian government pays a small portion of the hospital fee, whether or not the patient belongs to a private insurance fund. If he *is* insured, the government provides a further subsidy, which, together with the payments from the insurance fund, is intended to cover the full cost of hospital care. Contributors can insure themselves for one of three grades of accommodation at different contribution rates.

The insurance premiums of families whose gross income in near the minimum wage are paid by the government, upon application. Those families which are slightly better off are entitled to benefits at a reduced subscription rate.

The pharmaceutical benefits scheme was originally started to allow doctors to prescribe expensive "life-saving drugs" free of charge to the patient. As it turned out, however, these drugs were often prescribed simply because they were free, when some less expensive alternative, which would have had to be charged to the patient, might have been used. In 1959, therefore, the list was greatly extended to allow doctors to prescribe the cheaper drugs, and the patient was charged a moderate sum. Since then, the cost of the scheme has increased steadily until now it costs more than all the hospital benefits schemes together and as much as the medical benefits scheme.

THE PROVISION OF WELFARE SERVICES FOR MIGRANTS

In the last 25 years, permanent arrivals in Australia have exceeded departures by more than two million people. For the most part, this has been the result of policies designed to encourage large-scale migration. Migration is a complex phenomenon and often results in social and economic stresses not experienced to the same degree by members of the dominant culture. For this reason, special services must be provided to compensate for the disadvantages suffered by migrants.

Types of Services

Education. In the area of education, assistance is mainly in the form of language instruction. Since 1946, approximately 47% of new arrivals have not been able to speak English. (Such instruction is also available to non-English speaking migrants already established in Australia.)

Preembarkation language programs exist in many countries of origin, and language instruction is also provided on all regular migrant vessels. In Australia there are a wide range of course, including full-time intensive and accelerated courses, part-time courses, correspondence lessons, and radio and television broadcasts. Special courses are conducted for migrant workers in industries, and the Home Tutor Scheme provides individual tuition for women migrants in their homes. All these classes are available free of charge to migrants over the school-leaving age. Migrants who qualify for the full-time courses receive a living allowance, and for most of the other courses, basic textbooks, tapes, and other items are provided free of charge or at reduced rates.

In contrast to the early establishment of English classes for adult migrants, teaching English to immigrant children was completely ignored until the mid-1960s. Special teachers now provide English instruction, and the arrangements may be in the form of full-time intensive instruction for one or two terms or withdrawal of children from their normal lessons two or three times a day. A 1972 survey of 63 schools in Melbourne revealed that only one-third of the migrant children assessed as in need of special instruction were attending special English classes. Approximately 40% of the children attending special classes were not receiving sufficient instruction (Australian Parliament, 1973b).

Migrant education centers have recently opened in the major capital cities and these provide a focal point of reference and administration for migrant education programs in each state and a point of social contact for migrants.

Health. The subsidized Health Benefits Plan (to avoid the necessity of a "waiting period") assists newly arrived migrants with the cost of health insurance. Under this scheme, migrants are insured with a hospital and a medical insurance fund for the first two months that they are in Australia, all at the cost of the Australian government. In addition, pharmaceutical benefits are provided at reduced rates. However, only a small proportion of migrants take advantage of this scheme, probably because of lack of comprehension of the health system in Australia. In 1973, arrangements were introduced to provide most new settlers with information cards printed in their own language.

Accommodations. The Australian government provides migrants with temporary accommodations in hostels and flats at low rents. The maximum period of stay in a hostel is 12 months, and in a self-contained flat six months.

Hostels provide a number of advantages. They offer reasonable accommodation and time to adjust to a new environment while looking for permanent quarters. Welfare service officers are available; English classes are often conducted in the hostels; and housing advisory officers are available to give free assistance in finding homes and flats for rental or purchase. Hostels are located in cities, but families preferring to settle in country towns can get rental subsidies from the Australian government.

Social Services. It is important that migrants be eligible to receive social service payments as soon as they arrive in Australia. Barriers have been progressively lowered during the past years, and migrants now have immediate access to unemployment benefits, sickness benefits, maternity allowances, and child endowments. Still, there are some areas in Australia's social service scheme in which migrants see themselves at a disadvantage. To receive old-age, widow, and invalid pensions, persons must still satisfy residential qualifications. However, the government can award "special benefits" to migrants who are otherwise not eligible for certain types of social service.

The migrants' problems are partly compounded by the fact that many of them have not only to support their family members in Australia but also relatives in the home country. Government assistance does not take that into account.

Legal Aid. Migrants, along with certain other groups (e.g., Aborigines), qualify for special legal assistance provided that they satisfy certain flexible requirements. This legal assistance is provided free or at reduced rates by the Australian government and covers federal and state matters.

Interpreter Service. Migrants have never been supplied with a sufficient number of interpreters, adequate multilingual application forms, adequate translation services, or adequate literature in languages other than English. A 24-hour telephone interpretation service was recently established to handle such emergencies as calls to hospitals, doctors, and the police. But already the service has come to satisfy not only emergencies but everyday needs for general interpretation and communication.

Grant-in-Aid Scheme. A number of voluntary welfare agencies working with migrants can apply to the Australian government for grants to cover the salaries and ancillary costs of social workers. In general, the social workers provide casework or counseling services for migrants who are faced with a variety of social and emotional problems.

Repatriation. The Australian government recognizes that, in a large-scale migration program, there are bound to be casualties for a variety of reasons. The Australian government has a liberal plan for repatriation and sometimes receives supplementary aid from governments overseas. Assistance generally consists of tracing relatives, arranging departures, and arranging the receptions on return.

General Policy

There has been some ambivalence in government circles both about the ideal size of the immigration program and about what should be the general pattern of provision for those who settle in Australia. In the late 1950s and early 1960s the Department of Immigration, for example, arranged for most of the migrant services and had its own substantial social work service for this purpose. In the mid 1960s these separate services were reduced, and attempts were made to integrate the immigrant populations into the normal range of social services. These attempts were only partly and temporarily successful, and several of the separate provisions that had been reduced had to be renewed. More recently, however, with ethnic organizations themselves providing more and more services to their members, the Department of Immigration has been abolished, and its services have been distributed to other departments, principally Labor and Social Security.

THE PROVISION OF WELFARE SERVICES FOR ABORIGINES

In describing the organization of welfare services in Australia, one must discuss the Aboriginal population as a special category. Aborigines constitute less than 1% of the total population, and they have suffered a fate similar to that of indigenous minorities in many other countries, being exploited by the general community and consigned to the lowest social ranking. Aborigines in Australia are faced with limited and substandard housing, an ill-equipped educational system, inadequate health care, an uncomprehending and foreign legal system, and limited employment opportunities. All the social welfare provisions open to Australians generally are open to Aborigines; however, extra facilities and special policies have been developed to accommodate their special needs and to compensate for and redress existing inequalities.

If special provisions are to apply to the Aboriginal population, such persons have to be legally defined. An Aborigine is a person of Aboriginal descent who identifies as an Aborigine and is accepted as such by the community with which he is associated. The number enumerated at the 1971 census was 106,288 persons; their rate of natural increase is about 3% per annum, i.e., twice the national rate. Few Aborigines have a nomadic life, and, although the majority live in rural areas, a large percentage live in urban areas.

In a referendum of May 1967, a majority of valid votes favored two amendments to the Constitution, one of which gave the Australian government power, with the states, to legislate for Aborigines in the states. In April 1973, the Australian government assumed full responsibility for policy and finance with respect to Aboriginal affairs, but the transfer of certain powers from the various state governments to the Australian government has not been finalized. The Department of Aboriginal Affairs is the Australian government authority responsible for the development of national policy in Aboriginal affairs and for the coordination of federal and state programs and those of other agencies involved. In general, the same welfare authorities that provide services for Australians generally also provide assistance to Aborigines—e.g., social services, health care, and education. In 1973-1974, extra welfare assistance provided by the Australian government to Aborigines amounted to approximately $866 per capita. This was in addition to the welfare services provided to Australians generally and legally open to individual Aborigines. These basic types of assistance are described below: assistance to individuals and assistance for community development.

Individual Assistance

Education. All Aboriginal secondary students are eligible to receive textbooks, uniforms, and personal and living allowances. Allowances are also paid to cover certain school fees, fares, and boarding charges. Aboriginal tertiary students are eligible for living allowances and a dependent's allowances for financial assistance for textbooks, equipment, travel, and all compulsory fees.

Health. If an Aborigine does not belong to a Medical Benefit Fund, he or she may attend a general practitioner or specialist free, and the state government will reimburse the doctor concerned. If an Aborigine is unable to pay his hospital debts, the Australian government can assume responsibility for the amount outstanding. The government also pays for the first year's enrollment in an Ambulance Insurance Fund and makes community nurses available specifically to care for Aborigines.

Housing. An Aborigine may apply for accommodation under the Special Homes for Aboriginal program administered by the New South Wales Housing Commission; the rents charged are lower than those otherwise levied. Low-interest loans are available for the purchase of homes, for the renovation of existing dwellings, and for the purchase of furniture whose value does not exceed $500.

Aboriginal hostels have been established mainly for the benefit of single persons.

Employment. Job assistance, given particularly to young Aborigines who wish to move to obtain work, consists of living-away allowances (for those persons under 21), payments of the first week's rent, clothing grants, and far allowances.

Vocational training is offered at the Sydney Technical College, designed exclusively for Aborigines; and the government offers subsidies for on-the-job training up to 60% of the prevailing wage.

Legal Aid. Aside from standard legal aid facilities, an Aboriginal in N.S.W. can obtain free legal aid from the Aboriginal Legal Service. Free counseling and representation are given irrespective of the seriousness of the crime.

Aid for Community Development

In addition to personal assistance provided by the various authorities concerned with Aboriginal affairs, numerous organizations and Aboriginal communities have received assistance for various projects. The aim is to assist Aborigines to solve their problems through self-help.

Housing and Property. Grants have been provided to Aboriginal housing associations, which help individual communities to plan, organize, and administer programs for building or purchasing houses. In April 1973, a grant was given to the Redfern Aboriginal Housing Project in Sydney for this purpose.

In recent years there has been a greater recognition of the Aborigines' desire to secure land titles which would be valid and safe and would freely allow

Aboriginals as individuals or communities to use land for economic and social purposes. Financial assistance has been provided to help purchase properties; in 1972, for instance, such assistance allowed an Aboriginal community to purchase and thus own and control a Western Australian pastoral company.

Education. In 1973 the Australian government provided financial assistance to a volunteer all-Aboriginal women's association in an inner Sydney suburb to enable the group to continue and expand its preschool and cultural education and breakfast service for Aboriginal children.

Health. An Aboriginal Medical Service, established in Sydney by the Aboriginal community, offers free medical service. The Australian government finances the running costs. A similar center in Brisbane has also received government assistance.

Summary

To describe the services to which Aborigines are entitled does not, unfortunately, answer questions about how many Aborigines can take advantage of the extra provisions or how adequate the provisions are. There is little doubt that in some areas Aborigines receive more than their share of unemployment benefits, for example, but this says little more than that they have more than their share of unemployment.

Table 1 shows the amounts spent in 1972-1973 for the whole Australian population by all levels of government and the additional amounts spent for the Aboriginal population. Bearing in mind that the Aboriginal population is approximately 1% of the total population, the figures mean that, for education and social security, the Aborigines get a sum per capita about equal to that of the general population; they receive about one-third extra on their health services, and about twice as much extra on their housing.

PROSPECTS AND PLANS

In February 1973, in a statement of the intentions of his government in the welfare field, Prime Minister Edward Gough Whitlam listed four main areas in which significant developments were planned: the National Health Service, a

Table 1: Total Government Expenditures (1972-1973 fiscal year)

	Total Australian Population (in millions)	Aboriginal Population (in millions)
Education	$1,979.0	$15.3
Health	1,470.2	4.5
Social Service and Welfare	2,108.9	20.9
Housing	87.3	13.9

SOURCE: Australian Bureau of Statistics, 1973-1974a.

National Compensation and Rehabilitation Scheme, a National Superannuation Scheme, and the Australian Assistance Plan. It is now possible to see what was intended and what is likely to happen in these four areas.

National Health Insurance and National Health Services

The Australian government has announced a new health insurance scheme to start in 1975, which would provide everyone with health insurance benefits. Previously, only about 85% of the population was covered by the government-subsidized private health insurance funds. The new scheme, entitled Medibank, is financed by a levy on each person's income, plus a government subsidy. (The levy is expected to provide 40% of the necessary funds.) The program also involved abolishing the means test for public ward treatment, so that everyone is entitled to free hospital ward treatment, including free medical treatment by doctors and hospital staff. Medical benefits are based on standard fee schedules, with several alternative methods of participation by doctors. If a doctor bulk-bills the government for his services, the patient will have no more to pay. But if the doctor bills the patient directly, the patient will receive up to 85% of the fee from the insurance commission.

Some benefits not currently covered by the voluntary insurance schemes —e.g., eye refraction tests—are being brought into the new benefits scheme. Other services such as pathology and radiology services and diagnostic screening, which were previously treated and paid for on roughly the same basis as medical consultations, are excluded from the new scheme. Instead, institutions providing these services, whether hospitals or incorporated organizations, are supported directly by the Australian government through a program of health program grants rather than through fees-for-service.

In the past, hospital services have been overseen by state bodies, with financing based on a combination of hospital fees and state and commonwealth subsidies. Most patients of course insure themselves against their share of the costs by joining one of the private insurance schemes, which in their turn are also subsidized from government funds. The intention of the new scheme is that all patients should be able to receive treatment in public wards without charge and regardless of means. If they wish to claim more private or expensive accommodation within the hospital, they must pay the extra charge. If they also wish to be treated by doctors of their choice with whom they have contracted separately for medical attention, they will be able to do that too, with some portion of the fees being paid by the government.

The most controversial part of the scheme concerned how the ordinary finances of the public hospitals would be handled. Eventually, the Australian government agreed to meet 50% of the net operating costs of public hospitals. This is done partly by a payment to each hospital with respect to the number of beds and occupancy and partly by payment to the states, which are the owners and operators of the public hospitals. Medical treatment, on the other hand, is largely covered by cost-sharing agreements concluded between the states and the federal government. Thus, patients no longer must continue to insure themselves privately against hospital costs. The whole Australian population is now covered for both medical and hospital services by Medibank.

National Compensation and Rehabilitation Scheme

A report of the National Committee of Inquiry (1974) recommended the establishment of a comprehensive range of rehabilitation services to be made available to every handicapped person irrespective of the cause or nature of his handicap or where he lives. These services should be available as soon as the disability is recognized and should continue until optimum recovery is achieved. The Australian government should accept overall responsibility for coordinating and financing the services including financial assistance to applicants.

The main instrumentality for carrying out this scheme will be a Rehabilitation Division of the Department of Social Security, which will make funds available to state governments to run medical rehabilitation units, sheltered workshops, day activity centers, special schools, etc. The medical units will be independent of hospitals as regards their staffing, but integrated as regards treatment. The other units in the scheme (for vocational assessment, day care, sheltered employment, etc.) will be established where needed. Where the process of rehabilitation does not reach the point of enabling the handicapped person to pursue employment, schooling, or whatever in the open community without help, the Rehabilitation Division will provide domiciliary services, aids, and appliances or secure the services of a voluntary body.

The scheme also includes a variety of transport allowances for special driver training and grants to purchase or modify vehicles to meet individual needs.

The same organization will also have responsibility for community aspects of the care of the handicapped: persuading employers to employ handicapped persons (if necessary, via a subsidy), working for redesign of buildings to reduce any barriers to use by handicapped persons, and, of course, encouraging the training of suitable personnel to run the various services.

National Superannuation Scheme

Currently, old-age pensions are awarded men over 64 and women over 60; a means test is applied up to age 70. Payments are laid down in legislation, and, within the terms of eligibility, pensioners have a statutory right to their pension. The scheme is very much the same as it was in 1909, although it has been liberalized in terms of qualifying conditions and level of payment. The present government is committed to abolishing the means test and to raising pensions to one-quarter of former weekly earnings. Today nearly 100% of all persons over 75, almost 79% of all persons between 65 and 74, and 50% of women between 60 and 64 receive pension benefits of some kind. For the rest of the population, it is difficult to find out how many are supported by nonstatutory pensions. However, for those not yet of retirement age, there are a large number of superannuation schemes, most of which receive concessions; they cover upwards of 760,000 persons, including 678,000 government employees. These figures suggest that about 22% of the present work force will have retirement provision alongside or instead of the statutory provision.

A National Superannuation Committee of Inquiry, appointed in 1973, has proposed a pension which would be available to all and would have two components. The first would be common to all aged persons, and the second would be related to each pensioner's accumulated contributions. It also recommended that the basic part of the pension be adjusted automatically for changes in the general price level by being tied either to an index of earnings or to a retail prices index.

Australian Assistance Plan

This program, not yet determined by legislation, did begin in 1972 as a national experimental program instituted by the newly elected Labor government (Parliament, 1973a). The aim eventually is to cover Australia with a network of "regional councils" operating community-based programs. These regional councils will have representatives from, and be financed by, local voluntary agencies and commonwealth and state governments and will integrate the work of all local welfare organizations. Consumers will also be represented.

These Regional Councils for Social Development, either planned or operating, will each serve a population ranging from about one-quarter to half a million people, all within a region having some measure of economic, social, and political unity. The tasks of each council are (1) to work with other regional planning bodies concerned with physical planning, education, and housing, (2) to evaluate and monitor the social needs of the region and to report these to the state and Australian governments, (3) to devise plans for welfare services to meet the needs of the region, (4) to advise and assist statutory and voluntary agencies in carrying out appropriate welfare policies, and (5) to advise the Australian government on the development of its own services in the region and on the allocation of grants and subsidies.

According to the Australian Welfare Commission personal welfare services that may receive grants under the plan include information centers, citizens advice bureaus, youth centers, etc. Many such services exist already, of course, and are run by local authorities, by ad hoc bodies, and sometimes by more general social welfare agencies. What is novel about the new ventures is that they will be part of a pattern of services planned and sponsored by the Regional Councils, and therefore they will probably be better located and better integrated with other services. The region, it is claimed, will be more appropriate for this purpose than the smaller locality or the larger state.

NOTES

1. A recent report (Australian Council of Social Service, 1972), calling for a "national inquiry into social welfare," distinguished six developmental stages in the history of the evolving structure of social welfare in Australia. The opening paragraphs are drawn mainly from that report.

2. Since federation, the national government of the whole of Australia has variously been referred to as the "commonwealth" or "federal" government. The present usage is the "Australian government." Whichever title is used, the meaning is exactly the same. The terms used here are the ones used in the documents referred to. Whenever the reference is not a quotation or a paraphrase of some other discussion, the term employed is "the Australian government."

REFERENCES

Australia, National Committee of Inquiry (1974). Compensation and rehabilitation in Australia. Canberra: Australian Government Publishing Service.

Australia, National Superannuation Committee of Inquiry (1974). Interim report. Canberra: Australian Government Publishing Service.

Australia, Parliament of the Commonwealth (1973a). Australian Assistance Plan (Parliamentary paper no. 18). Canberra: Australian Government Publishing Service.

——— (1973b). Report on the survey of child migrant education in schools of high migrant density in Melbourne (Parliamentary paper no. 31). Canberra: Australian Government Publishing Service.

Australian Bureau of Statistics (1973-1974). "Outlay on Aboriginal affairs by authorities of the Australian government." In Public Authority Finance. Canberra: Author.

Australian Council of Social Service (1972). "A national inquiry into social welfare." Australian Social Welfare, 2(2).

DAVIES, D., and ENCEL, S. (eds., 1965). Australian society. Melbourne: Cheshire.

HENDERSON, R.F., et al. (1970). People in poverty in a Melbourne survey. Melbourne: Cheshire.

KAIM-CAUDLE, P.R. (1973). Comparative social policy and social security. London: Martin Robertson.

6

DENMARK: HUMAN SERVICES IN THE "SERVICE STATE"

HENNING FRIIS
ANDERS FROM

INTRODUCTION

Development of a Modern Social Service System

From the end of the 19th century until World War II a Danish system of income-maintenance was gradually built up with the aim of securing an acceptable minimum level of living for all population groups in case of loss of income. This was done by widening the coverage of various social insurance schemes (covering illness, unemployment, employment accidents) and by the development of national pension schemes for invalids and people of old age, financed by general taxation and not, as in most other countries, through individual contributions. During the same period, various kinds of social services had been organized by central and local governments. The public health system had been expanding since the beginning of the century, aiming at a national coverage of public hospitals and of general practitioners. All urban and most rural municipalities had built homes for old people. A national care program for the mentally handicapped was developed, and day-care institutions for children had been established. At the end of the 1930s mothers' aid institutions were established as a public service for mothers with small children. Simultaneously a system of visiting nurses supervising the health of small children was introduced.

Recent decades have shown major extensions and new approaches in the various income-maintenance schemes (Friis, 1969), but the development in the field of social services has been quite remarkable too. Just to mention some examples: The number of children in day-care institutions for children has more than tripled since 1960; youth clubs have been introduced in most communities; services for the old living in their own home have shown a spectacular expansion and diversification; a new system for rehabilitation of the handicapped has been established; the special care for the mentally handicapped has been modernized.

The expansion of the social security system and the social services has been based on one of the main principles in Danish social policy: that social policy measures shall be universalistic with regard to coverage and equal standard for all groups in the population irrespective of employment status or income. Whereas, formerly, old-age assistance and institutions for the old were not much more than poor relief given to old people with no other means, today's "peoples' pension" goes out to the whole population from 67 years of age, and all classes use institutions and home services for the old. And while the kindergartens in the first half of the century were mainly catering to children from socially deprived families and single mothers, today's thousands of day-care institutions provide a broad coverage. Recent research even indicates that they are preferably used by high-income families. The "Welfare State" is developing into a "Service State" with improved standards of the services in quantity as well as quality.

The expansion of the social welfare system has caused a large increase in expenditures. When the total expenditures for social security and social services including health services are seen in relation to the Danish net national income, the percentage has been increasing from 9.9% in 1950 to 12.8% in 1960, to 22.9% in 1970 and to 25.5% in 1973, the latest year for which comprehensive statistics are available.[1] The cost of social services in kind accounts for about half of the expenditures, while the other half is due to the costs of social security cash benefits and pensions.

Economic Background

The rapid expansion of the Danish social policy programs during the 1960s must be viewed on the background of the general economic and social changes in Danish society. The first decade after World War II was characterized in Denmark by a rather small rate of economic growth and by relatively high unemployment. Denmark was at that time primarily an exporter of agricultural products, and the Danish economy had a larger agricultural sector than was the case in most other countries in northwestern Europe. When international economic conditions changed for the better toward the end of the 1950s, Denmark thus had a large reservoir of manpower which could be transferred rather smoothly into an expanding industry. Industrialization, economic growth, and urbanization progressed rapidly from the end of the 1950s to the beginning of the 1970s, a period of 15 years which has been called Denmark's second industrial revolution. Economic progress measured in per capita income increased the level of living in all social strata, though it only to a small extent moderated the inequalities between them. The employment rate was probably the highest in Europe, and a very considerable increase took place in the employment of married women. At the same time the economic growth made it possible to carry the cost of the expansion and improvement which took place in nearly all kinds of social services. After this period of economic boom, the international economic crisis from 1974 caused a severe setback for Denmark, and the level of unemployment is now higher than it has been since the early 1950s, particularly among youth and women. The colder economic climate has also made its impact on the social services where the tendency at present is to avoid any further expansion. The influence of socioeconomic events on the Danish social services can be illustrated by examples from developments in the areas of family policy.

A deliberate Danish family policy began in the middle of the 1930s, with the particular aim of bringing down the number of abortions and the high infant mortality rate through preventive social and health measures benefiting low-income families and unmarried mothers and their children. The impetus for this sudden interest was to a large degree to be found in the general fertility decline of that decade which was looked upon as undesirable.

The economic developments in the 1960s gave an impetus to new developments in the area of family policy. The increased demand for married women on the labor market increased the need for day-care services for their children. A rapid expansion of these services was met with general acceptance, and new day-care institutions were initiated by parents groups, which received municipal and state support, and by the municipal authorities. In the recent economically leaner years, the expansion of day-care services for children has suddenly become one of the main targets for criticism. It has been argued that the state and municipal subventions given to these institutions are to the benefit of only a selected group of families, namely, those with children in the institutions. Another argument presented is that there is no need to encourage women to work outside their home by subventions for day-care services during a period of high unemployment. The practical consequences of this shift in political attitudes have been a decision of the Parliament to increase parent's payments for day-care and a 10% cut in the number of personnel employed in day-care institutions.

THE DANISH "SOCIAL REFORM"

The Ideas Behind the Danish "Social Reform" of the 1970s

In 1964 the Danish Parliament unanimously passed a proposal that a government commission should be set up to make proposals for an overall reform of the organizational, administrative, and financial structure of the social welfare system. In the proposal it was stated that:

> The Commission shall hereby have in view that the social administration —to benefit those who receive services—must be shaped to ascertain and develop the effectiveness of the preventive, therapeutic and rehabilitative

activities, and must be suited to furthering the best possible coordination of the various programs. . . . [The Commission shall investigate] whether it is desirable and possible to change the regulations of the general social security programs with a view to greater adaption to the goals of our time—prevention, rehabilitation, security and well-being. In this connection, the Commission shall not only investigate whether these regulations can and shall be better coordinated than hitherto, but it shall also consider whether there is a necessity in modern society to improve existing programs in order to reach real security of the individual in every situation of need.

Simultaneously, with the Social Reform Commission another commission has been dealing with the training of personnel for social administration and social work, a prerequisite for future improvements in these fields.

In order to establish a factual basis for its work, the Social Reform Commission requested the Danish National Institute of Social Research to carry out a major research project concerning the functions of the Danish social security and social service system (Andersen, 1972). A national sample of several thousand people covering the population in general as well as a sample of social welfare clients were interviewed during the years 1966 and 1967. The research project had three main aims. The first aim was to find out how many people were hit by so-called "social accidents" (illness, unemployment, loss of bread-winner, etc.) and how many of these actually came in contact with the authorities because of the "social accident." It was shown that by far the most common "social accident" was illness of varying duration. Most of the people hit by illness did not come into contact with either medical personnel or social authorities. Those few who did mainly contacted the sickness insurance societies to obtain sickness allowances. These societies, being semi-independent agencies, rarely referred the clients to other agencies, even in cases of need for further social services.

Second, the surveys obtained information concerning a sample of those clients who did have contacts with any official agency. It was shown that even in comparatively simple cases—such as an uncomplicated illness—it was quite normal to establish contacts with more than one agency, and in many cases four or more agencies became involved in the case. Very often the services given by these agencies were uncoordinated.

Third, a sample of persons with more complicated case histories were followed as their contacts with the social welfare system developed. About 15% of the clients took up more than half of the services provided by the social agencies.

On this background the Social Reform Commission formulated the basic ideas behind the reform which can be highlighted by two "code words" that have often been used in the Danish debate: *integration*, as regards the treatment of individuals and families, and *decentralization*, as regards the administrative structure. The commission found that integration and decentralization could best be obtained by the introduction of what was called the one-stringed system of social welfare, according to which income maintenance programs as well as social services will be administered inside one administrative structure. That integration in the treatment had become a necessity was quite clear, not only from the above-mentioned studies by the Institute of Social Research but also from numerous complaints from clients and social workers. It was very difficult for any one agency to get the full knowledge of the problems of the client, since the same client might, in some cases, simultaneously receive assistance from the municipal social office, the health insurance society, and the mothers' aid institution, quite apart from his or her contacts outside the field of social welfare proper, i.e., with doctors, hospitals, and tax authorities. For several reasons this situation could hurt the clients. There was a risk that the clients might not get the help they were entitled to, simply because of difficulties in finding the right contacts. Moreover, the fact that each single agency only had the duty to make the legal checks to see if a concrete claim was justified meant that in many cases there was no agency which had the responsibility for the general guidance and rehabilitation of the client. The mothers' aid institutions and the rehabilitation centers had been established under the central government with the exact purpose of assuming such responsibility. They had well-trained staffs of social workers and medical doctors and did an important service in their area of competence, though they had been given rather insufficient resources. The reason for their establishment as separate agencies had been the unappealing public image of the municipal social welfare offices and the mainly legalistic treatment which these offices gave the clients. The commission felt, however, that the mothers' aid agencies and the rehabilitation centers were too isolated from the other social welfare agencies and that their experiences and personnel could be more useful in an integrated system.

The legislation which forms the background for the "Social Reform" is contained in five acts which have entered into force between 1970 and 1976. They are:

Act of 1970 in Administration of Social and Certain Health Matters. This act introduced the administrative structure necessary for the establishment of a one-stringed system of social welfare.

Public Health Security Act of 1971 (entered into force in 1973). This act abolished the health insurance societies, transferring their functions to the municipalities.

Daily Cash Benefit (Sickness or Maternity) Act of 1972 (entered into force in 1973). This act governs the conditions of certain benefits in cases of short-term needs.

Act concerning the Social Appeals Board of 1972. This act established a central board of appeal for social cases and abolished several independent boards for specialized fields.

Social Assistance Act of 1974 (entering into force in 1976). This act can be seen as the last building-block, which is completing the legal basis of the Social Reform. It lays down the detailed rules for activities of the municipal social welfare and health administration and provides the basis for its new central role in the system.

Taken together, these five acts provide a system where one single agency—the municipal social and health administration—is responsible for the total sum of services and cash benefits given to each individual and family. The idea is that most clients will only need to get into contact with this local administration, even those who may require rather intensive guidance and support. This should be made possible also for small municipalities because the regional (county) administration, according to the new legislation, has established a central team of specialists which will be available as consultants to the municipal social administration. The county authorities have certain new powers as regards planning, supervision, and coordination of the municipal activities in the social welfare field.

There are, however, some exceptions to this trend toward integration of the social services. Although the new health security system is an integral part of municipal welfare, the persons responsible for medical aid—the general practitioners—are not directly integrated into the system itself, even though most of their income will be channeled through the system. There is no automatic or legal mechanism which will secure the cooperation between the local doctors and the social welfare authorities. This will probably be an important issue for further discussion considering that the studies by the Institute of Social Research have shown that 80% of the clients with more complicated social case histories had been in contact with a medical practitioner in connection with their present difficulties. Also the trade-union-affiliated unemployment insurance programs as well as the state-run labor exchange offices are outside the system, mainly because of political pressure from the trade unions who have a fear of losing a hold on their members if municipal authorities get too involved in labor market affairs.

Municipal Reform

As mentioned above, decentralization of the administration of the social services is the second code word characterizing the Danish Social Reform. The principle of decentralization is nothing new in Danish social administration. Although rules regarding benefits and administration of services have been laid down in the legislation, the actual operation of the programs has been delegated to local bodies. The social welfare boards of the municipalities have administered pensions, public assistance, and large areas of child welfare; health insurance societies have administered the health insurance benefits; the counties have been responsible for the general hospital system. However, a number of important programs have been operated as branches of the central government, such as most residential institutions for children and the handicapped, including the care of the mentally handicapped and the psychiatric hospitals. From the end of the 1930s new types of social services were established under the central government, in particular, as earlier mentioned, the mothers' aid institutions and the rehabilitation centers. The administrative changes inherent in the Social Reform mean that the responsibility for most of the social service programs under the central government, the primary health services and the psychiatric hospitals, is being transferred to the municipal and county authorities. When this transfer is finished during the forthcoming years, Denmark will probably be the country in Europe which has the most decentralized social welfare system with regard to planning as well as administration.

A precondition for this development has been some rather wide-ranging changes in the Danish system of administration at the local level. Around 1970 the total number of municipalities in Denmark was reduced from about 1,300 to 275, which of course meant a considerable increase in the average population of the municipalities, which now is 18,000, with practically no municipality having less than 5,000. The number of regional authorities (counties) was at the same time reduced from 25 to 14. Along with these administrative reforms, various measures have been introduced making the municipalities and the counties more independent and responsible in their expenditure decisions. Even though the local authorities have always to a certain extent been depending on local taxation, the larger share of their expenditures has been covered by governmental subsidies. These subsidies have until now normally taken the form of percentage reimbursement, with percentages ranging up to 85% (in special cases, where the municipalities acted only as agents of the central government, 100%). This meant that some programs were very cheap from the municipal point of view. In the future, governmental subsidies will still constitute the larger part of the total revenues of the municipalities (and counties), but the subsidies will mainly be given as general "block grants," their size being related not to expenditures of individual programs but to certain criteria in each municipality such as number of inhabitants in various age groups and the total amount of taxable income and property in each municipality.

Since the enactment of these legislative changes, the 275 municipalities have had the direct responsibility of aiding clients with a social need, a fact which has meant that the municipal social office is now often called "the municipal social supermarket." The counties have the responsibilities for most of the hospital system and, together with the central government, for certain specialized services, but the main responsibility of the counties lies in the sphere of coordination and planning.

An important goal of the Social Reform has been to construct a social planning system which makes it possible for local planning to operate as independently as possible inside the wider framework of general social policy. Arrangements have been made for planning to take place in cooperation between all three levels in the social welfare system: state, county, and municipality. In this system the state authorities have the role to work out the general guidelines and, when feasible, maximum and minimum standards. The 14 counties have been assigned the task of coordinating the municipal plans and integrating them into a framework laid down by the state authorities. The municipalities have the primary responsibility for making plans for social service development and for fitting these plans into the financial framework inside which they operate. To facilitate this process, a system of annual "Social Reports" has been introduced. Every year each municipality has to deliver a report to its country specifying its resources in the social field, the demographic data which will be of relevance in estimating future needs, and its plans for the coming years. The county uses these municipal reports for an overall report which is submitted to the Ministry of Social Affairs as a basis for national planning of the social services. A problem which is not solved by the municipal reform concerns the relationship between the social welfare officials and the elected members of the municipal social and health council, which is the politically responsible organ for social welfare under the municipality council. When municipalities were smaller, the local councillors traditionally played a great role concerning decisions on individual social cases. Formally, the responsibility for individual decisions still rests with the elected councillors, but in later years this responsibility has increasingly been delegated to the officials. Because the obligations of the municipalities are increasing, it is expected that a more clear-cut division of labor will be worked out. The elected councillors will primarily have the responsibility for policy and planning, while officials will make decisions on most of the individual cases.

TRAINING OF STAFF FOR THE SOCIAL SERVICES

The main prerequisite for the social service system is manpower, and in particular manpower with relevant training. In the health field this has from the early beginning been recognized in Denmark, but in other areas of social services the recognition came rather late. Training of teachers for day-care centers for children began early in this century, while the first school of social work was established in the 1930s. Later came training of staff for residential care of children and the handicapped. By the 1960s the Danish government felt the need of a systematic policy for training of personnel for the social services. Parallel to the Social Reform Commission the government constituted another commission which would survey the training activities and the quantitative and qualitative training needs for social services and social administration. Though training for the health services was outside its mandate, the territory of the commission was very wide, covering 125,000 employed persons or 5% of the total Danish labor force. The commission submitted its final report in 1972.

The commission noticed that there was a broad spectrum of training activities of very different structure and duration. The various activities followed the institutional divisions in the social welfare field. Their theoretical content was often rather modest compared, for instance, to training in the educational field. The programs of the schools of social work and for training of staff for institutions for children and the handicapped were relatively well developed, while training for work with the aged was totally neglected. Most staff in the municipal social welfare administration had only clerical and administrative training. Nearly all types of training had far more applicants than they could receive. For the purpose of its work the commission defined two main categories of workers in the social welfare field. One category the commission called "social pedagogers" or "social educators," working in day-care and residential institutions. This category includes the large majority of those working in social welfare. The other category was called "social formularies," covering those dealing with social work and social administration. For "social educators" it was found that there were nine different basic training specializations with a great deal of common ground. The commission proposed an integrated training for all social educators lasting three years, including one year of common basic training, one year of practice, and one year of specialization.

In the area of social casework and social administration, the commission did not find it possible to propose a consolidated system encompassing the training at the schools of social work as well as training of social administrative personnel. Considering the urgent need for improvement of the qualifications of the staff in the municipal social welfare offices under the new Social Reform, the commission recommended that the capacity of the schools of social work should be increased and that substantial training programs should be established for the clerical and administrative staff of the social welfare offices. The proposals of the commission have until now resulted in an integration of the training for staff for residential institutions following the lines suggested by the commission, while its proposal to integrate the training of teachers for day-care institutions for children has not been accepted. The capacity of the schools of social work has been expanded, and courses for municipal social welfare staffs have started. It should be mentioned that in spite of the obvious need for using trained social workers to a much greater extent that hitherto in the municipal social welfare offices, many municipalities have not been so interested in employing professional social workers as was expected by the commission. They prefer staff which have their training through the municipal training system, which has a dominantly clerical and administrative content. The increased output of graduates from the schools of social work has therefore resulted in considerable unemployment among this group.

DANISH SOCIAL SERVICES

This section attempts an overview of the more important elements in the Danish social service system. It is by no means exhaustive, but an effort is made to present branches of the service which offer aid to major groups of the population.

Family Planning

Denmark has traditionally pursued a rather liberal policy in family planning matters. For many years the state has given financial aid to private organizations providing advice on family planning, and such advice has also been provided by the state-run mothers' aid institutions. Legal provisions require doctors to offer women free advice on contraception at their first postnatal examination, and such advice may be given to any woman, even to minors over 15 years of age, without their parents' consent. The Danish abortion legislation has for many years been rather liberal. Since 1973 legal abortion can be performed without special permission if it is done before the termination of the 12th week of pregnancy. Since then the number of induced abortions has been rising steeply, but the general impression is that the number of illegal abortions has been declining to a similar extent. In 1974 about 24,000 abortions were performed, as compared to 72,000 births in the same year. Abortions usually take place at the general hospital and are performed free of charge.

Services Around Childbirth

During pregnancy all women are entitled to nine preventive examinations, three by the doctor, seven by a midwife. All assistance during childbirth is free, whether the birth takes place at a private clinic or a hospital (90% of all births) or in the home, assisted by a midwife. After the child is born, the family is visited by a municipal health nurse, usually about once a month during the child's first year of life. Her job is to give general advice concerning nutrition and the health care of the child, but she also acts as a kind of unofficial municipal "supervisor" of the family and is able to get in touch with relevant authorities if the situation of the child calls for further assistance. All municipalities are obliged by law to establish such health nurse supervision. If the child is born out of wedlock, the mother will get official assistance to carry through a lawsuit to establish paternity of the child. For unwed mothers there are also possibilities of getting special housing and aid to further education.

Services for Children and Youth

Health Services and Dental Care. From birth and until school-entering age, all children are entitled to nine free medical examinations, which are carried out either by a general practitioner or at specialized child health centers. During school age the child will be examined at the school by a doctor and a health nurse, usually once a year. If any case of illness or anomaly is found, the child is referred to his or her general practitioner or to one of the institutions for the deaf, blind, crippled, etc. Since 1972 a system of free dental care for children of school age has been gradually introduced.

General Services for Children and Young People. The responsibility for establishing the necessary child welfare institutions and services is, according to the Social Assistance Act, vested in the municipalities. This act contains a general provision stating, "It shall be the duty of the local social welfare committee to supervise the conditions under which children within its area live and to support their parents in the upbringing and care of them"; and it includes several special provisions, among them one relating to day-care institutions: "The local council shall provide for the necessary number of places to be available in day-care institutions for children and young persons, including socio-educational leisure facilities." The municipalities have interpreted the legislative requirements concerning the establishment of a sufficient number of day-care institutions in very different ways. The result is that some of the 275 municipalities have no institutions at all, while in other municipalities such institutions provide room for more than 60% of the children in the appropriate age groups. In addition to crèches, kindergartens, recreation centers, and youth clubs, most municipalities organize and control the placement of children under school age in private day-care. All of these activities—whether public or private—are heavily subsidized by both state and municipality, but except for families of very small means, parents are obliged to pay part of the cost. The payment is graduated according to the income of the parents.

Crèches. These institutions admit children from the age of a few weeks. The maximum age is not rigidly fixed, but the children will usually leave the crèche when they are allowed to enter a kindergarten—about the age of 2½ years. The crèches are mainly aimed at children of single mothers or families in which both parents are employed outside the home. Most people consider it a doubtful solution to the problems of child care to place children in this age group in institutions, away from their parents most of the day. In 1974 the crèches had room for 8% of all children in the age group from birth to 2½ years.

Kindergartens. These institutions cater to children from the age of about 2½ until school age (6 or 7). Increasing attention is given to the functions that they may perform as educational or socializing agencies for the children in this age group. In 1965 the kindergartens had room for 10% of all children in the age group 2½ to 6 years, while in 1974 the corresponding percentage was 30%.

Day-Care in Private Homes. As already mentioned, there was a sharply rising demand for day-care institutions in the 1960s. Many municipalities had difficulties in keeping up with this demand, and a scheme was introduced whereby the municipal authorities undertook to organize the placement of children under school age in private day-care. Families offering private care are checked by the municipal authorities, and payment for the service is also made by the municipality, which collects an income-graduated contribution from the child's parents. In 1974 about 5% of all children under school age were receiving such private day-care.

Nursery School Classes. Such classes became very common during the 1960s. They are intended for children of about 6 years of age, that is, the last year before they enter the school system proper. The work in the classes closely parallels the work in the kindergartens, but the classes are run in connection with the school system. The children stay in the classes only for a few hours a day, which means that they may in many cases still have to frequent a kindergarten. In 1973 almost 50% of all children in the 6-year-old group participated in such classes.

Recreation Centers. These centers can be seen as an extended form of kindergarten, catering to younger children from 7 to 12 years. More than the kindergartens, they are intended to meet the needs of children from socially and educationally deprived families. Like the kindergartens, they have facilities for work and play, and the children may also prepare their homework under supervision. In 1974 such institutions could accommodate 5% of all children in the age group.

Youth Clubs. In Denmark the youth club movement started in the years after the Second World War. Most clubs are set up by the welfare authorities, often in connection with the recreation centers, while others are linked to the educational system. Youth clubs are mainly seen as informal meeting places for young people, but considerable efforts are made to activate the members toward amateur theater, music, games, and various hobby activities. The clubs mainly cater to the age group from 13 to 18 years of age. A count made in the spring of 1974 showed that about 10% of all young people in the relevant age group visited such clubs.

General Municipal Activities in the Field of Family and Child Welfare

Besides their activities concerning day-care institutions for children, the municipalities have—as already mentioned—general responsibilities concerning child welfare. This means that it is the duty of the municipal authorities to provide help and guidance to troubled families and, if necessary, take steps to protect children who are not being treated properly—in extreme cases, by removing them from the family. The methods used by the municipal authorities to accomplish this task have changed considerably during the last half-century. In former days the municipal activity in this field was almost exclusively of a controlling nature, and the removal of children from their families was quite often used as a measure in such cases. In the years since the Second World War, there has been increasing emphasis upon prevention, counselling, and guidance for troubled families. During the 1960s most municipalities established family counselling programs. The job of the "family counsellors" has been to coordinate the various kinds of help and services being offered, such as placement in day-care, monetary assistance, medical treatment, or help by a psychologist. As a last resort, the municipality has the possibility of placing the child or young person away from its home, either at a traditional "children's home" or (as is increasingly the case) in private care with foster parents. Such placement is usually done with the parents consent, but may in extreme cases be done against their will. Many of the placements are made because the child is without support, because of either the sickness or the absence of the parents. Several "children and youth pensions" have been established, providing a somewhat protected environment for youngsters who cannot stay in a parental home. Also, building societies and semiprivate organizations are providing housing (single rooms) catering to the needs of this age group (Kahn and Kamerman, 1975).

Health Services

Through the national social security system and the public hospitals, the Danish population receives free medical attention. The treatment of illness outside hospitals is centered in the general medical practitioners who are spread evenly throughout the country and who normally are the gatekeepers to medical specialists, physiotherapy, and hospitals. The vast majority of families choose a general practitioner from the local panel of doctors, while a minority use the option to choose their doctor without being attached to one particular practitioner. For the first group the use of a general practitioner and specialists is free, and the doctors are directly paid by the health security system according to the number of their patients. The latter group pay the fee of the doctor whom they have used directly and then claim reimbursement of part of the fee from the health security office. For essential medicines a reduction is paid by the health security system. Similarly, a part of dentists' bills are paid directly to the dentists by the system. Hospitals provide all services free of charge, including bed and board, operations, X-ray, etc. The main carrier of the general hospital system has always been the counties. Until 1976 the psychiatric hospitals were under the state, but they have now been transferred to the counties. The primary health services have until recently been closely connected with the semipublic health insurance societies, which have been subsidized by the state since the end of the 19th century. By the Public Health Security Act of 1973, the health insurance societies were abolished, and their work was transferred to the municipal social welfare authorities, and the cost is now financed through state and municipal taxation. The costs of hospitals are shared between the state and the counties. The general practitioners and the specialist doctors outside hospitals work on a private basis, but they receive most of their income from the public health security system. The hospitals have their own medical and nursing staff, which is part of the public service. Per 10,000 of population Denmark has 16 practicing doctors, 8 dentists, and 54 qualified nurses and midwives. There are 90 beds per 10,000 of population in general hospitals. In addition, there are 13 mental hospitals. The number of patients corresponds to 20 per 10,000 of population.

Rehabilitation Services

The rehabilitation and education of the handicapped have played a great role in Danish social policy from the second half of the last century when the foundation was laid for the private institutions caring for the needs of persons with special handicaps: the blind, the deaf and hard of hearing, the speech defectives, the cripples, the mentally handicapped, etc. Today it is the state that provides for the education and care of these groups. A handicapped person receives training and care in a state institution or lives with a private family, if possible with their own family. Physically handicapped children whenever possible attend normal or special classes in the primary schools. Parents with children having handicaps will normally contact their local doctor, or they make direct contact with the proper agencies themselves. It is, however, the duty of midwives, doctors, health nurses, staff in day-care centers, schoolteachers, and municipal social welfare officials to notify the specialized agencies if they encounter children with special handicaps. The training and education of the blind, the partially sighted, the deaf, the hard of hearing, speech defectives, and cripples takes place inside the normal primary school system and the educational system, if that is at all possible. The child will be able to obtain technical aids and specialized educational materials (books in Braille, tapes, etc.), and many teachers in the primary school system have attended courses from which they have obtained qualifications necessary to give specialized instruction. For the more severely handicapped there exist several state-run and semiprivate institutions (clinics, treatment centers, boarding schools, etc.), where more intensive training and care may be given.

The Mentally Deficient. The service for the mentally deficient covers more patients than any other branch of special care services. The number of persons receiving help from the national service for the mentally deficient has doubled in the course of the past 30 years, the number of patients now amounting to some 22,000. If the parents agree, it is in many cases possible for the child to stay at home. The authorities in such cases provide the parents with the necessary guidance concerning the upbringing of the child, and, when the child comes of school age, he or she will have the opportunity to attend one of the state-run day schools for mentally retarded children. About two-thirds of all mentally deficient children are thus able to stay at home, outside the specialized institutions. The aim of the education of mentally retarded children and young persons has increasingly been to prepare them for a life as close to normal as possible. The majority of the adult mentally deficient live outside specialized institutions. In 1972 almost 60% of all mentally deficient thus lived outside institutions, about half of them in supervised family care.

General Rehabilitation Services. Rehabilitative measures are not confined to persons with the above-mentioned, readily identifiable handicaps. In the 1950s some labor exchange offices established employment services for the handicapped. Rehabilitation clinics and workshops were also established. In 1960 these efforts were coordinated on a nationwide basis after the enactment of the Rehabilitation Act. The rehabilitation services—consisting of training, retraining, medical treatment, and advice concerning job opportunities—were administered by 12 rehabilitation centers throughout the country. Clients were referred to the centers by doctors, hospitals, social welfare offices, etc., but clients might also apply for assistance on their own initiative. In 1972 there were 81 rehabilitation institutions with a total number of about 7,000 clients. In the first years after 1960 most of the clients at the rehabilitation centers were physically handicapped. Because of the general shortage of labor, reemployment of the handicapped was rather easy. Later in the 1960s a rather large proportion of the physically handicapped had been rehabilitated. The clients of the centers to a large extent consisted of persons with various degrees of mental handicaps and persons with so-called social handicaps. Occupational rehabilitation of these groups was often very difficult in spite of the situation of full employment which still existed at that time. One of the results of the Social Reform is that the rehabilitation centers are being abolished and their work taken over by the municipal social authorities (from April 1, 1976). Many of the larger municipalities are able to carry out rehabilitation work in much the same way as it was done by the former rehabilitation centers, but there is some concern about the ability of the smaller municipalities to give the necessary guidance. The counties have for this reason established teams of specialists who will be able to give advice to the municipal social offices in such cases.

Services for Invalid Pensioners and Other Disabled Persons. If rehabilitation proves to be impossible, the client has the possibility of obtaining an invalid pension. There are about 150,000 invalid pensioners, and the number has been rising steadily during later years, a fact which has been much discussed, though no general explanation for this tendency has been found. Many kinds of specialized social services are available to pensioners. The services to a great extent parallel the services given to the aged described below, such as pensioners' flats, collective housing, and home-help services. Persons with physical handicaps—whether they are receiving pensions or not—can obtain assistance toward the purchase and maintenance of technical aids. These aids can be orthopedic or medical, or they may consist of technical changes in their dwellings. These aids are provided free of charge or at a nominal cost. Substantial grants may also be given toward the purchase of motor vehicles, if they are of importance for the employment of the handicapped.

Services for the Aged

Everybody from the age of 67 is entitled to the so-called "peoples' pension," which is generally considered (also by the pensioners themselves) to be sufficient for a life well above minimum. Persons of old age—as everybody else in Denmark—are covered by the Public Health Security Act, which means that they have access to free medical care in and outside hospitals. The responsibility for social services for the aged is vested in the municipal social welfare authorities. The Social Assistance Act makes it obligatory for each municipality to provide a sufficient number of places in sheltered flats, nursing homes, or day-care centers. As most older people prefer to stay in their own homes as long as they are able and at least partly to manage for themselves, the municipality has a duty to assist them in their homes by offering various services. The most important of these measures is the home-help service, which is now obligatory for all municipalities. The work of the home-helps consists in assistance with cleaning, washing, cooking, shopping, mending of clothes, personal hygiene, dressing, and similar services. Actual nursing, which is not included in this work, is done by the home nurse service, which is well developed in all municipalities.

With regard to housing for pensioners, the municipal authorities can take various measures. A pensioner living in a flat is covered by special provisions in the Rent Subsidy Act, which in most cases makes it economically possible for him to pay his rent. About one-fourth of all pensioners receive such a subsidy. For a pensioner living in his own house or in a hired room, the municipality may award a rent allowance as an individual supplement to the pension. If minor technical alternations of the flat or the house will make it possible for the pensioner to stay there, aid may be given to that end. If the pensioner has to leave his former home, several possibilities are open. Local municipalities have since the 1930s built blocks of small flats for pensioners; and, in addition, there are small flats designed for pensioners in the normal housing projects of the nonprofit building societies. These flats, called "pensioners' dwellings," are designed especially for pensioners, but they are essentially normal flats, and the pensioner living there is expected to be able to care for himself (with home-help service if needed).

So-called "old peoples' homes" had already been introduced in Denmark by the turn of the century. With the development of the "pensioners' dwellings" and the home-help service, the trend now is to abolish these institutions or change them into nursing homes. When the pensioner becomes so frail that he or she is in need of intensive treatment (often after treatment in a hospital), a room in a nursing home is provided. Some of these homes are placed in the immediate vicinity of hospitals and function as long-term treatment centers. The capacity in nursing homes has increased substantially, and the number of places in old peoples' homes and nursing homes now correspond to 10% of the population over 70. However, there are not enough places in the various homes to meet the needs. Many older people, therefore, have to stay at general hospitals for longer periods than necessary.

A compromise between staying at home and going to a nursing home has been introduced in some municipalities through service flats. In blocks of these, each resident has his own flat, but there is a common restaurant where the residents may take their meals if they do not want to do their own cooking. Most of these blocks have a unit for nursing home patients, and the residents can move from the flats to this unit if they are no longer able to manage for themselves. In recent decades, private and semiprivate organizations have increasingly begun to organize services for the aged with considerable financial support from the municipalities. Some organizations are providing nursing homes which are run in cooperation with the municipal authorities. Other private activities, appealing to a wider group of aged, include pensioners' clubs and organizations which sponsor lectures and excursions. Several Danish folk high schools are arranging special courses for the elderly. A travel agency, specializing in arranging travels to other countries for the aged, has been set up.

NOTES

1. A comprehensive comparative report on expenditures and scope of social security and services in Denmark, Finland, Iceland, Norway, and Sweden is published biannually in Scandinavian languages and English under the title *Social Security in the Nordic Countries* (Nordic Statistical Secretariat, Post Box 2550, DK-2100 Copenhagen).
2. For detailed information on the social condition of the aged in Denmark and the services for them compared with those in Britain and the U.S.A., see Shanon et al., 1968.

REFERENCES

ANDERSEN, B.A. (1972). "A Danish study of the functioning of the system of social security." Journal of Social Policy, 1(4):331-344.
FRISS, H. (1969). "Issues in social security policies in Denmark." Pp. 129-150 in S. Jenkins (ed.), Social security in international perspective. New York: Columbia University Press.
KAHN, A., and KAMERMAN, S.B. (1975). Not for the poor alone. Philadelphia: Temple University Press.
KOCH-NIELSEN, I., SCHMIDT, G., and USSING, J. (1975). "Law and fertility in Denmark." Pp. 199-217 in M. Kirk (ed.), Law and fertility in Europe. Dolhain, Belgium: Ordina Editors.
SHANON, E., TOWNSEND, P., WEDDERBURN, D., FRIIS, H., MILHOJ, P., and STEHOUWER, J. (1968). Old people in three industrial societies. New York: Atherton.

7

FINLAND: COMMUNAL CONTROL
OF SOCIAL SERVICES

MARITA V. LINDSTROM

To understand the social welfare system of Finland requires some historical background. Finland achieved independence in 1917 and became a republic in 1919. As a result of the Finnish-Russian War (1939-1940) during World War II, however, every ninth citizen lost his home to the Russian invaders. Ninety percent of Lapland, north of the Arctic Circle, was destroyed in a "scorched earth policy." Although Finland maintained its independence, the terms of the peace treaty with the Soviet Union were not good. The U.S.S.R. received the country's most valuable province, Karelia, and the northern ice-free port of Petsamo. The U.S.S.R. also demanded reparations amounting to 80% of Finland's peacetime exports. Also Finland had a debt to the United States, for food sent to her during the 1919 famine of World War I. The combination of these demands was a crushing blow to Finland's economy. By 1949 the war debt to the United States was repaid, and on September 19, 1952, the last of the reparation payments to the Soviet Union was paid.

AUTHOR'S NOTE: *I wish to thank all the people in the field of social work who have so warmly received me and so graciously given of their time to help me obtain comprehensive understanding of the social welfare system in Finland. Especially, I would like to extend my sincere gratitude to the following: Mervi Ahla, Lector at the School of Social Policy, Helsinki University; Riitta Auvinen, Assistant Professor of the School of Social Policy, Helsinki University; Ahti Hailuoto, Director of the Central Union for Child Welfare, Helsinki; Marja-Liisa Heiskanen, Inspector of Rehabilitation Affairs, National Board of Social Welfare; Tuula Laiho, Deaconess of the Special Youth Office, Finnish Evangelical Lutheran Church, Helsinki; Siv Renlund, Psychologist, Folkhalsan Policilinic, Helsinki; Pastor Wille Riekkinen, Assistant Director of the Young Men's Christian Association, Helsinki; Olavi Riihinen, Director of the School of Social Policy, Helsinki University; Helena Vapaaralta, Chief Social Worker, Children's Castel Hospital, Helsinki.*

Today Finland stands 13th among the developed countries of the world in gross national product per capita. With industrialization has emerged the social problems that are common to industrialized nations. Finland is encountering inmigration from forests to factories, urbanization with severe housing shortages in the cities, breakdowns in the traditional family structure, income insecurity, increasing health problems, mechanization of forestry and farming methods, unemployment in rural areas, a flight of youth to the towns, increasing poverty for the aged, longer dependency periods for children, and the need for highly skilled and educated citizens to meet the demands of modern society.

A critical problem has been the shrinking population, resulting from a decreasing birth rate[1] and the emigration of workers to Sweden (Finnish Delegation, 1974:27). Most emigrants have been leaving the impoverished rural regions of Lapland for Sweden, where wages are 40% higher than in Finland. By the year 1950, more than 70,000 citizens had left for Sweden, and in the next decade, another 100,000 left. As of 1970, the figure had swollen to 300,000. In a population of 4.5 million people, this loss of labor has been critical.

In 1950, 68% of the population was rural; by 1974, the figure was 49%. In a land of 130,000 square miles, one-half of the population had settled into one-tenth of the land area. In Helsinki and its surrounding areas, there are 56.5 persons per square mile, whereas in the northern section of Finland the ratio is 4.9 persons per square mile. From 1951 through 1970, an average of 274,263 persons moved to urban areas.

Today Finland is making special efforts to meet the social needs of the people. In 1963, a Research Committee for the State was established. Pekka Kuusi (1964) published *Social Policy for the Sixties*. Both events had much influence on efforts to adapt social welfare to rapid social change. Kuusi stated that "sound social welfare promotes economic growth by mobilizing human resources and creating a firm body of consumers." He believed that society should be collectively responsible for the social security of every citizen in the nation and that buying power should be assured also to the unproductive—the aged, the young, and others incapable of contributing to the economy. He claimed that the only method of achieving this was by the redistribution of the national income, transferring the income from the active to the inactive. His goal, ideally, was for social security to absorb 26% of the gross national product, but he conceded that 20% was a more realistic aim (Kuusi, 1964:10).

ADMINISTRATIVE ORGANIZATION OF SOCIAL POLICIES

Finland allocates 20% of its national budget to the Ministry of Social Welfare and Health. Most social programs receive financial aid from the state, whether they are sponsored by public or private organizations.

In 1968, the Ministry of Social Welfare and Health was organized by combining the Ministry of Health and the Ministry of Social Welfare. Under this

new ministry, a National Welfare Board was created, and the country was
divided into 11 districts, with each district headed by a district supervisor. The
National Welfare Board exercises central control and is charged with (a)
supervising and promoting social welfare, (b) controlling the distribution of
social allowances, (c) managing the administration of state institutions, and (d)
supervising the activities of communal and private institutions. Several administrators have expressed the opinion that the National Welfare Board needs further
decentralization, because the staff has increasingly become "bogged down with
paper work and wrapped in red tape."[2] From the top come final decisions on
minor matters, such as determining the client's eligibility for a wheelchair, rent
allowance, or emergency housing. These and similar decisions could be more
expediently handled by a local communal board, some argue.

There are seven departments under the jurisdiction of the Ministry of Social
Welfare and Health:

(1) The Administrative Department draws and controls the budget, supervises personnel, coordinates international activities, and conciliates labor
and court disputes.

(2) The Department of Labor Protection sponsors social legislation and
decrees concerning occupational safety and health.

(3) The Department of Insurance sponsors legislation and handles pensions,
unemployment insurance, sickness insurance, disability insurance, etc.

(4) The Department of Social Welfare sponsors social legislation, supervises
the National Welfare Board and other social administrators and oversees
family costs compensation, the upbringing and care of children, old-age
care, and the rehabilitation of the abusers of narcotic drugs and
alcohol.

(5) The Temperance and Alcohol Department sponsors alcohol legislation
and controls the monopolized state alcohol company.

(6) The Research Department handles research.

(7) The Health Department directs and supervises public work and medical
care.

Politically, Finland is divided into 512 communes,[3] consisting of 82 cities
and boroughs and 420 rural areas. They levy their own taxes and have their own
councils, which are elected for four-year terms by popular vote. The councils
appoint communal boards for various tasks. The power base of the communal
administration is the local citizens, who are elected to the communal boards,
each of which consists of six members (two men and two women, plus a
chairman and a vice chairman). For each communal institution (e.g., Home for
Aged) a separate board of administration is often appointed. However, in most
communes there are two boards: the "general board" handles family, child, and
youth matters and administers social assistance, vocational training, and
disability aid; the "welfare board" handles public aid and the problems of

vagrants and alcoholics. Separate child welfare boards have been established in three of the larger cities, Helsinki, Turky, and Pori. Communes receive state subsidies for day care, for managing children's homes, for providing care for the mentally subnormal, and for other social services. Generally the state pays two-thirds of the cost of a service; the remainder must be raised by the local commune; thus, the level of service depends on regional affluence and the local government's priorities. The disparity in the quality of the services is one of the strongest criticisms leveled at the social welfare system.

SOCIAL SECURITY

Finnish social security is divided into three areas: (1) social insurances, (2) social allowances, and (3) social welfare.

Social Insurances

The first area of social security is the social insurances: National Pension, Statutory Sickness, and Unemployment. The largest is the National Pension Insurance, which assures every old or disabled person a basic buying power not dependent on previous income or on the number of years of employment. Every person aged 65 or over is eligible. A change of employment does not jeopardize an employee's entitlement to the basic pension. It is based strictly on the assessment principle, whereby funds from active citizens are transferred to the inactive old and disabled. This basic plan has been enhanced by amendments:

(1) The National Basic Support is given those aged 65 or over. There is no upper income limit, and every individual, regardless of his past earning power, receives this basic allotment. However, if there is no other income available to the individual (if he is needy), he may collect a maximum amount, depending on need. The minimum figure is 108 Finn marks (about $28) per month for every pensioner. As of September 1, 1974, the maximum rate for a needy individual was raised to 546 Finn marks (about $142) per month.

(2) The Employee's Pension Act provides benefits dependent on former wages, length of service, and actuarial percentages. Costs are borne by the employer, amounting to 5% of the employee's wages.

(3) The Communal Employees Pension Act covers communal employees at the retirement age of 63. It grants full pension after 30 years of service (66% of income). It is financed by employers and coordinated by communal authorities.

(4) The Amendment to the Basic Pension, 1965 provides pensioners aged 80 years and over with help at home and provides pensioners aged 85 and over with nursing care if needed.

(5) The 1966 Civil Service Act grants state employees, teachers, etc. the same retirement benefits as those given to communal employees.

(6) The Evangical Lutheran Church Act of 1967 granted churchmen the same benefits as those given to communal employees.

(7) The Housing Supplement Act of 1970 leveled differences due to variances in housing costs.

(8) The Farmer's Pension Act and Self Employed Act of 1970 provides state subsidies on a farmer's insurance premiums (up to 60%), according to need.

(9) The Privileged Incomes include minimal basic pensions, veteran's pensions, war-wounded pensions, etc., which are not calculated as annual income in determining the beneficiary's total support pension.

The majority of citizens who have left the labor market are covered by two pension plans, the National Basic and the Employees Pension.[4] Some social policy experts criticize the pension system because it is not universal, has no coordination, has been assembled through a series of legislative acts, and is the result of piecemeal development. Some pensioners maintain that their benefits are inadequate to provide a livelihood, whereas others receive a pension greater than the standard of living that they maintained before retirement.

Statutory Sickness Insurance. The Statutory Sickness Insurance covers every person in the country, regardless of age or income, whether he or she is employed or not. The only test of eligibility is that the person be a citizen of Finland. Citizens need not reside in the country. Benefits are available even while abroad.

The program has been praised because it promotes adequate care for the noninstitutionalized and more intense assistance to the more critical cases. Its benefits cover the cost of treatment, the loss of earnings due to illnesses, and the expenses of maternity care (women are granted 72 working days' leave). This insurance partly compensates beneficiaries for medical examinations, medicine, and travel (the patient paying only the first four Finn marks). Full compensation is paid to the chronic invalid. The hospitalization costs the patient 15% of the total bill. The Sickness Plan is financed by the insured and employers, through local and state taxes. It is administered through the National Pension Institute. In 1971, over three million people, two-thirds of the population, received Statutory Sickness benefits.

Unemployment Insurance. Employment has been affected by the seasonal changes in economic conditions. It is difficult to maintain employment with such varying working conditions year-round and even more difficult to enforce a universal law of unemployment insurance. Although most men in rural areas work partly on their own small farms and several months of the year as lumbermen, unemployment in these areas has been as high as 6%. The Employment Act of 1963 created more permanent jobs. The average rate of unemployment (1974) was 4.5%, and as low as 1.9% in 1970 in the southeastern section of the country (Finnish Delegation, 1972:15).

Unemployment coverage involves two systems, compensation and insurance. Unemployment Insurance is a voluntary activity administered by the Unemployment Benefit Societies, which operate in conjunction with their respective trade unions. The benefit is paid for five days a week, maximum of two years, at which time it terminates for six months. Supervision of the Unemployment Insurance programs is the responsibility of the Ministry of Social Welfare and Health. The financing of the insurance scheme is undertaken by the state, the Central Fund of the Unemployment Benefit Societies (financed by the employers), and the members of the societies. The state support is 50%, the Central Fund 43%, and the member's share 7%.

According to the Employment Act of 1960, unemployment compensation is available to every person above 16 years of age who is not entitled to receive assistance from an Unemployment Insurance Plan (apparently most wage earners are involved in employer compulsory unemployment insurance plans with their place of employment). It must also be impossible for the individual to find work or training, and he must be in need of economic support. The compensation is paid for a maximum of five days a week, 120 days within a year. The program is under the jurisdiction of the Ministry of Labor. The benefits are granted by the public employment board in each commune and is funded by state taxes.

Social Allowances

Social Allowances are allocated from state funds that are given to local communes to distribute. Allowances have contributed much to improve the health, vocational skill, and working capacity of various social groups and to level the extra costs of raising a family. The most important leveler of family expense is the Child Allowance.

Child Allowance. With the birth of the first child, a family receives 268 Finn marks a year, with the second, 320 Finn marks, and with each subsequent child, 380 Finn marks. These sums are paid quarterly to the mother. Child Allowances are also paid to mothers of children born out of wedlock, if it has been possible to ensure the child's maintenance from the father, who is liable. The state bears 75% of the cost; the remainder is subsidized by the commune.

Maternity Allowances. Maternity Allowances were initiated with the Maternity Benefit Act of 1941, which assures all future mothers medical examinations, advice, and some financial assistance toward the cost of childbirth (50 Finn marks in 1968). These benefits are granted only if the applicant has seen a doctor or midwife or has been to a maternity center for a checkup. In 1967, benefits were granted to 72,527 mothers, accounting for 94% of all babies born that year.

Family Allowances. Family Allowances are directed to large families of limited means, who have four or more children and whose income does not exceed the upper limit set by the commune. The limit varies between 65 and 76 Finn marks a year per child, depending on the local cost of living (Central Union for Child Welfare in Finland, 1968:24). In 1969, there were 61,409 families who were beneficiaries at an expenditure of 7.6 million Finn marks. By 1971, benefits had been paid to 78,737 families.

Holidays for Housewives. Holidays for housewives are granted from state funds and administered locally. Two-thirds of the cost of a two-week vacation for a needy woman with three or more children is paid by the state; the remainder is met by the commune or a private organization. Often, less affluent communes cannot provide this service.

The holiday is available to mothers with three or more children under the age of 16, who are existing within limited means. The purpose is to give women freedom from family obligations. No children are permitted to accompany mothers. In 1970, this benefit was received by over 10,000 mothers.

Housing Allowances. Housing Allowances were enacted in 1962 to attempt to relieve the severe shortage of dwellings, particularly in the towns and cities. In 1963 there were 9.7 dwellings built per 1,000 inhabitants, but by 1968 there were only 7.6 dwellings built per 1,000 inhabitants. This decrease is due to the spiraling costs of construction that must be sturdy enough to meet the demands of the severe winter climate. Not only is there a shortage of dwellings, but the existing dwellings are small by international standards. In the 1950s, one-third of the population lived in households with more than two persons per room, and by the 1960s the density of inhabitants had only decreased to 1.31 persons per room. Of all the dwellings built in Finnish cities and towns, 70% contain a maximum of two rooms and a kitchen. Many are simply one-room flats.

The Act of 1962 provided rent subsidies of 20% to 70%, depending on the income of the family with two or more children. The apartments are required to have at least two rooms and a kitchen. In 1968, communes paid a monthly subsidy to 20,000 families; by 1972 the figure had increased to 28,000, costing the state 42.8 million Finn marks.

As of 1974, the state provides loans of up to 60% of the cost of the purchase of an apartment, at an interest rate of 3%, for those with limited incomes. Also, several communes are developing housing projects for the aged to promote independent living rather than institutionalization. Despite all these efforts, it is apparent that housing policy must be integrated with other societal planning in order to ease the housing shortage.

Social Welfare

The Public Aid Act of 1956 states:

Every individual is absolutely liable for the maintenance of himself, his spouse, and children under the age of sixteen. In cases of need and to the extent of his ability, every person is also conditionally obliged to support his parents and children of sixteen through twenty-one years of age and in some cases his grandparents.

Financial aid was considered a loan, which had to be repaid, by labor detention in a workhouse if necessary. In 1971, an amendment was enacted to change some of the severe implications of the law. It required repayment of benefits received only in exceptional cases. It also removed the "criminal stigma" of labor in the workhouse.

In 1966, approximately 6.8% of the population received public aid. Of that total, 44.5% collected monetary aid, 55% received support in institutions. There are no statistics on the duration of the benefits, but it appears that the monetary assistance is of short duration, while the institutional care is generally long term. The monetary aid does diminish or become more stringent the longer it is given. No required length of residence is necessary in the commune in order to receive aid.

SOCIAL SERVICES

In Finland, social services are defined as those that "don't entail the distribution of money."[5] Services are seen as necessary supplements to the transfer-of-income schemes and other intangible assistances, not goods exchangeable for money. It is felt that all must be entitled to the benefits of the programs, that they are socially acceptable to everyone, and consequently readily available to all.

Finland has not established any one particular system to fill social service needs. Some programs are directed at social problems (alcoholism, marriage disintegration, cerebral palsy, etc.), whereas other programs target in on special groups needing services, such as children, adolescents, or the handicapped. Some services are delivered from all three levels of administration—state, communal, and voluntary agencies. Others are delivered from only one level or from various combinations of the three.

There are more than 100 voluntary organizations. Most of these are held accountable to the state authorities because they receive state aid or economic support from public funds. Despite this, they tend to maintain freedom and flexibility to adapt their activities to the needs which are most urgent. Whereas the private agency has the opportunity to experiment with new ideas and approaches to social problems, the state agencies are burdened by the legislative machinery which is presently too slow to meet the rapid changes and vacillating needs of today (Finnish Delegation, 1972:7). As the role of the state became more predominant in the dispensing of services, it took over the administration of many of the voluntary agencies. In turn, the private agencies have been exploring other areas of social need and making the public aware of these. The private agency is also a significant influence on legislation, when it combines with others to form pressure groups. Some of the major volunteer agencies in Finland are the Central Union for Child Welfare, the Lutheran church, the Mannerheim League, the Save the Children Association, A-Clinics (comparable to the American Alcoholic Anonymous), and the Salvation Army.

Child Welfare

One of the major concerns of the social services of Finland has been the welfare of the child. In 1811, the first children's health organization was founded, known as Collegium Medicii.

During World War II, between 1941 and 1946, the Ministry of Social Affairs arranged for 48,628 children to be evacuated to neutral Sweden, and an additional 15,174 were sent there privately. This movement was deemed in the best interest of the child, to save them from the bombings and ravages of war.[6] A school Feeding Act was initiated in 1943 to make certain that every school-aged child received at least one substantial meal a day. Mr. Ahti Hailuoto, Director of the largest child agency in Finland, the Central Union for Child Welfare, states:

The purpose of child welfare is to undertake a broad spectrum of activity within the limits imposed by the prevailing economic resources, in order to create the best possible environment for children in general to grow into physically and mentally healthy, well-balanced, responsible and constructive adults who will adapt themselves to a society that is constantly on the move.

The surveys of 1965 showed that 45.3% of the population was aged 25 years or under. Those under 15 years of age represented 26.7% of the population. In 1971, child welfare cost 10.6% of the budget allotted to the Ministry of Social Welfare and Health. It covered the care of 11,183 children.

Child Day-Care. In the cities and boroughs of Finland, the day-care of children is an acute problem. The rate of employment of women and mothers in this country is one of the highest in Europe. Of all urban mothers, 46.2% hold jobs. Of mothers with children aged six years and under, 27.1% have full-time employment. In 1970, 284,000 children of that age bracket had working mothers. Only about half of these working mothers could make satisfactory arrangements for the care of her children.

Compulsory education does not begin until the age of seven. The kindergartens are for children aged three to seven. There is no federal financial aid for establishing kindergartens; however, if an operating kindergarten is approved by the government, it may receive aid for 25% of its annual expenses. These arrangements are administered by the Department of Social Welfare, since kindergartens are not considered part of the educational system.

Crèches are day-care centers for children aged six months to three years. They receive no state funds and operate solely on funds from meal payments,[7] made by the parents or municipalities.

There are day-care voluntary services where the poor have first priority, based on their income. For every admission, there are 10 applicants.[8] Private day-care activities are mushrooming, whereby a mother may take care of one or more children in her home for a fee. In 1970, the Child Day-Care Regulation Committee ordered stricter supervision of the private homes for day-care.

Play schools and playground programs are also coming into existence. These are conducted for shorter periods of time and their programs are of lower standard than kindergartens. The majority are conducted by churches, factories, and individuals.

Communal day-care institutions and programs with public assistance are supervised by the National Welfare Board. In 1974, legislation mandated that every commune provide day-care in its district. The commune must draw up a five-year plan to be approved by the National Welfare Board. The communes receive 35% to 80% state subsidies, based on the needs of the commune. At the end of 1964 there were a total of 608 day-care institutions. Of these, 83.9% were in receipt of public funds. By 1972, the figure had grown to 879, servicing 40,731 children. At least 5,000 more day-care establishments are needed (Auvinen, 1969:34).

Home Helper Act. The Home Helper Act of 1966 was introduced to provide additional stability to the child in the family setting. Rather than "farm" a child out to neighbors or strangers if the mother of the household becomes sick, or is in childbirth, or has to take a necessary vacation, the home is kept intact, through an experienced worker coming into the home. This avoids disruption in the family; meals are prepared, and even the cows get milked.

Every commune is obligated to have at least one home helper, determined by the size of the commune. This helper is especially trained for a period of one to two years. The fee is determined by the client's financial status. In 1965, this service was rendered to 41,800 families. The demand for these services is far beyond what the state can provide. In 1971, there were 2,327 home helpers.

Child Psychiatric Services. The municipality of Helsinki conducted a survey of six-year old children in 1956 to determine if there was a need for psychiatric services in Finland. Out of a random sampling of 5,800 children it was discovered that 10% needed psychiatric treatment and 2% needed hospitalization.

In 1973, there were 39 child guidance clinics in Finland. Although they form the principal network for preventative mental health, only one-third of the demand is being filled. The great obstacle to opening more clinics is the shortage of trained professionals.[9] A Child Guidance Bill that granted 35%-80% financial support from the state was passed in July 1971. It helped formalize the status of clinics and began to alleviate the shortage.

A new and innovative approach to treatment, which first appeared in 1960, is the teenage poli-clinic. Teenagers receive treatment through a team approach. The team consists of a general practitioner, endocrinologist, psychiatrist, psychologist, and social worker. Treatment includes medical and hormonal treatment, psychotheraphy, and group therapy. The original, and most widely known, poli-clinic is Folkhalsan, established by the Swedish-speaking community. It was supported solely at first from their contributions. Now Folkhalsan has entered into contract with approximately 20 communes, located within the vicinity of Helsinki. Its services are free to Finnish and Swedish teenagers.

The poli-clinic handles medical as well as psychiatric symptoms. A major problem that faces the teenager in Finland is the rigorous demands of the educational system. The system is now in the process of change, but it has been excessively achievement-oriented, requiring the passing of a series of difficult examinations. With the failure to meet the requirements comes the shattering of the young person's self-esteem and the termination of educational pursuit.

In 1970, there were eight teenage poli-clinics, not nearly enough to meet the growing need for these services.

The teenager with a problem may also go to the Evangelical Lutheran church for help, for it provides extensive youth work throughout its parishes. In Helsinki there is a central parish for young alcoholics and drug addicts. Work is done both in the drop-in center and in street outreach programs. The young person is helped to help himself in seeking employment, housing, and alternate methods of handling his emotional problems. The staff consists of one psychologist, one minister, three deaconesses, one youth leader, an ex-addict, and one student in training. In 1972, there were approximately 2,000 youngsters under the age of 18 abusing drugs. Approximately 200 youngsters are being reached from this parish.

Drug programs are also sponsored by child welfare and social welfare offices, child guidance clinics, outpatient clinics of mental-health-care centers, and alcohol foundations. The two mental hospitals have special wards for the young drug abuser. The A-Clinic has a halfway house in Helsinki. Collaboration between these agencies is mostly informal.

Juvenile Delinquents. Much of the responsibility for helping socially maladjusted minors falls on communal authorities. According to the Child Welfare Act of 1936:

> The child welfare board must take steps to secure the care and education of a child if he is neglected or if he has committed an offense against the law.

In 1964, there were 23,256 prosecutions for crimes and 37,151 for infringements of other laws (mainly traffic offenses), by minors aged 15 to 20 (Central Union for Child Welfare in Finland, 1968:73). Of all registered criminals and offenders in that year, 25.9% were persons aged 10 to 20 years. However, the rate of crime is decreasing.

All police juvenile cases must be reported by the court to the Ministry of Justice and then to the Criminal Welfare Association, when under the jurisdiction of the Ministry of Justice. The Criminal Welfare Association names a supervisor for the youth, who is responsible for providing guidance and advice. The Criminal Welfare Association's services also arrange probation, administer boarding homes and work camps for ex-prisoners, and establish employment exchanges.

Of all young people aged 15 to 17 years who were prosecuted and found guilty in 1963, 3.4% were not sentenced. In the same year, of these youths sentenced to imprisonment in courts of the first instance, 70% of those 15 to 17 were granted probation. The imposition of the sentence is postponed for a period decided by the court—a minimum of two years and a maximum of five years. When a youth is sentenced, he may be sent to a "state labor colony" for isolation from society or a juvenile prison if he is considered a more "difficult" case. In prisons, some attempts at therapy are undertaken. The Lutheran church runs five therapy groups in two prisons, the Kerava Prison for men and the Nunmenkyla for women.

Illegitimate Children. The communal board is responsible for the child born out of wedlock. The board must appoint a "communal godfather," who looks after the child's rights, interests and legalities and helps the mother through advice and practical assistance. He also checks on the mother's suitability for guardianship. Often a board member is assigned this responsibility.

Youth Programs. The main purpose of the state and communal organizations for youth is to assist and coordinate programs. Each commune has a Youth Work Committee within the Ministry of Education, which trains youth workers and initiates youth activities. Communal boards also provide summer holidays, summer camps, and summer visits to private country homes and farms. Summer holidays and recreation programs are made available by voluntary agencies such as the Lutheran church, the Mannerheim League, the YMCA, and the Best for the Children Association. There is Mustasaari, a leisure island for youth, which is sponsored by the church. There young people learn to raise pigs and sheep and study the art of building. Various sports are offered, and there are a discotheque for the evenings and church services on Sunday.

Youth Funding. The government claims that 24.5% of all social expenditures are directed toward children's welfare, including the tax deductions declared by families. The latest census available shows that, in 1970, there were 1,189,329 children under the age of 16, who constitute 25.2% of the total population of Finland (a 2% decrease from the year 1965).

There are several unique means of funding child welfare programs. Linnanmaki is an amusement park in Helsinki that is operated by the Children's Day Foundation. All profits from the park are distributed between its founder, the Central Union for Child Welfare (a totally self-funding organization), and member voluntary child welfare agencies. The Slot Machine Association, another means of financing voluntary agencies, was decreed legal by President Uhro Kekkonen and is administrated by the state. Machines are placed at obvious locations, beckoning the passerby to try his luck. All profits go to the voluntary agencies. The final decision on the distribution of the funds is decided by the state.

Family Services

The major emphasis on aiding families as a unit has been through financial aid, through the social insurance plans. Actual personal services are few, basically consisting of family counseling and Home Case Assistance (home helpers).

The present rate of divorce in Finland is one out of every five marriages. In the cities, the rate increases, with a ratio of one out of two in Helsinki. Marriage counseling is compulsory by law as a preliminary to legal separation and is conducted by the local social welfare board, by the Lutheran church,[10] or by voluntary agencies. From a religious orientation, the church attempts to resolve the marital conflict and endeavors reconciliation. The Population and Family Welfare League has marriage counseling in four cities and also provides information on birth control, family problems and abortions and attempts to resolve sexual difficulties between marriage partners.

The Aged

Services for the elderly are focused on noninstitutional care, referred to as "open-care." Home-help was enacted in 1966 through the Communal Home Helper Act, which required communes to provide home care for the aged. Under state supervision, health care, legal assistance, and leisure programs are also available to the aged.

The majority of the direct services to the elderly are dispensed by voluntary agencies, who receive no financial aid from the state. The Lutheran church, Salvation Army, Red Cross, Central League for Welfare of the Aged, and other agencies organize programs of meal services, friendly visits, and Golden Age Club activities. The Red Cross operates 23 day centers for the aged.

The national government supplies employment agencies for the aged in 20 cities, where they can obtain information and guidance on part-time or additional jobs and information on hobby clubs that are available. The communes administer these services under state supervision.

Culturally, the Finns have always maintained reverence and respect for the older person. (At a family dinner, the elders are always served first.)

INSTITUTIONAL CARE

Today, institutional care is considered secondary to "open care," although at times it is the only alternative available. The total number of institutions in Finland is 860, serving 40,700 residents. The majority are administered by local communes, some are state managed, and the remainder are conducted by private associations. All are under the supervision of the National Welfare Board. The National Welfare Board must approve the architectural plans of a building and the proposed administration's regulations. District inspectors check facilities before they are put to use. The director and the nursing staff also must be given approval before they are employed.

An analysis of the expenditures on public welfare in 1967 shows that institutional care is by far the most expensive form of social welfare. Seventy-five percent of the total budget is allotted to institutionalization, even with the policy of "open care."

Children's Homes

Communes are not obligated by law to establish children's institutions, but, if they do, state assistance is provided. There are 85 voluntary children's homes, out of a total of 213. The average number of residents per home is 23 children, although the trend is toward providing a more "homelike" atmosphere with no more than 10 children per home. Such a home is usually managed by a married couple.

In most cases, efforts are made to place children in foster homes, rather than in institutions. Yet the feeling does prevail that it is preferable for the child to remain in a stable institution, rather than a series of foster homes, especially if the child displays adjustment problems. In 1974, 11,183 children were placed in outside care. In actual practice, the welfare board often delegates the work of the placement of a child in a foster home to the Save the Children Association.

For the mentally subnormal, 14 institutions have been established. The mentally subnormal constitute .15% of the population. The institutes provide examinations, treatment (case study), care, education, training and supervision, and slowly expanding psychiatric care. Open care is the desired goal, to cut down on the expense of institutional maintenance. In 1969, the Mental Subnormal Act Amendment established state aid for open-care centers. Today there are 39 such day-care establishments, which provide training and occupational therapy to the mentally subnormal.

Homes for the Aged

Homes for the Aged provide services for 28,500 elderly persons, who constitute 6.3% of the population aged 65 or over. The number of persons requiring such services is on the increase.

There are three levels of care for the elderly. The first is for the healthy individual who needs lodging and perhaps a small amount of home care. In 1966, there were 541 such establishments, 34% privately managed. The second level is for the invalid who needs nursing care. There are very few such institutions, but special wards within the homes for the aged provide such health services. The third level is for the chronically ill. They are also treated in the nursing wards and often in general hospitals.

Hospitals

The majority of hospitals are almost totally subsidized by the state. The patient pays approximately 10% of the cost. The ratio of beds to persons is exceptional according to European standards, 10.6 beds per 1,000 inhabitants. Open-care health service provides patients with free shots and free maternity benefits. Most hospitals have clinics as part of their open care facilities. The Children's Castle hospital in Helsinki offers one of the most comprehensive programs of health care in the country. It specializes in investigational and therapeutic activities, both mental and physical. The hospital was founded in 1921 by the Mannerheim League for Child Welfare. In 1952, a special association of communities was established to support the league in the administration of the constantly expanding services. It has a unique method of funding, for in 1968 the possession and maintenance of the institute were transferred to a Communal Federation. This federation is an association of local communes, presently numbering 103, located in the southern and central sections of Finland. The total number of residents residing in these communities is approximately two million.

The Children's Castle hospital maintains 170 beds, of which 80 are for psychiatric patients. The medical and nursing staff consists of 379 workers, including 9 social workers. The service personnel comprises 115 persons, making a total of 406 personnel in the Children's Castle hospital. There are 10 psychologists. They are the only ones that provide treatment for the children. Social workers interview and give consultation to the parents. The total expense per day per patient in 1974 was 180 Finn marks (about $48). The patient pays eight Finn marks; the state support is 10%; and the remainder is paid by the Communal Federation.

Penal Institutes

With the focus on open care, the number of people contained in prisons is on the decrease. According to the 1971 census, 4,991 persons were in prison. The census of 1973 showed a slight decrease, with a total of 4,706 persons imprisoned.

Most social services available to prisoners are under the jurisdiction of the National Welfare Board. Financial aid is given to the families if needed. Attempts are made at some form of rehabilitation. In two of the largest institutions, education is made available for those who never completed their schooling. They may either complete their secondary level of education or opt for vocational training in order to prepare for a trade at the time of their release. Psychiatric services are practically nil, but a prisoner feeling disturbed may speak with a priest.

Prison after-care is given both by the state and by volunteer agencies. While serving their term of conviction, the prisoners earn a meager salary. Part of it is saved and returned to them at the time of their release to help them reenter society and meet the cost of living until they are able to find employment. Aid is also provided by the volunteer agency Kriminaalihuolto R.Y. (Criminal Care, Inc.), which assists released prisoners to become adjusted to society and their freedom. This agency is 90% state-funded.

Of all persons arrested and imprisoned, 23.7% are charged with drunkenness.[11] The Alcoholics Welfare Act of 1936 established a state institute solely for the abusers of alcohol. Today there are nine such establishments, three state-owned, and six privately owned. The communal-administered institutes are two-thirds supported by the state, one-third supported by the commune. Alcohol abusers may be placed in such institutes against their will, according to the decision of the local communal board. The Welfare for Abusers of Intoxicants Act of 1961 states that the maximum sentence permissible for such an offense is two years. During that period of time, guidance and counseling must be provided. Unfortunately, because of a lack of trained personnel, this act has not been enforced effectively.

In an effort to restrict the consumption of alcohol in Finland, the government has placed high taxes and tariffs on the sale of alcohol. An Alcohol Monopoly, which maintains strict control of the production and distribution of alcohol, has also been established by the government. The profits from the Alcohol Monopoly go to the state welfare authorities. These funds are distributed to needy alcoholics and deprived families.

SOCIAL WORK

Education

Since August 1970, Finland has been undergoing a total educational reform. Previously, it had been necessary to pass certain examinations to move from the primary to the junior secondary level of education. Now the two levels have been merged, permitting all children to have an opportunity for a higher education. This process of change will take at least 10 years for total transition in all communes and cities. In 1969, the number of students continuing their education into the university level was 11.4 per 1,000.

Within the hierarchy of learning, the time spent at a certain level of education is inconsequential. It is the series of examinations that must be completed, whether it takes two years or six years. Three degrees are offered at the university: the master's degree (equivalent to the bachelor's in the United States), the licentiate, and the doctorate. The student is required to have a specialty in at least three disciplines and reach the level of "laudatur" in his major field.

Social work training at the university level was established in 1942 at the University of Helsinki (which awarded the licentiate degree), but such studies were known as Social Policy and dealt strictly with theory. It was possible for a student to receive five years of education and never come in contact with a client. In 1965 there was a split in this school, with a branch moving to the city of Tampere to establish a school of social welfare. After three years of training the school awards a certificate to work in the state social welfare system. Presently this school is considering an undergraduate B.A. program in social welfare.

In addition to the two university-level schools, there are several schools that award certificates upon graduation, but are not considered of academic status and have no university accreditation. One of the finest of these schools is the Svenska-Social-Och Kommunalhoskolan, which was founded in 1942. Its program lasts three years, with two years of theory and one year of practice. The curriculum includes the study of law and medicine, as well as psychology and casework. Upon completion, a certificate of social work is awarded.

The Lutheran Institute is another school that trains social workers, but it also has no university recognition. Its program began in 1953 with emphasis on group work as well as casework and on much field practice in social agencies and welfare institutions. The training is religiously oriented, with deaconesses receiving certificates in social work upon the completion of the three-year program.

Apparently there is a gap in the education of social workers in Finland. On the one hand there are students who are university educated with an excellent exposure to social planning, politics, law, and research, but with no exposure to the client and his personal needs. On the other hand there are students who are educated solely to administer welfare and to understand the client's needs, but receive no preparation in methods of long-term planning, politics and its importance, or the significance of statistics and record-keeping. Added to these shortcomings is the great lack of schools to train social workers. There is a need for reform in the education of social workers, and, although there is a movement toward dovetailing the basic practical training with university level training, nothing as of yet has really been changed.

Staffing and Manpower Patterns

For centuries, charity work was considered the obligation of the church parish, so the professional social worker is a fairly new phenomenon. Not until the Social Welfare Administration Act of 1950 were communes obligated to hire social work officials.

Today, there are approximately 3,000 full-time professional social workers in Finland. They hold positions as directors, secretaries, inspectors, and case-workers. (According to the statistics of 1966, the percentage of directors who had university level education was 73%; the percentage of secretaries was 52%; and the percentage of all inspectors was 53%.) In order for a worker to hold a national social work position, such as in a bureau of the National Welfare Board, it is necessary to have an academic degree. The majority of administrative positions of state and communal offices are held by those with a university education. Although women predominate in the field of social work in terms of numbers, men usually hold the executive positions. Some employees with a three-year training certificate plus some experience time may advance to an administrative position. Generally the students of the social policy program obtain the executive positions, as well as placements with the national government and with research firms.

Field social workers are hired by the larger communes. Since field-workers are paid by the local government, a poor commune may not be able to afford a social worker. In 1967, the city of Helsinki employed 188 field-workers. The total number of field-workers for the country was 634.

The shortage of social workers is one of the primary problems. Many social workers are burdened with both field work and administrative red tape. Placed in a one-man office, the social worker may find himself saddled with getting state subsidies for the commune, for recovering welfare costs, and for many other budgetary items, as well as being responsible for the welfare of the client. He may never have time to discover the real problems of the client. The criticism leveled at the social welfare worker is that he has been educated to implement welfare laws and that he embraces legal procedures and principles that have a patronizing and moralizing attitude toward the client. Additional criticism is directed at the field-worker who is not trained to handle social planning and is uninformed of the influence that his participation in political activities can bear.

Social Work Association

In 1962, a National Association of Social Workers was formed, which is comprised of seven associations, each representing a separate branch of service. The association is under the jurisdiction of the Union of Akave, which protects the salaries and work conditions of such professional people as doctors, dentists, and administrators. The union's journal is called the *Akateeminen.* The journal of the National Social Worker's Association is called *Sosiaalityontekija.* Finland joined the International Council of Social Welfare in 1963. The Finnish sector of this council disseminates information and translates literary material regarding conferences, negotiations, and activities in Finnish.

RESEARCH

The earliest effort at research in the field of social policy was undertaken by Eino Kuusi in 1931. Social research remained dormant until Pekka Kuusi's book of 1961. No comprehensive research for social development was undertaken by the government until the establishment of the State Research Council in 1963. Social planning, it was said, should

(1) Answer special needs and relate to gaps in reality and social standards,

(2) Review alternative actions and evaluate effects on the community,

(3) Observe and assess the effects of current trends.

In 1968, there were a total of 548 state committees involved in the research of social development. There are also many institutes conducting research. They include:

(1) Research Department of the Ministry of Social Welfare and Health

(2) National boards

(3) Academy of Finland (draws up contracts and distributes funds for scientific research)

(4) Universities

(5) National voluntary agencies (Mannerheim League, Central Union for Child Welfare, etc.)

(6) Three major unions (Akava, Central Organization of Finnish Trade Union, Central Organization of Employers Union)

SUMMARY

In the past three decades, Finland has experienced tremendous growth, both industrially and socially. Twenty percent of the National Budget is allocated for the social needs of the people. The social security system is sound despite the ever-rising cost of living (the inflation rate reached 18% in 1974). Although, as in any other modern and complex nation, new problems are constantly emerging, growth continues.

The major debate concerning the delivery of social services presently is whether the services should become more dispersed or more centralized. Some experts argue that with the widening scope of redistribution of income through government expenditures, more power has been added to Parliament, which has consequently encroached upon the old tradition of local self-government. Others contend that programs must be more centrally administered in order to ensure equality, both quantitively and qualitively, to all communes, regardless of residence or income.

There are clear gaps in the Social Service delivery system. Social insurance, social assistance, and public welfare are not being adequately supplemented by social services. The services that are available are not sufficiently coordinated. Apparently there is difficulty in informing the public what services are available. Since the present system of delivering services is provided on three levels, there is overlapping and confusion.

There has been an intensification of regional policies to develop the growth of centers in underdeveloped rural areas and to alleviate the congestion of the

Southwest. Many offices, universities, and research centers have decentralized and established themselves away from Helsinki in the hope of remedying the disequilibrium. Presently Helsinki University is preparing plans to establish a branch at Rovaniemi, a city located on the Arctic Circle.

Social workers must have the opportunity to receive higher education to better qualify them to service clients in a rapid-moving, complex society. Social workers must have training in social planning and must learn to move into psychotherapy, as well as into the current existing services.

Near future goals include (1) equality of family and housing costs, (2) increase in noninstitutional care and preventative activities, particularly in hospitals, (3) systematic procedures in the field of administration, (4) improved activities and planning with regard to the day care of children, and (5) decrease in the disparity of living standards among pensioners.

NOTES

1. At the turn of the century there were 30 births per 1,000. In 1947-1948, during the postwar boom, there were 28 per 1,000. By 1972, the rate was 12.9 per 1,000, one of the lowest rates in the world.

2. This is the view of Ms. Marja-Diisa Heiskanen, Inspector of Rehabilitation Affairs, National Welfare Board.

3. Originally the communes were the parish districts of the Lutheran church. Now they represent the areas of the local governments.

4. Inflation is considered by tying pensions into a wage and salary index and adjusting quarterly.

5. This is a remark by Ms. Riitta Auvineen, Assistant Professor of the School of Social Policy, Helsinki University.

6. Child psychiatrists have since researched the emotional after-effects of the separation period of one to three years. In most cases it has proven to be detrimental, with adverse psychological results. Of the children evacuated, 10,000 were not returned to Finland.

7. The meal payments are for a midday hot meal for the children, prepared by the proprietor. The fee is for this service and not for caring for the children.

8. It has been noted that due to the severe shortage of day-care centers, some women are participating in the trend of not marrying legally, in order to qualify economically to obtain communal day-care.

9. Centers are for the diagnosis of the child and counseling of the parents. There is an attempt at psychotherapy, but inadequate training and staff shortages make this virtually impossible.

10. Ninety-two percent of the nation embraces the Lutheran faith. Through state taxation, it is compulsory for citizens to pay 1% of their taxable income to the church. This enables the church to provide free social services.

11. In 1970, 1,936 persons were institutionalized for the abuse of alcohol. Driving while intoxicated is a criminal act; in fact, not one drink is permitted to be consumed before driving. Offenders are often placed in workhouses for hard labor.

REFERENCES

AUVINEN, R. (1969). "The repercussions of scientific and technological development on the status of women" (Report of Finland to the United Nations). Iasi, Rumania: Vaestopollutinen Tutkimuslaitos (Population Research Institute).
Central Union for Child Welfare in Finland (1968). "Child welfare in Finland." Kohopanio.
Finnish Delegation (1972). "Developing social policy in conditions of rapid change." Report to the 16th International Conference on Social Welfare, The Hague, August.
――― (1974). "Development and participation: Operational implications for social welfare." Report to the 17th International Conference on Social Welfare, Nairobi, July.
KUUSI, P. (1964). Social policies for the sixties: A plan for Finland. Helsinki: Finnish Social Policy Association.

8

YUGOSLAVIAN SELF-MANAGING
COMMUNITIES

NADA SMOLIC-KRKOVIC

The central problem of the socialist construction of Yugoslavia after World War II was the question of the new conception of socioeconomic relations. Instead of the traditional administrative system, a new system of self-management had to be constructed which would enable a more rapid, just, and equitable development of social relations. The decision to hand over the management of economic organizations to the workers was adopted in 1950. The system of self-management quickly expanded to work organizations in noneconomic activities. Self-management was introduced to the field of social insurance in 1952, to health institutions in 1953, and to educational and cultural institutions in 1954. In accordance with the new Constitution of 1974, the self-management system is to be introduced in all fields of social life and established in law.

The basic document governing social organizations and services is the Law on Social Welfare. There is no single Law on Social Welfare for all of Yugoslavia, but every constituent republic creates the law according to its own development, needs, and possibilities. The main provisions of such a law can be seen in the example of the Law on Social Welfare of Croatia.

THE CONCEPTION OF SOCIAL WELFARE

According to the Law on Social Welfare of Croatia, social welfare is defined as

organized societal activity which on the basis of solidarity and mutuality contributes to the satisfaction of the social welfare needs of the working people and citizens. It also aims to diminish causes and consequences for these needs. [Paragraph 1]

The law goes on to identify a social welfare need as the particular situation of a person or group which creates an inability to ameliorate one's problems without societal help. Satisfaction of such a need is provided through various social welfare functions: discovering root causes; providing material conditions, organizations, and personnel for improvement; studying social problems and related phenomena; applying scientific knowledge to such activities; proposing measures for early detection and prevention; and undertaking any other necessary measures which might contribute to the actualization of social welfare objectives.

The principle of socialist self-management is fundamental to Yugoslav social welfare activity. The Croatian law states:

> Working people and their self-managing organizations and communities, as well as socio-political communities and humanitarian social organizations, determine the policy in the sphere of social welfare. They decide upon the forms, scope and terms of the satisfaction of social welfare needs. On the basis of solidarity and mutuality, they provide and associate means for carrying out social welfare policy in accordance with the range of their material abilities. [Paragraph 4]

The identified needs are cared for through voluntary contributions and through funding of self-managing organizations of associated labor in health, education, child care, retirement and invalid insurance, employment insurance, and other measures for the carrying out of social welfare. Financial means are provided on the basis of social compacts and self-management agreements. Judicial bodies and institutions also organize and carry out social welfare measures in collaboration with other carriers of such functions, within the scope of their responsibility.

The Croatian law recognizes the following categories of people in particular need of organized social welfare aid: (1) minors without parental care; (2) minors who live under unfavorable conditions of upbringing; (3) persons entirely incapable of earning and deprived of necessary funds for living; (4) persons with disturbances of psycho-physical development and other handicapped persons; (5) persons needing advisory or other services of professional social work or related professional fields; (6) persons with socially non-adjusted behavior, such as vagabonds, beggars, prostitutes, delinquents, alcoholics, and drug addicts; (7) persons who need social welfare services because of any other circumstance. The law ennumerates the following as applicable aspects of social welfare: guardianship and adoption, observation by specialists, probation, aid in vocational training, employment, financial aid, placement in social welfare or other institutions, placement in foster care, social welfare services.

Financial Allowance

The Croatian law delineates three broad categories of eligibility for regular financial allowance: deprivation of necessary funds for living, incapability of earning a living, and holding one's domicile on the territory of a commune while submitting a claim. The law stipulates that a household shall be considered a unit of persons living together on joint earnings and consumption.

Deprivation of necessary funds for living occurs when personal income, regular income of household members, and other earnings do not exceed the amount prescribed by the communal assembly. Persons considered entirely incapable of earning are women age 60 or over, men age 65 or over, children under 15 without parental care or under 19 if in school, children and youth with psychophysical problems until the age of 21 or until getting a job, persons with severe disturbances in psychophysical development.

An unemployed mother is entitled to financial aid during pregnancy and after delivery for 180 days, if living on the territory of the commune where the claim is submitted. A self-supporting unemployed mother is entitled to a financial allowance for one year, or up to three years if it is beneficial for a child to remain with the mother instead of being placed in an institution or foster care.

The regular financial allowance for a person deprived of necessary funds for living amounts to at least 40% of the lowest worker's income regulated by law. Extra allowance may be provided to those who must be under the care of other persons, whether or not assigned by the social welfare service. Some persons are entitled to an allowance during a period of training for work.

Adults incapable of self-reliant living and earning may be placed with other families or in a social welfare or other institution—provided that they have no family or, for justifiable reasons, cannot stay with their own family. Minors without parental care, as well as minors who live in such social, economic and family circumstances that threaten their psychophysical development, have the right to be placed with another family or in a suitable institution.

While deciding about the aspect of social welfare measures to be applied in a particular case, preference is given to those that can be carried out in the place where the need occurred in order to avoid displacement of a person from his own environment.

SELF-MANAGING COMMUNITIES OF INTEREST

The self-managing community of interest is a legal entity and must be registered at the authorized court of commerce. The Croatian law states:

In order to satisfy certain personal and common needs and interests in social welfare on the principles of solidarity and mutuality, working people and citizens through their self-managing organizations and communities associate themselves and with the working people in the organizations of associated labor in the self-managing community of interest in social welfare. Working people in the organizations of associated labor in the sphere of social welfare render social welfare services to the citizens with social welfare needs on the basis of societal solidarity, performing the duties of special societal importance. [Paragraph 45]

The three types of self-managing communities of interest in social welfare are the basic community, the communal community, and the republic community.

Basic self-managing communities of interest carry out specific activities of some institutions, and the needs satisfaction of one or more local communities. Self-managing communes can operate singly or can associate themselves into a community of communes. Self-managing communes and associations, however, are obliged to associate themselves with the republic's self-managing community in social welfare.

All participants are equal, and the procedure for arriving at agreements is public. A self-management agreement is adopted only when it has been accepted by the majority of working people. It is obligatory only for those participants who have adopted it or have entered into it. However, by the decision of the communal assembly, obligatory membership may be prescribed for those participants who have not adopted the self-management agreement.

The self-management agreement of the self-managing community determines:

—Activities of common interest for the members of the community.

—The program of activities, the scope of rights, and needs which will be satisfied, as well as financial means which will be joined in the basic, communal, and republic self-managing communities of interest.

—Socioeconomic relations in the exchange of labor and other mutual relations.

—The mode of joining and decisions on financial means.

—The mode of decision making on the rights, duties, and responsibilities in mutual relations.

—Basic rights and duties of delegates and delegations.

—Procedures and the composition of the assembly of the community.

—Spheres of action and power.

—Foundation of the other bodies of the community, their spheres of action, and responsibilities toward the assembly of the community.

—The manner of control of the members of the self-managing community over the assembly and the community's professional services.

—The procedure for issuing statutes for the self-managing community. [Paragraph 54]

The delegations are formed by working people in their basic labor organizations; by working people who are in agricultural, artisan, and other similar occupations where the means of production are individually owned and who are organized in associations or cooperatives; by working people organized in state administrative bodies and socio-political organizations; by active military cadres and other persons working in the armed forces; by working people and citizens in local communities; by working people and citizens in humanitarian social organizations; and by recipients of social welfare services. Members of the delegations are elected for a period of four years. The number of delegates to an assembly of the basic self-managing community has to be stated in the self-management agreement; each delegate should represent approximately equal numbers of working people and citizens.

The assembly of delegates consists of two chambers, having equal rights. One chamber consists of working people from self-managing organizations, local communities, humanitarian organizations, and communities of recipients of social welfare services. The other chamber consists of working people from organized labor and from working organizations in the sphere of social welfare. The assembly issues statutes, work programs, financial plans, and financial accounts; decides upon associating in wider communities and with the republic; issues decisions on collaborating with other communities of interest; and accomplishes other duties prescribed by law, the self-management agreement, and various statutes. The activity of the assembly is public, and it is obliged to issue announcements of its agreements and decisions through the mass media or other fashion.

From among the delegates to the assembly an executive body is elected to carry out the decisions of the assembly and to report on other aspects of its work. In smaller self-managing communities the president of the assembly is charged with such functions. A business manager is also elected by the assembly for a period of four years.

The republic also has an assembly, which is composed of delegates from the communal assemblies, from the Republic Conference for Rehabilitation and Social Welfare of Handicapped Persons, and from the Republic Council of the Red Cross of Croatia. The assembly is composed of two chambers, and its organization, mode of work, and decision making are regulated by a self-management agreement. It issues statutes and other legislation and performs other duties as regulated by the self-management agreement.

Certain social welfare needs are cared for principally on the republic level; they include the protection of the victims of fascist terror and civil victims of war, as well as their family members; the protection of persons of unknown domicile; partial financing of social welfare in the republic; international obligations in the sphere of social welfare; participation in building, adapting, and maintaining social welfare facilities; and development and promotion of the activities, methods of work, and other aspects of social welfare which contribute to the satisfaction of social welfare needs in the republic.

Relations Between Self-Managing Communities of Interest in Social Welfare and Socio-Political Communities

In order to promote the prevention of social problems, the assembly of the self-managing community of interest collaborates with the competent chambers of the socio-political community in the issuing of social policy measures in the sphere of personal and common consumption, health care, housing, employment, upbringing and education, child care, taxation policy, penal policy, and other spheres of public policy. [Paragraph 74]

A self-management agreement must be ratified by the assembly of the socio-political community of the territory in which its activities take place. The assembly of the socio-political community has the right to dissolve the executive bodies of the self-managing communities of interest and suspend the person holding the post of business manager, as well as workers in the professional service jobs, if self-management relations have been disturbed, societal interest has been damaged, or the community has not performed its duties as established by law. Temporary bodies may be appointed with rights and obligations as stated in the law.

Self-managing communities of interest in social welfare collaborate with communities of interest in other spheres of societal concern. With communities of interest in the field of upbringing and education they decide on social welfare measures for persons or groups whose unfavorable socioeconomic status or personal disturbances prevent them from acquiring satisfactory upbringing and education. With communities of interest in the field of health care they work on matters concerning social and health measures. With communities of interest in the sphere of disablement and pension insurance they try to satisfy the social welfare needs of those persons who need enlarged benefits. With self-managing communities of interest in the sphere of employment they collaborate on matters of vocational advice, training, and employment. With self-managing communities of interest in the sphere of child care they work on matters of care and protection of children who, due to social, economic, and cultural factors within the family, as well as personal disturbances, need special attention. With communities of interest in the field of housing they assess measures for individuals and families whose financial, family, or personal disadvantages give them an unfavorable role in the distribution of dwellings, housing loans, and rents.

Financing of Social Welfare

To finance social welfare, workers and others join in contributing from their personal earnings. The assembly of the socio-political community may also appropriate funds for social welfare. Self-managing communities of interest in social welfare which are not able to provide financial means for the satisfaction of minimum social welfare performance are entitled to receive funds from the republic self-managing community of interest in social welfare. Self-managing communities of interest may also acquire funds from socio-political communities established for specific purposes, from humanitarian social organizations, from transfers of ownership, and from random contributions.

Procedure for Awarding Social Welfare Benefits

The procedure for securing social welfare benefits starts with a claim submitted by a person or his legal representative or by an official of the social welfare service. Diagnosis and certification of need are made by a medical team or other professional team appointed by a social welfare service. The fulfillment of social welfare rights is considered urgent; decisions must be made in 15 days if there is no need for a special examinatory procedure, which must take place within 30 days after the claim is entered. The decisions are then executed by the social welfare service. Financial allowances are paid monthly and in advance.

A self-management workers' control unit evaluates the work of the assembly of the self-managing community of interest in social welfare, its executive body, and the social welfare service.

Social welfare institutions and services decide on the mode of carrying out defined measures concerned with psychophysical development, education, resocialization, and vocational training. Their activities are under supervision of social services of the commune, the community of communes, and the republic.

SOCIAL WELFARE INSTITUTIONS AND SOCIAL WORKERS

Tasks in the social welfare services and institutions are performed by social workers and other qualified persons in economics, social welfare, health, education, social insurance, employment services, the judiciary and corrections, humanitarian social organizations, and other social organizations. Professional social work is carried out by a social worker with a university degree or a degree of a higher school of professional training.

Social welfare service for the territory of a commune is managed from a Center for Social Work, which is the executive service of the self-managing community of interest in social welfare. It carries out other social welfare duties in the territory of the commune or the common duties of two or more communal self-managing communities. The business manager of the self-managing community of interest is the manager of the center.

The center performs early detection of social welfare needs and carries out social welfare measures, applying the principle of solving problems where they arise. It collaborates with citizens, with local humanitarian organizations and other social organizations, with labor organizations in health, education, and other fields; with employment services, with disability and pension insurance agencies, and with other organizations that can contribute to the satisfaction of social welfare needs. In the performance of such duties, the center keeps documents and records about persons with social welfare needs, handles the applied aspects of social welfare, and allocates funds.

The Center for Social Work represents the most important professional social service in the commune (Mladenovic, 1973:320). There are other institutions and services, however, as classified in the following sections.

Institutions and Services for the Protection of Children and Youth

1. Nurseries provide daily care, nutrition, medical care, and education for children from birth to three years.

2. Kindergartens provide daily care and education for children from three to seven years. Children can stay daily for 4, 5, or 12 hours if necessary (e.g., for families where both parents are working).

3. Children's Day Centers are for children of various age groups from birth to 15 years and offer programs similar to those of nurseries, kindergartens, and the schools.

4. Children's clubs provide hobby activities for children aged 10 or above.

5. Children's playgrounds are for children of varying age groups, and playing fields for young people.

6. After-school classes in schools offer children recreational activities and preparation for educational tasks (supervised learning).

7. Homes for children and youth are intended for children whose parents live in towns without schools. Those homes provide care, nutrition, and education.

, 8. Homes for children without parents and from deficient families are classified by age: (a) homes for babies and small children, (b) homes for children younger than either 14 or 18 years (e.g., until they are capable of leading independent lives).

9. Homes for educationally disadvantaged and delinquent children and youth provide protection, education, and professional training until they are able to participate successfully in life outside the home.

10. Institutions for the temporary observation of children and youth. The observation is made by a team of professionals (psychologist, psychiatrist, sociologist, educator, etc.) for the purpose of designing adequate care and education for the children and youth.

11. Homes for remedial education provides education for educationally and socially disadvantaged children and youth aged 10 to 18.

12. Disciplinary centers for minors provide short-term educational work for juveniles sent by courts collaborating with social agencies.

13. Educational-penitentiary homes for juvenile delinquents aged 14 to 21 are institutions where juvenile delinquents are sent by courts in collaboration with the social welfare service;

14. Special social institutions for physically and mentally disabled children and youth give care, education, and medical and professional rehabilitation for the blind, deaf, invalids, etc.

15. Rest homes for children and youth are provided in recreational areas.

16. Guardianship is organized by the Center for Social Work.

The funds for child care are defined by the law on social welfare and draw upon parents' contributions, contributions from worker's salaries, contributions from working organizations and such other sources as local communes, philanthropic citizens, etc.

Institutions and Services for the
Protection of Adults and Aged Persons

Social Welfare services and institutions encompass all those categories of the adult and aged populations who need help. This help can be in the form of (1) financial aid based on the Law on Social Welfare, (2) placement of adults and old people in institutions, such as homes for the aged or retired persons, (3) special homes for mentally disturbed adults, (4) clubs for aged persons for spending free time in hobbies, recreation, etc., (5) clubs for cured alcoholics, where social workers and physicians work with alcoholics and their families, (6) gerontological services for the aged or disabled adults in their homes (nursing, cooking, cleaning, etc.), (7) In-home service and care of patients, performed by medical and social workers of the Red Cross, (8) centers for citizens in a commune where a warm meal can be eaten, laundry done, and recreation provided (TV-viewing, reading, and participation in social and cultural activities).

Social Organizations

There are many social organizations. The most important for the social welfare of citizens are the following:

1. The Communist Union, the main political organization, devotes special attention to social problems, their causes, prevention, and cure, and to social policy and social planning.

2. The Socialist Union of Working People, the largest organization of citizens, devotes special attention to social policy and social problems.

3. The Union of Syndicates, the largest organization of workers, is also devoted to social protection of the rights of workers and their needs.

4. The War Veterans Organizations are concerned with the protection of war veterans and their families.

5. The Conference for the Social Activity of Woemn is concerned with social activity for women and children, help and protection of the family, etc.

6. The Youth Organization is concerned with the social life of youth, including their social problems.

7. The Red Cross, the largest humanitarian organization of citizens, is concerned with various tasks and also voluntary social work.

8. Caritas, a voluntary humanitarian organization of the Roman Catholic Church, is engaged in voluntary social assistance.

9. Our Children is a society which includes adults who are active in the field of social activities for children.

10. The Organization for Retired Persons is an important organization for the protection of the rights of retired persons. It also engages retired persons in various social activities.

11. Clubs for retired persons exist in working organizations where they once worked. They support free-time leisure activities.

12. The Organization of citizens in a commune is concerned with many social activities necessary to the communal life of children, youth, and adults.

13. Specialized social organizations include the Union of the Blind, the Union of the Deaf, the Union for Help for the Mentally Retarded, etc.

THE SYSTEM OF HEALTH CARE

Within the framework of the freedoms, rights, and responsibilities of the citizen, the 1974 Yugoslav Constitution, and the constitutions of the republics and autonomous provinces proclaim the following:

1. Everyone shall be entitled to health care. Cases in which uninsured citizens are entitled to health care from social resources shall be spelled out by statute.

2. Man shall have the right to a healthy environment.

3. Working people shall have the right to such working conditions as ensure their physical and moral integrity and security.

4. Workers shall have the right to health and other kinds of care and personal security in work. Young people, women and disabled persons shall enjoy special care.

5. The right of workers to social security shall be based on obligatory insurance, financed by contributions from workers' personal incomes, contributions from labor organizations, or contributions from other organizations or communities in which they work. On the basis of this insurance, the workers shall have the right of health care and other benefits in the case of illness; childbirth benefits; benefits in the case of diminution or loss of working capacity, unemployment, and old age; and other social security benefits. Worker's dependents have the right to health care, survivor's pensions, and other social security benefits.

Health institutions may be divided into three basic categories: outpatient clinics and poly-clinics, stationary health institutions, and public health institutions.

PROFESSIONAL SOCIAL WORK

In almost all countries of the world, the study of social work, regardless of its duration and program, is organized as an independent system of study; e.g., it is not a part of any other existing study, such as medicine, psychology, sociology. This is primarily due to the fact that social work is an interdisciplinary and integrative approach to man and his problems and represents a unique and special approach (Smolic-Krkovic, 1975:2). Its greatest asset consists of being close to the reality in which people live. Despite many dilemmas concerning specific methods, goals, practices and theories, social work has become an increasingly needed profession in Yugoslavia. Probably an important advantage of social work over other professions lies in its simultaneous variation and synthesis of knowledge about man.

The systematic education of experts for professional social work in Yugoslavia began in 1953 with the establishment of the first educational institution for social work. This was the two-year High School for Social Workers in Zagreb (Croatia). Today every republic in Yugoslavia (except Montenegro) has a two-year High School for Social Workers. Besides the two-year high school there is a four-year university level program for social work at the University of Zagreb (1971) and in the Faculty of Political Science at the University of Belgrad (1972).

Socioeconomic development has been quite rapid in Yugoslavia, and social problems brought about by industrialization, urbanization, and migration have developed faster than was perhaps expected. This rapid socioeconomic metamorphosis has demanded much more knowledge of coping with life's problems from social workers than perhaps from other professions. (People in trouble knocked first on their doors.) However, it soon became evident that it was necessary to single out the causes of sociopathological phenomena and problem behavior, utilizing knowledge from many disciplines and social institutions if real help is to be given, especially if prevention is a concern.

There followed an effort to raise the education of social workers to a higher level—to enable them to obtain scientific knowledge at the highest university level on a par with that of such other professionals as psychologists, sociologists, economists, and lawyers. Hence, several research institutions and organizations developed to offer research in social development. They include the Institute for Social Policy in Belgrad, the Institute for Social Work of the City of Belgrad, the Institute for Social Research (Ljubljana), the Institute for Social Work (Zagreb), the Institute for Social Research (University of Zagreb), the Center for the Investigation of Migration (University of Zagreb), the Institute of Geography (University of Zagreb), the Yugoslav Conference for Social Activities (Belgrad), and the Union of Societies for Social Workers (in each republic).

Interdisciplinary education and research for social workers affords a quicker exchange of knowledge from the various fields that are concerned with man's environment.

REFERENCES

MLADENOVIC, M. (1973). "Rad." Drustvena zastita porodice i dice. Belgrad.
SMILIJKOVIC, R. (1973). Workers' self-management in Yugoslavia. Belgrade.
SMOLIC-KRKOVIC, N. (1975). "The interdisciplinary approach in the education of social workers." Paper presented to the eighth Regional Symposium of ICSW, Opatija, Yugoslavia.
Zakon o Socijalnoj Zastiti SR Hrvatske (1974). Narodne novine. Zagreb.

9

PEOPLE SERVING PEOPLE: HUMAN SERVICES IN THE PEOPLE'S REPUBLIC OF CHINA

RUTH SIDEL

The changes which have taken place in the health, well-being, and spirit of the Chinese people over the past 25 years have been truly astonishing. Within one generation the world has seen the metamorphosis of a nation—from one living in abject poverty, plagued with disease, natural disaster, and mass illiteracy, to one which appears to be healthy, well-nourished, vigorous, and, perhaps most important, confident of its ability to mold its destiny. To understand this complex process of change and the current ways in which China provides human services for its vast population is extremely difficult, in part because of China's ancient and complex history and culture and in part because of elements in the organization of contemporary Chinese society.

Contemporary Chinese society is highly decentralized, with services provided at every level of organization. Great variety therefore exists in the provision of services from one area to another, particularly from urban areas which are more highly developed to rural areas which are invariably poorer. Statistics on a national scale are essentially nonexistent, and they are only occasionally available at the local level. The provision of human services has been integrated at all levels with the social, political, and economic structure of the society and cannot be understood apart from that larger structure. Human services are provided, in large part, by nonprofessionals and paraprofessionals in the place of work, in urban residential neighborhoods, and in the production teams and brigades of China's communes. Thus, to describe the organization and provision of human services in the People's Republic of China, one must also describe the

AUTHOR'S NOTE: *Portions of this chapter have been adapted from the author's book,* Families of Fengsheng: Urban Life in China *(Baltimore: Penguin Books, 1974), and from a book coauthored with Victor W. Sidel, M.D.,* Serve the People: Observations in Medicine in the People's Republic of China *(Boston: Beacon Press, 1974).*

social, political, and economic framework in which the Chinese people live and work.

Because of these characteristics of Chinese society, I will attempt in this paper to describe social services as they are provided within their societal context. It must be stated at the outset that there are no social workers in China and that most services are provided by the family for its members, by ordinary people for one another, by the local collective for its members, by locally elected leaders with no professional training for their constituents, by paraprofessional medical workers, and by cadres and administrators who are frequently but not always members of the Communist party. "Professionals" provide social or human services only in cases of extreme need, such as in the treatment of psychotic patients—and then often in nontraditional ways.

THE "BITTER PAST"

A description of the current organization of social services in the People's Republic of China must be viewed against the backdrop of the extreme poverty under which the vast majority of Chinese people lived as recently as 25 years ago. This period before Liberation, before the Communists took power in 1949, is constantly referred to by Chinese people as the "bitter past," and a bitter past it was.

The characterization of China in the first half of this century as the "Sick Man of Asia" was largely metaphorical. It referred to China's technological backwardness, its inability to feed its people or provide them with other necessities of life, and its defenselessness in the face of economic and military onslaughts from the technologically developed nations. While, in its metaphorical sense, this characterization may have been overstated, in a literal sense China's sickness was very deep indeed. The country was riddled with almost every known form of nutritional and infectious disease, including cholera, leprosy, tuberculosis, typhoid fever, beriberi, scurvy, and plague. Venereal disease was widespread. One observer has estimated that China suffered four million "unnecessary" deaths each year. According to the economist John Gurley, "Undernourishment was common, starvation not unusual." Adequate housing, education, and medical care were reserved for the 2% of the population who made up the ruling classes: "the Emperor and his family and retainers, bureaucrats, landlords, money-lenders, and military officers" (Gurley, 1975:455-471).

Theodore H. White and Annalee Jacoby (1946:5-10), reporters in China during the Second World War, described conditions in Chungking during the 1940s:

The cities reeked of opium; cholera, dysentery, syphilis, and trachoma rotted the health of the people. . . . Sewage and garbage were emptied into the same stream from which drinking water was taken. . . . Dust coated the city [Chungking] almost as thickly as mud during the wintertime. Moisture remained in the air, perspiration dripped, and prickly heat ravaged the skin. Every errand became an expedition, each expedition an ordeal. Swarms of bugs emerged; small green ones swam on drinking water, and spiders four inches across crawled on the walls. . . . Meat spoiled; there was never enough water for washing; dysentery spread and could not be evaded.

Rewi Alley (1950:15), a New Zealander who lived for many years in China, described the condition of child laborers in a light bulb factory:

There are nine factories in the immediate vicinity of this one, each packed to capacity with child workers amongst whom skin diseases, such as scabies and great festering legs due primarily to bed bug bites, are very common. I was especially struck by the bad condition of two little boys whose beri-beri swollen legs were covered with running sores, and whose tired little bodies slumped wearily against the bench after they have moved to answer my questions.

China was a country with a woefully inadequate number of medical personnel and hospital facilities, and most of what did exist centered in and around the urban areas. While China did have a large number of practitioners of traditional Chinese medicine, the number of doctors of modern or scientific medicine were grossly inadequate—a reasonable estimate is one doctor for every 25,000 of China's people. Technologically developed countries at that time had one doctor for every 1,000 to 2,000 people.

It was a country, in Edgar Snow's words, with "child and female slave labor . . . twelve-to-fourteen-hour days . . . starvation wages and the absence of any protection against sickness, injury, unemployment and old age" (Snow, 1971b:97). In short it was a country in which the cycle of poverty, disease, and disability seemed to many to be endless and immutable.

While this paper will discuss the ways in which the new government has organized the society in order to provide basic human services, it must be stressed that the prerequisite for such a reorganization has been a revolution, a revolution that radically altered the basic social, political, and economic structure of the society. While this revolution attempted to lay the groundwork for the creation of a "new man" and a "new society," it is nevertheless a society which has been built in part upon principles from the past. Joseph Needham (1973) has discussed some of the patterns which have been part of the Chinese society for centuries and which still play a significant role in China's present: the tradition of a nonhereditary elite, the "unity" of rulers and the people and the respect for authority, the "mystique" of farming and of manual labor, and "social cohesion" within the family, among peasant farmers, within guilds, and within voluntary organizations. These characteristics from the past can be seen today, often in different forms, but are nonetheless evident in the organization of communities in modern China. One must therefore look briefly at the gradual development of China's current systems of social organization and the constant changes that these systems undergo in order to understand the human network that provides services for the Chinese people.

RURAL CHINA

China is divided into 22 provinces (including what the Chinese call the "as yet unliberated province of Taiwan"). In addition, there are five autonomous regions inhabited largely by minority ethnic groups that are relatively small in size compared to the dominant Han group, which comprises 90% of the population. China is still an overwhelmingly rural nation; 80% of the people live in the countryside. While the definitions on which such urban-rural statistics are based are not totally clear, the significance of the data can be appreciated when they are contrasted with those of other countries of comparable size. In the United States, for example, only 27% of the population live in what the Bureau of the Census in 1970 defined as rural areas (U.S. Bureau of the Census, 1971); in the Soviet Union the figure is 44% (U.S.S.R. Central Statistical Unit, 1969:7); in India it is 82% (Harth, 1972:715).

In some ways even more important than the total number of people living outside the cities is their distribution; most of the population is concentrated in eastern China. The provision of adequate services to the rural population is therefore complicated not only by the vast numbers but by areas of relatively high and of exceedingly low population densities.

Before Liberation the paucity of resources available to the rural population was further exacerbated by the despotic landlord and warlord systems that deprived the peasants of remuneration for their toil on the land and even of an adequate share of the food they produced. One of the first priorities in each area liberated from the Japanese or from the Kuomintang, therefore, was for the peasants themselves to distribute the land among those who worked and lived on it. In the period following Liberation, the land and the primitive tools for working it thus became the property of individual peasants.

During the 1950s, groups with increasingly collective ownership called "cooperatives" were formed. By the late 1950s and early 1960s much of the farmland had been converted into communes, with collective ownership of agricultural tools and of the land, except for small private plots on which the peasants could grow food for personal consumption. The communes were often large enough to include all the households of a township, whose government was then combined with the management of the commune. Unlike the cooperatives, which were purely economic organizations, the communes became units of both political and economic organization. Today communes are formal, self-contained political units with their own internal governments, usually reporting directly to the government of the county in which they are located.

The smallest subdivision of the commune is the "production team," with a membership of several hundred people. The team leadership is responsible for the day-to-day planning of the team's work. People on the same production team live close to one another, usually in small villages, and form the basic social unit in the countryside. Several teams combine to form a "production brigade," which usually has wider responsibility than the team with regard to health, transportation, and, in the North, the grinding and storing of grain. A typical commune is composed of 10 to 30 production brigades. The commune is the lowest level of formal state power in the rural areas, analogous to the "neighborhood" in the cities, and is responsible for overall planning, education, health and social services, and the operation of small factories that produce goods for its members and for outside distribution.

Many of the human services on the communes are provided by the people themselves for one another. "Mutual aid" and "self-reliance" are watchwords seen and heard throughout China. They are techniques which the Chinese Communists have used for a half century in organizing their vast population and which, furthermore, have roots in China's past.

Mutual Aid in Traditional China

The traditional Chinese family, while severely authoritarian and often cruel, functioned in some ways as a mini-mutual-aid group. Children worked on the land with their parents, and, when a son married, he and his new wife traditionally lived with his mother and father. Offspring were reared and nourished so that they might one day care for their old and, in all likelihood, needy parents. According to Solomon (1971:37), "The Confucian life pattern thus is 'cyclical,' for within the interdependence of the family the son reciprocates the nurturance he receives in his childhood dependency by nurturing his parents in the dependency of their old age."

Chinese rural society was organized on the basis of kinship, work, religion, and other ties. Clans organized the villages, and the villages, which were characterized more by self-organization than by organization from above, found links with nearby cities. Although agriculture was basically a family undertaking, extrafamilial elements of agricultural cooperation were used in farming.

During the Communist administration of the Kiangsi Soviet in the south of China (1927-1934) prior to the Long March, the Communists attempted to organize village cooperatives. In 1934 they organized production cooperatives, consumption cooperatives, food cooperatives, and credit cooperatives (Schurmann, 1968:415). But since much of the organization was from above rather than from below, it had limited success. It was not until the Yenan period that the Chinese Communists were able to utilize mutual aid with any substantial success. During this period they realized that, unless the basic problem of the transformation of the traditional village and of the peasantry was solved, China's most crucial problem, that of food production, could not be solved.

The Communists developed their techniques for organizing communities and mobilizing the population during their years in Yenan (1935-1946) following the completion of the Long March. They had special problems in Shensi Province as the villages were small and the peasants lived near the edge of starvation. They therefore needed creative economic measures to ensure survival and creative political methods of governing to bring about some form of socialism. Many of the methods and beliefs have remained with the Chinese to this time and are evident in an examination of the current rural and urban policies.

During 1942 the leaders decided to launch a campaign for rural cooperativization. An editorial that appeared on January 25, 1943, in the newspaper *Chiehfang Jihpao* (Schurmann, 1968:420) under the title "Let's Organize the Labor Force" explains part of the philosophy behind the cooperativization efforts during the Yenan days:

> Those who have labor give labor; those who have animals give animals. Those who have much give much; those who have little give little; human and animal power are put together. Thus, one can avoid violating the seasons and is able to plow in time, sow in time, and harvest in time.

But mutual aid was crucial not only as an economic technique but also as an organizational and educational tool in remolding the thinking of the Shensi peasant. The editorial continues (Schurmann, 1968:421):

> Because everyone works together life is active, morale is high, and there is mutual stimulation, mutual competition, and no one wants to be behind the others. The driving pace of work is just as the masses say: "Work for Work, Everyone Exerts Himself to the Bone."

It was during these days that the Communist leadership began to see the importance of developing and using indigenous leadership in governing the towns and the rural areas. Since kinship groups had been pivotal in the organization of traditional China, the Communists began recruiting indigenous leaders from the peasantry, from among the kinship groups, and brought them into mass organizations and eventually into the party.

In order to understand further the legacy of the Yenan period, one must consider the concept of *tzu-li keng-sheng,* usually translated as "self-reliance" but more accurately translated as "regeneration through one's own efforts." *Tzi-li keng-sheng* has been a key factor in Mao Tse-tung's foreign policy since the 1930s, when the Chinese were attempting to turn back the Japanese invaders. The essential meaning of *tzi-li keng-sheng* is that the Chinese must themselves transform China, must "stand up" in order to join the community of nations. The dual concepts of *tzi-li keng-sheng* and *yi kao tzu-chi li-liang* ("relying upon one's own strength") became key to the Communist domestic policy as well during the Yenan days and have become known as the Yenan Way. According to Selden (1971:210), the characteristic features of the Yenan Way "included a heavy reliance on the creativity of the Chinese people, particularly the peasantry, and a faith in the ultimate triumph of man over nature, poverty, and exploitation."

Combined with mutual aid and self-reliance is the Maoist concept of mass participation. Mao Tse-tung (1966:8) wrote in his essay "On Practice" in 1937:

> If you want to know the taste of a pear, you must change the pear by eating it yourself. If you want to know the structure and properties of the atom, you must make physical and chemical experiments to change the state of the atom. If you want to know the theory and methods of revolution, you must take part in revolution. All genuine knowledge originates in direct experience.

This theme of knowing by doing runs through essentially all aspects of Chinese life today. The mobilization of the mass has been the primary technique by which the Chinese have accomplished their great feats of engineering: the construction of their canals, bridges, large-scale irrigation projects, and dikes, and the damming of rivers. The mobilization of the mass has been the key mechanism in their feats of human engineering also. Han Suyin (1966:80-83) describes the process of education of the masses since 1949 as one that has included the "eradication of the feudal mind," and "getting the masses away from the anchored belief that natural calamities are 'fixed by heaven' and that therefore nothing can be done to remedy one's lot." She continues: "To bridge this gap between scientific modern man and feudal man, the prey of superstition, and to do it within the compass of one generation, is a formidible task."

Thus, the provision of human services in China as a whole but particularly in rural China must be viewed as a combination of mutual aid, self-reliance, and mass participation. The picture is not one of services being provided for people but rather of people collectively providing services for themselves and for one another.

The Role of the Family in Contemporary China

The smallest collective in both rural and urban China is, of course, the family. The family is often three-generational; family members are thus able to provide many essential services for one another. Grandmothers help to care for small children and therefore enable the younger women to go out to work; the younger people care for the elderly; and small children in the 1950s taught their parents and grandparents how to read and write by teaching them the characters they were learning in school. One physician has described the Chinese family as a "mini-collective," one in which "the old take care of the young and the middle-aged take care of the old."

While "homes for the respected age" do exist, most of the aged are cared for within the family unit—even if they are ill. Furthermore, since there is no fixed retirement age on the communes, older workers simply work fewer hours and are paid accordingly; their daily needs are guaranteed by other family members or by the commune.

Human Services Provided by the Commune

The collectivization of the land, the communal ownership of tools, and the ability to plan centrally for large numbers of people and large areas of the countryside all have been largely responsible for the well-being of the Chinese peasant today. The vast economic and political changes that have occurred in China over the past 25 years have solved many of the problems that other societies attempt to solve through their human service system. There is no necessity for a vast complex system of unemployment insurance since there is virtually no unemployment in China—in rural areas as well as in urban areas. Furthermore, inflation is nonexistent. According to Sweezy (1975:1-11), "Chinese economic policy has been to keep most prices stable, while allowing some of special importance to the people's livelihood to decline in step with decreasing costs of production." For example, the price of medicines has declined 80% over the past 20 years, and rent is held at between 3% and 5% of a family's income.

After the organization of the communes in 1958, the "five guarantees" were established: "enough food, enough clothes, enough fuel, an honorable funeral and education for [one's] children" (Myrdal and Kessle, 1972:52). These essentials were guaranteed by the collective in case of illness, old age, or death, but the basic principle was, and remains, that family members whenever possible will care for one another. The commune also guarantees a minimum level of essentials for all members by distributing a certain percentage of grain or rice and fuel to its commune members based upon the number in the family. Purchasing power is otherwise determined by income which is distributed on the basis of a work-point system.

Medical care is provided by all levels of the commune organization. The commune hospital is built, staffed, equipped, and maintained by the commune with help in terms of rotating medical personnel and training facilities from the county level and/or from the nearby city.

Education is also planned at the commune level, but primary schools and sometimes secondary schools are administered by the brigade. The registration of births, deaths, and marriages is handled by the administration of the commune.

Human Services Provided by the Production Brigade

Health Care. With the exception of cadres (administrators who work at every level of organization in China), health workers are the primary personnel who work specifically in the field of human services in China. Health workers are recruited and trained at every level and are seen as crucial links in the well-being of the people. Of the many levels and sorts of rural health workers, the barefoot doctor is undoubtedly the key link between the peasant and the society at large.

Barefoot doctors are peasants who are chosen by their production brigades to have a brief period of training and then to return to their brigades to combine agricultural work with medical work. Since the barefoot doctors are peasants, in planting and harvesting seasons almost all of their time is spent in farming work. In slack periods, however, a considerable part, often more than half, of their time is spent catching up on the health needs of their production brigades, particularly in the areas of environmental control and preventive medicine.

The barefoot doctors are considered by their communities, and apparently think of themselves, as peasants who perform some medical duties rather than as health workers who do some agricultural work. The term "barefoot doctor" originates in the south of China where such medical workers were originally trained. Peasants work barefoot in the highly irrigated rice paddies of southern China; the term is therefore used to emphasize their primary connection with agricultural work. China has reputedly trained over one million barefoot doctors (Yu Yang, 1974:6-10) and approximately half of these paraprofessionals are said to be women.

The barefoot doctors' tasks include health education, preventive medicine, the treatment of minor illnesses, and the supervision of "health workers" who work at the production team level. But the Chinese have attempted to develop something more than another medical paraprofessional. Joshua Horn (1971:135) perhaps best describes the kind of worker the Chinese are attempting to train:

> Throughout their period of training, emphasis was placed on developing those Communist qualities so stressed by Mao Tse-tung, of selfless service to the people, of limitless responsibility in work and of perserverance in the face of difficulties. The intention was not merely to impart medical knowledge, but to evolve a new kind of socialist-minded rural health worker who would retain the close links with the peasants and be content to stay permanently in the countryside.

While the barefoot doctors do not specifically have responsibilities in the area of social service, the respected role of the health worker, the emphasis on "serving the people," and the barefoot doctors' intimate knowledge of the social conditions and attitudes of their fellow peasants frequently leads them to become involved in far more than narrowly defined health issues.

For example, Horn describes the role of a barefoot doctor in interpreting a patient's feelings to a local physician who had only been in the countryside for a short period of time and did not know the village residents well. A dwarf, Fragrant Lotus, becomes pregnant and the local physician who feel she cannot survive the birth, wants to persuade the pregnant woman to have an abortion. The local barefoot doctor intervenes and gives the "social history" (Horn, 1971:157):

Of course, you know the medical aspects much better than I do, . . . but just now when you spoke about the facts, you mentioned only some of them. Another fact is that both Fragrant Lotus and Old Han [her husband] suffered greatly in the old society. Liberation has given them a new lease on life. If they have no child, both their families will die out. I don't know if they will agree to an abortion. Don't you think we should discuss it frankly with both of them before making up our minds?

Fragrant Lotus, of course, refuses to have an abortion, and the barefoot doctor and the fully trained physician together perform a Caesarean section in her home, which enables her to have her baby successfully.

But an intimate knowledge of social conditions is not the only extramedical role of the barefoot doctor. Barefoot doctors assume as part of their "medical" responsibility the provision of homemaking services to those in need (China Reconstructs, 1972), caring for the children of sick parents (China Reconstructs, 1974c), and health education both with regard to individual health care and environmental sanitation. Again, it is the barefoot doctor's intimate knowledge of his neighbors, their feelings, attitudes, and needs which enables him to play this special role.

Methods of payment for medical care in the communes vary widely. Peasants in many communes participate in a collective medical care system, each family paying into the fund an annual premium for each of its members. The entire family is then covered for all medical expenses except for payment of a minimal registration fee. In the Mai Chia Wu Production Brigade of the West Lake People's Commune outside the city of Hangchow, for example, a premium of one yüan (U.S. 40 cents) is paid annually for each person, including children; and all medical expenses, including hospitalization, are paid by the cooperative. The Shuan Wang Production Brigade near Sian also has a cooperative medical system under which each peasant pays 50 fen (U.S. 20 cents) a year into the fund; the brigade's public welfare fund contributes an equal amount. Patients must still pay a 5 fen registration fee each time they see a doctor, however; and, as is the custom in China, hospitalized patients pay for their food.

The Tachai Production Brigade in Shansi Province, on the other hand, has a very different system of payment for medical care. It uses a "three point system": (1) if a patient's illness is work-related, all medical care is free; (2) if the patient is seriously ill and cannot afford medical care, the brigade helps with the payment; and (3) if the patient has a "light disease" and can pay for treatment, he or she does so.

Whichever system is used, payment is minimal and is never a barrier if an individual needs care and does not have the money. On the other hand, the Chinese feel that they are not yet at a point either economically or ideologically where medical care can be totally free. They hope that that day will come, but for the moment they feel it is necessary for the individual to participate in the payment of medical care.

Day-Care. Child care in rural areas is more casual, less highly structured than in the urban areas. Since fewer children attend, units such as the nursing room and the nursery, or the nursery and the kindergarten, are often combined. These facilities are usually organized at the production brigade level and occasionally at the production team level.

Mutual aid among the mothers and grandmothers plays a large role in child care on the communes. For example, in one Shanghai production brigade the nursery cares for children from the end of the 56-day maternity leave to 4 years of age. However, there is no kindergarten in this production brigade; the grandparents take care of children from 4 to 7 years old, or the mothers care for each other's children.

The physical plants for rural day-care also vary enormously. One group of educators who visited China (Kessen, 1975:75) reported seeing a nursery and kindergarten in Canton which occupied a former landlord's villa and a kindergarten in Sian which occupied "two small, dark, and dirt-floored rooms of a new brick building."

Human Services Provided by the Production Team

Health Care. Sanitation work, health education, and the treatment of minor injuries are handled at the production-team level by "health workers," full-time agricultural workers who do medical work in their spare time under the supervision of the barefoot doctor. The work of these peasants is purely voluntary and is one of the ways in which voluntarism is encouraged in China.

Day-Care. Some day-care is provided by the production team. Kessen (1975:66) reports a commune 10 miles outside of Shanghai in which each of 88 production teams had a nursery attached. The nurseries were close to the homes of the residents, were located in small houses with one or two caretakers for 12 to 15 children. In a commune outside Peking (Sidel, 1973:84) each production team had its own nursery, which cared for children from 1 month to 6. However, most of the children in this commune were cared for by grandparents within their own families until they went to primary school.

What must be stressed not only about day-care but about all services in China's countryside is the great diversity. Services depend on the local conditions, the wealth of the particular commune or region, and the priorities set by the commune leadership. It is very difficult to generalize about rural China; an attempt has rather been made to indicate some of the patterns in the provision of human services.

URBAN ORGANIZATION

The history of China's cities stretches back nearly 4,000 years. Many of today's important metropolitan and industrial centers such as Shanghai, Kwangchow, Tientsin, and Taiyuan were old *hsien,* or county, capitals and have survived dynasty after dynasty, thus preserving a continuity from ancient times until today.

Urban dwellers in traditional China were ruled indirectly through urban organizations, guilds, occupational groups, family clubs, and clans. Rural-based people had migrated into the cities under the auspices of occupational associations and settled into neighborhoods in occupational groups; city officials could therefore maintain contact with the migrants through these associations and through indigenous neighborhood leaders. When the Kuomintang assumed power in the 1920s it essentially took over the existing forms of urban organization and extended city government further downward by dividing the cities into districts. Below the district level the only subdivisions were the police stations, which were established in various sections of the city and were responsible for supervising the people in those sections. In the summer of 1940 the Japanese occupiers introduced the *paochia* system (which had a long history in rural China) into Tientsin and later into other cities in occupied China. According to Franz Schurmann (1968:369), "Each group of ten households was organized into a *p'ai;* each ten *p'ai* formed a *chia;* each ten *chia* formed a *pao.* . . . Each unit had a designated leader who became the link between the local police authority and the population." The paochia was clearly thought of as an extension of the local police department and was used by the Japanese and later the Kuomintang solely to control the population.

Cities faced severe disorganization during the civil war which followed Japanese occupation. When the Communist government occupied the urban areas in 1949 they found chaos—inflation was rampant, food was in short supply, and human services had broken down. During the first decade after Liberation—the assumption of power by the Chinese Communists in 1949—the Chinese government faced severe problems in its attempt to govern the cities. These included the need to cope with ever-increasing rural to urban migration, to deliver human services to large numbers of people, to develop successful methods of social control over the urban population, to stem the anomie which seems to be endemic to modern industrial cities, and to involve people politically in their own governing.

The Communists were finally able to establish order in the cities with the assistance of both the local police and the military. They abolished the paochia system, until the establishment of residents' committees in 1952, no urban administration existed below the district level. Instead, local police stations began to take on civil responsibilities, and ad hoc mass organizations led by local party members or activists were formed to meet specific needs in health or sanitation. These efforts, however, were fragmentary since leadership in any one neighborhood was not unified.

In 1951 the first residents' committees were established in Tienstin and Shanghai, the same cities in which the Japanese-sponsored paochia had been most successful. The residents' committee was directly responsible to the neighborhood committee, which in turn was the administrative level that the city administration used to relate to the people. The tasks of the new residents' committees were very similar to the tasks of residents' committees today (Schurmann, 1968:376): (1) to serve as transmitters of government policies from higher urban authority to the people, (2) to perform public security functions and organize fire prevention, sanitation work, welfare work, mediation, and cultural and recreational activities, and (3) to serve as intermediaries for the transmission of ideas and requests from the people to the government level.

There was clearly some relationship between the functions of the old paochia system and the new residents' committee functions, particularly in the areas of public security. The residents' committees, however, moved far beyond the old public security functions of the paochia in attempting to meet the needs of the people and to mobilize them in determining the patterns of their own lives. Eventually the residents' committees moved into such areas as food rationing and the granting of certificates to people who wished to leave China. They therefore became the local branch of urban government closest to the people and were run by members of the masses themselves. From the start, women played an important role in the workings of the residents' committees, often gaining power at that level when they had little at higher levels.

The residents' committee system was not extended to all cities until 1954, when a series of governmental directives was issued. The standing committee of the National People's Congress on December 31, 1954, approved three directives which set out the administrative framework of police stations, neighborhood committees, and residents' committees. Neighborhood committees would be established as branches of the city government in all the major cities of China. They were mandatory in cities with over 100,000 population, optional in cities of 50,000-100,000 population, and not expected in cities of less than 50,000 population. Officials of the neighborhood committees were selected by the district city government and not by the residents (Schurmann, 1968:378). There were reports that the neighborhood committees and residents' committees were unpopular with the people because they were seen to some extent as an invasion of family privacy and as an extension of the local police system.

For a time in the 1950s the Chinese government experimented with the establishment of urban communes as part of an attempt to create an integrated way of life—one which would combine work and leisure, physical and intellectual endeavors. Although a variety of blueprints were used to guide the formation of urban communes, ultimately the ideal of an integrated way of life based around the work situation was to fail in China's cities.

Although China's urban neighborhoods today may seem to us in the West to be far more integrated than anything which we know, they are organized around the residential areas rather than around production. As Schurmann (1968:399) states, "The Chinese city remains today what it has been for a century, an area of concentrated human residence. Residence, not production, remains the foundation of city life." Thus in the 1960s the Chinese government was still left with the problems that it faced in 1958: the problem of creating economic capabilities to match the rising urban population and the problem of creating a sense of community which would reduce the feelings of anomie and alienation so characteristic of cities in both the West and the East. During the Cultural Revolution in the mid- and late 1960s the Chinese continued to grapple with these issues.

The Cultural Revolution was a time of massive political upheaval and of profound evaluation of both methodology and goals. During the sometimes bitter struggle of the Cultural Revolution, Mao's aim, according to Edgar Snow (1971a:15), was "to proletarianize Party thinking and, beyond that, to push the proletariat really to take power for themselves, and in the process to create a new culture free of domination by the feudal and bourgeois heritage."

The urban neighborhoods underwent profound change during this period. Residents began to protest what they felt to be abuses on the part of the local neighborhood cadres. It was felt that cadres had become entrenched groups that had subtle advantages over the rest of the population and that they had lost their contact with the people. It was also felt that cadres along with other Communist party members and professionals were becoming a new elite.

One of the primary goals within the urban neighborhoods during the Cultural Revolution was to democratize the leadership and assure greater participation on the part of the masses. Political study was encouraged; criticism sessions focusing on the merits and deficiencies of the leaders took place; and new, more representative revolutionary committees were elected to govern the neighborhoods.

Today approximately 20% of China's population live in the urban areas—an estimated population of 150,000,000 people. Three cities and their supporting countryside areas have been removed from the jurisdiction of the provinces in which they are situated and placed directly under the jurisdiction of the central government as independent municipalities. The largest of these is Shanghai, with a population of about 6 million in the city proper and about 4 million in its surrounding 10 counties. The other independent municipalities are Peking, with 4 million in the city proper and 3 million in its nine surrounding counties, and Tientsin, with a population of 4 million.

Cities are governed by revolutionary committees—formal governmental bodies. The next lower level of urban organization is the "district," which is also governed by a revolutionary committee. Hangchow, a city of 700,000 people, is divided into four districts, the city proper of Peking into nine districts, and the city proper of Shanghai into 10 districts. Districts are subdivided into "streets" or "neighborhoods," which are the lowest level of formal governmental organization in the city. The size of these neighborhoods varies from approximately 40,000 people to 70,000. The neighborhood is governed by a committee composed of representatives of the people in the area, cadres, and, in diminishing numbers since the end of the Cultural Revolution, members of the People's Liberation Army. The committee's responsibilities include the admin-

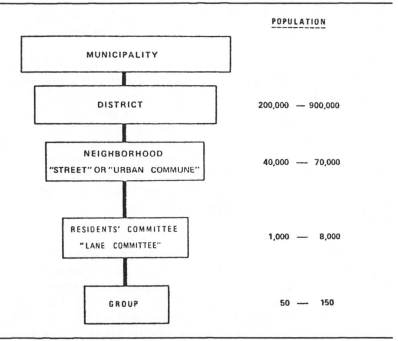

Figure 1: LEVELS OF URBAN ORGANIZATION IN THE PEOPLE'S REPUBLIC
OF CHINA

istration of local factories, primary schools and kindergartens, a neighborhood
hospital or health center, repair services, and a housing department, the
provision of certain social services, and the organization and supervision of
"residents" or "lane" committees. The smallest units in the urban areas are these
residents' committees, with from 1,000 to 8,000 residents. Some lanes are
further divided into groups—for example, the residents of a single large
·apartment building—headed by a group or deputy group leader. The lane is
governed by a committee chosen by, and from among, the "mass" living in the
lane.

Human Services in the Urban Neighborhood

In keeping with the Chinese belief in decentralization and mass participation,
the provision of human services is diffused throughout the levels of urban
organization. The West District of Peking, for example, has nine neighborhoods,
one of which is the Fengsheng neighborhood with a population of 53,000.
Within the Fengsheng neighborhood's jurisdiction are 6 factories, 8 shops, 10
primary schools, 4 kindergartens, and a neighborhood hospital. Fengsheng is one
of the older neighborhoods of Peking. It consists entirely of one-story dwellings
rather than the four- or five-story apartment buildings found in newer

neighborhoods. Courtyards, with several families living in each, are entered through doorways in the walls lining Fengsheng's 132 lanes. The people are grouped into 25 residents' committees, each of which encompasses about 2,000 people.

The Fengsheng neighborhood has a revolutionary committee of 27 members. There has been an attempt to balance the committee somewhat according to age and sex—the elderly, the middle-aged, and the young are represented, and 16 members are women. Ten of the 27 members are government cadre members selected by the district level and sent to the Fengsheng neighborhood to work. In addition to the 10 government cadre members on the committee there are two members from the People's Liberation Army and 15 representatives of the "mass" who have been selected by the units in which they live or work.

Employment. The Chinese have attempted to deal with unemployment not by the mechanism of unemployment compensation but by the organization of small locally run factories which may employ and train unskilled women. These factories serve the function not only of employing a segment of the population that was unemployed but also of integating the workers, usually women, more thoroughly into the life of the community. They often begin as simple workshops and gradually expand as their production and income grow. Rather than receiving any financial help from the government, the factories are expected to flourish because of their "self-reliance" and "hard work." Many of the health and welfare needs of the workers are handled within the factories themselves.

The Printing and Binding Factory in the Ching Nian Lu neighborhood in the midwestern city of Sian illustrates the organization and functioning of small satellite factories. The factory was organized in 1966 at the beginning the the Cultural Revolution. According to the director,

> The women themselves requested work. A large printing factory nearby needed to have work done and a few of the women went to the factory for one month full-time to learn the work while the others remained here and prepared space and a few simple tools. There was no working shop then nor any equipment; the women just worked under a roof. Then the four or five came back and trained the others. They all worked together under the roof folding paper, cutting covers, and binding simple books with a plastic cover. Back in 1966 the housewives earned only 7 *yüan* per month as they could only earn what their production was worth. As they produced more, they earned more. Now the housewives earn 35 *yüan* per month.

The factory is completely self-sufficient; it pays the workers out of its earnings and uses any profit to enlarge the factory. The factory even provides a form of health insurance for its workers—each worker pays 3 yüan per year and then receives free medical care at the local health station. The factory also handles some welfare problems; if a worker becomes ill for a long period of time, she will receive her full salary for six months, but when the six months is over she will then receive no further salary. Furthermore, if a worker or her family has financial difficulties, they can get help from this factory. Recently one worker had financial problems because her husband was sick for a long period of time. All the workers met together and decided "by open discussion" to give the worker 15 yüan. This decision was then approved by the leading group. This situation, however, was said to be quite unusual.

Health Care. Health care in China has been viewed in its broadest context particularly at the level of the urban neighborhood and the residents' committee. The urban neighborhood generally has a hospital to care for the health needs of its residents. These hospitals frequently resemble neighborhood health centers in the United States in that they often do not have in-patient services. The functions of the neighborhood hospital include preventive medicine, curative medicine, health education, and the training and on-going supervision of Red Medical Workers. Red Medical Workers are paraprofessionals, usually former "housewives," who are recruited from among the "mass," given short periods of training, not long enough to alienate them from their peer group, and then sent back to the residents' committee to give first-level medical care. The Red Medical Workers are the urban counterpart of the rural barefoot doctors.

The Fengsheng neighborhood hospital serves one-half of the population of the Fengsheng neighborhood, approximately 20,000 people. Some 1,500 preschool children, the children who attend four primary schools and two middle schools, and the workers in five factories are included in the population served.

Public health is a key focus within the neighborhood hospital. The emphasis is on educating the people about prevention, on the importance of immunizations, on the management of infectious disease, on the health of children, on family planning, on the management of occupational diseases in the factories and on the importance of sanitation. Immunizations, for example, are given to neighborhood children jointly by a public health doctor and a Red Medical Worker. The Fengsheng neighborhood hospital has an astonishing record of children immunized: 86.9% of the children, for example, have been immunized for smallpox, 99.6% have been immunized for measles.

Methods of payment for health care in the cities vary widely, from total subsidization by the patient's factory to payment by the patient for individual services. An official Peking publication, *For the Health of the People* (1963:2-3), stated:

> Free medical care is extended to government employees, industrial workers, miners, university and college students, and to the entire population in some of the national minority areas. To those who are unable to pay for treatment, the local authorities ... grant allowances according to their specific conditions.

Workers in most industries have all medical care paid for by their factories; their families are subsidized for half the cost of the services and must pay the balance themselves. Members of a workers' family must pay a registration fee plus half the cost of the medicine.

In Kwangchow, urban "cooperative medical care systems" are being tried experimentally. By contributing 1 yüan a month, the patient's ambulatory care is given free at the time of service, and only one-tenth of the cost of inpatient care is paid directly by the patient.

The Chinese hope to see the elimination of all medical care payments "when there are sufficient resources to make this possible." Apparently this will be done, as is so much else, on a decentralized basis. The cost of individual service and of prepayment premiums is extremely low, not only by American standards but as a percentage of a Chinese worker's income; the payments are therefore felt to be little or no barrier to access to care.

Family Counseling. Marriage and divorce are both dealt with at the neighborhood level by a "cadre of basic state power." The Chinese are currently advocating late marriage, 24 to 26 years of age for women and 26 to 29 for men. If the couple is much younger, the cadre will try to dissuade them from marrying at that time. According to Chen Pi-chao (1975:320-322), "Delayed marriage is vigorously encouraged and promoted through intense peer pressure and 'thought work' and the available statistics all indicate that age at marriage is rising."

Although divorce was legalized for both men and women by the 1950 Marriage Law, it is currently being discouraged in China. If a couple wants a divorce, the cadre official will ask the reason. He may then consult with the work units of both husband and wife and with the residents' committee where they live; he might do some marital counseling—first seeing the husband and wife separately and then together. The cadre official will often see the couple three to five times, perhaps as many as ten times. If they still want a divorce in spite of the cadre official's urging them "to unite," he can issue them a divorce certificate. During the first nine months of 1972, for example, out of a population of 9,100 families in the Ching Nian Lu neighborhood in Sian, 17 couples requested divorce but only 11 couples were divorced; the other six "united." Marital problems are also handled at the place of work and at the residents' committee level.

Day-Care. Prior to the assumption of power in 1949 by the Chinese Communists there were very few preschool facilities and essentially none for the vast majority of the poor and near-poor. By 1957, out of 140 to 150 million children under the age of 7, one and a half million children were attending some form of preschool (Orleans, 1960:29). There was another sharp increase in the number of preschool facilities between 1957 and 1958 at the time of the Great Leap Forward, when in rural areas as well as in the cities women went to work in large numbers. By 1975, Hsinhua News reported that Peking alone had 4,500 kindergartens and nurseries serving 200,000 children and infants (Hsinhua, 1975:7-8). These are run by the state, government institutions, army units, factories, and neighborhood committees. Although reliable statistics do not exist at this time, it is estimated that at least 50% of the children under the age of 3 are cared for at home, usually by grandparents, and 50% are cared for in nursing rooms and nurseries usually located in the place of work. From the age of 3 until the beginning of primary school at age 7 the number attending kindergarten rises to 80% in the cities. The percentages for all age groups are far lower in the countryside.

At 3 years of age children move into the kindergarten, which is generally located in the neighborhood rather than in the place of work. The funds for kindergartens are generated by the neighborhood, and the policies, teaching content, and methods are under the jurisdiction of the neighborhood committee. Kindergartens are larger establishments than nurseries, with more equipment, particularly outdoor equipment—swings, slides, seesaws, jungle gyms. The teachers usually have had special academic training.

The children usually attend kindergarten for 8-9 hours while their parents are at work. They have outdoor play, meals, naps, a snack, and an occasional excursion to a place of historical interest. But Chinese kindergartens are also attempting to develop children whose "class consciousness has been raised" and who will through "socialist education and socialist culture be the successors to the socialist cause." The children are taught to love Chairman Mao and to love their country; they are trained to love the workers, peasants, and soldiers and to love physical labor; they are taught to "keep only the public good in mind." And above all they are taught *Wei renmin fuwu*—"Serve the people."

Children are taught these principles through Mao Tse-tung Thought classes, through revolutionary songs and dances, through their interaction with the teachers and with each other, and through productive labor. As early as age 3, the children wipe off their tables or wash out their own towels. By 5 or 6 they are helping to tend a vegetable garden and doing jobs such as folding boxes in which crayons will be exported or folding containers in which light bulbs, made by their mothers in a local neighborhood factory, will be packaged. These jobs are on consignment from a large factory; the kindergarten is paid by the factory and uses that extra money to buy extra equipment. Thus the children simultaneously learn the value of manual labor and contribute to their society.

Since the initiative and funds for preschool care come from the local neighborhoods and factories, preschool facilities develop at different rates and provide services to varying numbers of children. In the Fengsheng neighborhood, for example, the Ta Cheng Nursery and Kindergarten was organized by four "housewives" in 1955. It began with 40 children in three rooms, but in 1958, when many women went to work, the demand for preschool care greatly increased. By 1972 the nursery and kindergarten employed 44 teachers and staff members to care for 230 children. Nurseries and kindergartens are generally open 12 hours a day; most children arrive at Ta Cheng at 7:30 in the morning and leave at 6:00 in the evening.

The Chinese also provide a few 24-hour or "full-time" kindergartens for children whose parents work odd hours and cannot care for their children at night. At these kindergartens the children arrive on Monday morning, stay until Saturday afternoon, and spend the weekend with their parents. One such kindergarten is located in the Ching Nian Lu neighborhood in the city of Sian. When it was organized in 1952, two teachers cared for 30 children. By 1972, nine teachers and 13 "staff members" were caring for 100 children from the ages of 3 to 7. The cost is 16 yüan ($8.00) per child per month including food, three meals a day plus snacks. The goals of the kindergarten are stated by the chairman of the school's revolutionary committee:

> Our main task is to educate children from three to seven years. Our main focus is on language—telling stories, reading poems—but we also want to help the children to know society and nature. They sing songs and do dances, have physical exercises and active play. They study simple arithmetic to learn their numbers and they paint, sometimes special subjects and other times whatever is in their minds. We also train the children to love the Communist Party, to love Chairman Mao and to love the socialist motherland. We stress politeness and sanitation and want them to have a good ideology. We want them to have good health and basic knowledge to prepare them for entering primary school.

The kindergarten is built around a series of courtyards; equipment is minimal though adequate. The teachers here, as in preschool facilities in general, are enthusiastic, warm, and loving with the children and seem extraordinarily involved with their work. The children here, as in all preschool facilities visited, appear to be happy, healthy, lively, self-assured, and cooperative. Although the usual ratio for teachers to children is low by Western standards—approximately one teacher to every nine children—the children appear to receive individual attention, and behavior problems appear to be rare.

Preschool facilities are supported both by fees from the parents and by a subsidy from the unit that administers the facility. "Part-time" urban day-care, whose facilities open 12 hours a day, generally cost the parent from 3 to 6 yüan ($1.50-$3.00) per month per child, excluding food, which is an additional cost. Twenty-four-hour care in kindergartens and nurseries at which the children remain from Monday morning until Saturday afternoon cost the family from 7 to 10 yüan ($3.50-$5.00) per month, again excluding food (Hsinhua, 1975:7-8). These "full-time" facilities are exceedingly rare at the present time.

Teachers at both the preschool and the primary-school levels do not confine their activities to the intellectual sphere but rather are concerned about the physical, emotional, political, and social well-being of the child. They see home visits as part of their responsibility; teachers from the Shanghai Experimental School, a primary school, report making routine home visits prior to the start of school in order to "learn about the family situation—who the primary caretakers are, their general views about child care, the adequacy of space and other physical conditions for homework—and the nature of the child's friendship ties and the 'strengths and weaknesses' of the child" (Kessen, 1975:44).

Other reports indicate that teachers concern themselves with such social matters as whether a child has had breakfast or not and how best to help a boy who has been known as a "troublemaker" (China Reconstructs, 1973a:7-12). In the latter case the teacher made a home visit, "tried to get close to" the child, worked with the parents, visited the child when he was sick, "gave him individual help after school," "encouraged every sign of progress," and made him a bowl of soup when the student was ill at home and there was no one to fix him lunch.

In addition, fellow students help to solve one another's problems. Little Red Guards, a group of students selected by their fellow classmates and adult advisors because they are "honest, courageous, lively and promote unity among their classmates" (China Reconstructs, 1973b:10-11), help to mediate disputes among the children, help slower students with their work, help sick children catch up with their work, and help to maintain discipline in school. In this way, mutual aid is fostered among the children, and the helper gains as much from the experience as the helped.

Services for the Handicapped. Relatively little is known about services for the handicapped in China. An effort is made to integrate the handicapped—both the mentally and the physically handicapped—into the general society. Retarded children, for example, are integrated whenever possible into classes for normal children (Science for the People, 1974:293), and handicapped adults are given work in regular factories.

It is the responsibility of the neighborhood committee to help its handicapped residents to find suitable work. In recent years in a Sian neighborhood five deaf mutes were aided in obtaining work, one as a carpenter, two in a metal factory, and two in the neighborhood's printing and binding factory. Local workers stress that handicapped workers are able to choose the kind of work they prefer.

Services for the handicapped are also provided at the municipality level in Peking. An article in China Reconstructs (1974a:40-42) describes a factory that specifically employs deaf, dumb, and blind workers. The factory encompasses a medical clinic, a dining room, a kindergarten, and housing for some of the workers. Thus, the needs of the workers are met within the framework of the workplace and are not seen as separate welfare needs. Furthermore, it is not uncommon for a place of work to function as a total environment—even for people who are not handicapped.

Human Services at the Residents' Committee Level

Residents' committees are led by local residents who have been elected by the people whom they serve. The residents' committee leaders are often middle-aged women or retired male workers. The primary tasks of these leaders are to organize the health and welfare work for the residents, to function as a link or intermediary between the residents and the neighborhood committee, and to mobilize the masses to fulfill the tasks handed down by higher governmental levels.

For example, 466 families live in two lanes which comprise the Min Kang (People's Health) Residents' Committee in the Fengsheng neighborhood. Of the total population of 1,658, the residents' committee is actively responsible only for the 265 older housewives, the 118 men over the age of 60, the 513 students, and the 18 women of working age who remain at home as housewives. Working men and women are under the aegis of their groups in their places of work. The head of the Min Kang Residents' Committee is Chang Sheng-eh, a 43-year-old mother of four whose husband is a factory worker. Comrade Chang has lived in Min Kang for 10 years and was elected to her present position in April 1971 after having been a group leader for one year. Comrade Chang and her family live within the same courtyard at right angles to the Min Kang health station.

The position of head of Min Kang became open when the former head moved to another residents' committee. At that time the retired workers, cadres and housewives met in one of the courtyards to discuss the situation with a cadre official from the neighborhood committee who led the meeting. Usually all the people who are eligible to vote come; only the very old or the ill stay away. After the neighborhood committee cadre official explained the situation, the residents then discussed likely candidates for the position of head of the residents' committee. According to the vice-head of the residents' committee, the residents try to choose

> those who will serve the peole whole-heartedly. The people know who worked very hard as group leaders. First many names are suggested and because more people are always nominated than are needed to fill the jobs, the attempt is made to narrow down the list. Then everyone votes. The vote is not by secret ballot; it is taken by a show of hands as each name is called. The person who receives the most votes becomes the head. Another vote is taken for the vice-head. Neither the head nor the vice-head receive any pay or do any other work.

Chang Hsin-kuan, the 45-year-old vice-chairman, is the mother of five children; her husband is also a factory worker. Comrade Chang and her family have lived in this neighborhood for 10 years, and, prior to being elected vice-chairman, she had been a group leader for three or four years.

Group leaders are chosen through a similar selection process. In Min Kang there are about 50 families in each group, and each group has a leader and vice-chairman, many of whom are housewives. Both the group leaders and the chairman of the residents' committee are responsible for organizing study sessions, for organizing sanitation work, and for settling disputes.

Mediation of Disputes. Mediating disputes is a primary responsibility of local leaders. They know local conditions well, know the residents intimately, and have their confidence. And, as Jerome Alan Cohen (1971:29) has pointed out, "For millennia the Chinese have preferred unofficial mediation to official adjudication." After the overthrow of the Manchu dynasty the republican government attempted to enact legislation to institutionalize extrajudicial mediation and in 1913 created a Commercial Arbitration Bureau to mediate commercial disputes. The Nationalist government further attempted to modernize traditional mediation techniques, and the Communists "made popular mediation a major instrument of its legal policy" (Cohen, 1971:30). Local mediators and mediation committees have taken on added importance with the paucity of laws enacted during the decade between the Great Leap Forward (1958) and the Great Proletarian Cultural Revolution (1966-1969).

In one Shanghai neighborhood (Science for the People, 1974:297) interpersonal disputes were described as falling into four categories: "those between neighbors, between husband and wife, and between mother-in-law and daughter-in-law, and conflicts over property." An example of local mediation work is described by a group that recently visited China (Science for the People, 1974:297-298):

> One of the conflicts between neighbors involved two women in the same building who had sons of different ages. The boys started fighting, and their anger spread to their mothers, who quarreled over the use of water in the building and ended up fighting physically. At that point a comrade from the local neighborhood committee tried to help. She began by getting both women to sit down and study the works of Chairman Mao and to engage in self-criticism. Since the Chairman says the people must unite to win greater victories, she asked, how could those women think they should fight each other? She pointed out that before Liberation people lived miserably in poor, small houses; but now they lived in decent, adequate buildings: all the more reason for less quarreling and more unity. Eventually both women engaged in self-criticism, stopped their dispute, and agreed that each should pay more attention to the social education of her own child.

Marital problems are handled in a similar fashion. If a couple is having problems, a member of the local committee might be called by any family member, even by one of the children. The local leader will go to the home and discuss the problem first with one partner, then with the other. Later the mediator will gather together the entire family, including the children and the elderly members of the family. They will all discuss the problem, and the mediator is likely to "urge the couple to unite."

In attempting to understand relationships between family members and the techniques used to mediate disputes, it must be stressed that the individual in China sees himself quite differently in relation to his environment than does the individual in the West. While the Chinese are clearly concerned about their personal lives, they see themselves at the same time as part of a larger scene—as part of the society, as part of the revolution—and, consequently, one's obligation is not merely to achieve a "happy" or "fulfilled" life for oneself but also to participate actively in the larger world.

The Role of the Elderly. The elderly play a significant role in the management of the residents' committees and as group leaders. The Chinese utilize the continuing respect that people have for the elderly by giving them key roles within the community. The elderly, for example, teach about the "bitter past" in schools, and they help to organize after-school activities (Science for the People, 1974:173).

The Ching Nian Lu Residents' Committee is divided into six groups, each with a group leader. An Fu-kuei, a retired machine tool worker, is a group leader and, as part of his work, he organizes "the masses to study." Out of the 180 people in his six courtyards, only 30 housewives and one retired worker are at home full-time and therefore do not belong to a group elsewhere. He meets together with these 31 residents twice a week. The two or three residents who are literate will take turns reading the *Sian Daily* aloud, and then everyone will discuss the content and meaning of what has been read. They also discuss the sanitation work which needs to be done.

Chang Chung-hsiu, another elderly group leader organizes study groups and literacy classes; those who know how to read and write teach the rest. They study Mao's "Three Constantly Read Articles" ("Serve the People," "In Memory of Norman Bethune," and "The Foolish Old Man Who Removed the Mountains"), which Comrade Chang feels are "easy for the masses to understand." In addition they study somewhat longer, more complex essays of Mao's, "On Contradiction" and "Combat Liberalism." Current political issues are also discussed, and these study groups become a vehicle for helping older neighborhood residents remain involved in local as well as national affairs.

Health Care. Health services at the residents' committee level are provided by Red Medical Workers who work in health stations located in the residential courtyards. Red Medical Workers, usually former "housewives," are selected for training because of their closeness to the people and their desire to be of service.

The major functions of the Red Medical Workers are prevention, the treatment of minor illness, health education, and sanitation work. Three paraprofessionals serve the 1,500 people who live in the Wu Ting Residents' Committee, located in the western part of Peking's Fengsheng neighborhood. Although he is not a health worker, the chairman of the residents' committee serves as the director of the Wu Ting Residents' Committee health station, thus pointing up the close connection between the functions of the residents' committee and the provision of health services.

The Wu Ting health station is located in a single room off one of the courtyards. Its fairly typical equipment includes a bed for examination or treatment, a table with chairs at which consultations may occur, and a cabinet with both Western-type and traditional Chinese medicines. On the walls are a picture of Mao Tse-tung, an acupuncture chart, and health education posters.

One of the Wu Ting's Red Medical Workers, Yang Hsio-hua, is 38 years old. After her marriage she worked briefly as a saleswoman until age 19, when her first child was born. Since then she has been home taking care of her children, now ages 19, 15, and 11. In 1970, responding to a call to "Serve the People" which grew out of the Cultural Revolution, she volunteered for one month of training in the Fengsheng neighborhood hospital. During the training period she and her fellow housewives learned history-taking and simple physical examination techniques such as blood pressure determination. They were taught the uses of a number of Western and herbal medicines and techniques of acupuncture and of intramuscular and subcutaneous injection. Preventive measures, such as sanitation, immunization, and birth control techniques were an important part of the curriculum. But the most important part, according to Comrade Yang, was that she and her colleagues were taught that there are no barriers between them and the acquisition of medical knowledge other than their own fears. Once these are overcome, in part by sessions in which the "bitter past" and the feelings of the students are shared and discussed, the housewives feel it is indeed possible to become medical personnel.

The health workers are paid a modest sum for their work, about 15 yüan per month, roughly one-third the wages of a beginning factory worker. These wages come in part from the small payments made by patients visiting the health station and in part from the collective income from the neighborhood factories. The fee paid for a patient visit to the health station is never more than 10 fen, and usually far less. If the patient is a retired worker, he or she may present the bills from the health station to the former factory, where reimbursement is made in full. If the patient is a dependent of someone who is now working or a retired worker, the factory will reimburse half the health station charge. People who are currently working are rarely seen in residents' committee health stations because their primary medical care needs are taken care of at their place of work.

The Public Health Department supervises the Red Medical Workers in providing immunizations, which are usually given in the residents' committee health station. The Red Medical Workers will often go to the homes to bring the children to the health station for immunization and, if it is necessary for some reason, may give the immunization in the home. It is considered the responsibility of the health workers as well as of the parents to make sure that all those eligible for immunizations are, in actuality, immunized. Perhaps it is this mutual feeling of responsibility on the part of both the citizen and the health establishment which accounts for the incredible immunization rate and subsequent drop in infectious disease in China.

The Red Medical Workers also have as their responsibility the provision of birth control information. They give out oral contraceptives directly; intrauterine contraceptive devices are available, and insertion is performed by trained personnel in the neighborhood hospital. The Red Medical Workers make periodic visits to all the women of the residents' committee area, encouraging the use of contraception and discussing with them the need to lower China's birth rate and the importance of "planned birth" in the liberation of women. There is some evidence that couples of child-bearing age are being asked to decide collectively what the target birth rate of their neighborhood should be and then to allocate the births among themselves in a rational organized fashion. Red Medical Workers are key to this intensive effort in "planned birth," as the Chinese have termed their birth control efforts. It is their integration with the people in the residents' committee, their intimate knowledge of their concerns, their hopes, and their problems that enable these medical paraprofessionals to have such a crucial role in the Chinese attempt to lower the birth rate.

Because of these intensive, person-to-person efforts, the birth rate seems to have been lowered significantly in certain urban areas. In a Hangchow neighborhood in 1972 the birth rate was reported to be an almost unbelievably low 7 per 1,000 per year (Sidel and Sidel, 1974:60) and the estimated crude birth rate for the entire Shanghai City Proper in 1974 was 6.1 per 1,000 (Sidel and Sidel, 1974:252).

As part of their work in treating minor illnesses, organizing sanitation work and preventive medicine, and conducting the planned birth program, the Red Medical Workers, together with the leaders at the residents' committee level, group leaders, and leaders in the workplace, constitute the primary level of the mental health network in urban China. Although the Chinese do not describe the work of these local, indigenous activists as mental health work, it clearly functions as such. Interpersonal problems, individual needs, emotional disturbances, antisocial behavior are all handled by trusted untrained local leaders. When problems cannot be solved at the local level, they are referred step by step up the organizational ladder. Thus, emotional problems are first handled at the levels of the group, residents' committee, place of work, or neighborhood. If the problems remain, the individual may be referred to a district-level psychiatric prevention station. Finally, the individual may be referred to a mental hospital or to a psychiatric ward of a general hospital. It is only at a district-level prevention station and at the mental hospital that trained psychiatric personnel will be involved in treating the patient.

Services at the Workplace

The place of work in China is not simply where one goes to earn one's living; work is not kept separate or compartmentalized from one's home or private life. On the contrary, there has been an ongoing attempt to integrate living and working, and the provision of such services as medical care and day-care at the place of work aids in this integration.

Some places of work are total environments. The Institute for Biological Products in Peking, for example, which produces pharmaceutical products, is a self-contained neighborhood which includes laboratories for scientific work, dormitories for single workers, quarters for married workers, dining halls, a kindergarten, and a primary school. Many large factories provide housing and dining halls for the workers and their families, day-care for their preschool children, and medical care for both the workers and their dependents.

In addition, all workers belong to a study group in which political matters, personal problems, and issues of productivity are handled. The workplace in China, therefore, provides the opportunity for belonging to yet another primary group. Study groups have been a particularly important socializing force in China. As Victor Li (1973:150) points out:

> With the exception of young children, everyone is a member of one or more "small groups" which are composed of about twenty persons who are closely affiliated through their employment, place of residence, or other ties. In addition to other activities, those groups engage in a number of hours of "study" each week; a substantial portion of the study sessions deal with matters falling under the rubric of law. . . . Moreover, an effort is made to apply the general principles examined to the actual living and working conditions of the members of the group.

Not only is the study group instrumental in communicating current norms to the general population but it is also a key to enforcing those norms. Li points out (1973:151) that group members know each other so well that incipient antisocial behavior can be spotted early and dealt with immediately. For it is considered one's responsibility to help one's neighbor or one's co-worker correct deviations in thought or in behavior.

> If a person truly loves his neighbor or truly is his brother's keeper, then he has a moral and social duty to correct his brother's shortcomings. If truly no man is an island and the actions of each person directly affect the lives of all others, then the "group," however defined, has a real and direct stake in controlling the actions of its members.

Thus local leaders, the organizers of these groups, become extremely important in the functioning of Chinese society.

It is through the mechanism of study groups *(hsueh hsi hsiao tsu)* that the attempt is being made to teach the Chinese people a different way of relating to their world, to "remold their world outlook," as the Chinese say. It is in the study groups, in the factories, in the neighborhoods, and in the schools, that the Chinese citizen is encouraged to think scientifically about the world around him, to attempt to put aside superstition and "subjective reality." It is in the study group, surrounded by co-workers or neighbors, that he is expected to examine his attitudes and behavior honestly and attempt to evaluate whether he is still motivated by self-interest and individualism or whether he is attempting to contribute to the common good. These meetings are punctuated by bouts of "criticism and self-criticism" as members struggle to function within their society according to current norms.

These small study groups are characterized by a level of intimacy rarely shared in urban America outside of, perhaps, therapy groups. As one American (Tannebaum, 1973) who has lived in China for many years has observed, "Study groups are composed of people with whom you work every day or of neighbors whose life is intimately linked with your own. . . . Everyone is well versed in the others' personalities, traits and expressions, and this makes the atmosphere for criticism and self-criticism a little easier."

Health Care. Many factories provide medical care through small clinics, and some are even equipped with a small ward. Medical care is usually provided by a worker doctor, the counterpart to the barefoot doctor in the countryside and the Red Medical Worker in the urban neighborhood. Worker doctors have usually had one to two months of medical training and continue to spend most of their time doing factory work. Their tasks are largely preventive and educational, but they also care for "minor and common illness." In the larger factories there are large medical units run by regular doctors with the assistance of "middle medical workers" and worker doctors.

Day-Care. Many factories and other places of work provide nursing rooms and nurseries for the children of their employees.

After a guaranteed 56-day paid maternity leave, urban women generally return to work. Some mothers leave their infants at home with grandparents but since most Chinese women breast-feed their babies, the more convenient arrangement is for the mother to bring her infant to the nursing room in the factory or institution in which she works. The mother is free to nurse her baby twice during the 8-hour working day; the baby is given supplementary bottles if he is hungry between feedings. Infants remain in the nursing room from age 56 days until approximately 18 months. At 18 months the children, usually trained and weaned, move to nurseries, which are again found in most large factories and other places of work. Because the children are weaned, they can now, and often do, attend the nursery in the father's place of work. In nurseries, children can eat all of their meals, if their parents wish, and receive medical care, both preventive and acute. There is a fee for all preschool care, which is shared between the parents and the factory.

Welfare Services. According to China Reconstructs (1974b:35):

> The state system of labor insurance covers workers employed in all enterprises, undertakings and government offices, regardless of nationality, citizenship, religion, age or sex. Workers are entitled to benefits for sickness, injury, disability, childbirth, old age and death. There are no deductions from the workers' pay nor are they required to pay any premiums.

In case of a long illness, a worker may receive, in addition to free medical care, from 40% to 100% of his salary depending on how long he has worked until he has recovered and is back at work. A worker injured on the job receives his full salary during the period of treatment and recuperation. Medical and hospital expenses are free for female workers during childbirth, and they are entitled to 56 days of paid maternity leave in case of a normal delivery and 70 days in case of a complicated or difficult delivery.

Retired workers receive a monthly pension of from 50% to 85% of their salary depending on the number of years they have worked. If a worker dies as a result of an injury received while he was working, his funeral costs are paid by his place of work and his family will receive 25% to 50% of his salary until they are self-supporting. Many factories have welfare funds with which workers in special financial need can be helped. These matters are usually up to the discretion of the local factory committee.

Counseling. As in the neighborhood, the small group in the place of work is of utmost importance in helping to resolve personal problems. According to Victor Li (1973:152-153),

> a person might be sloppy in his work and consequently damage production. He is criticized for his carelessness, but also he is given additional technical training to improve his skills. Moreover, other aspects of his life are examined to find the root causes of his difficulties. Perhaps an unhappy marriage is adversely affecting his work; if so, the factory group must find means of "helping" his family life.

Fellow workers can become extremely involved in another's private life. In a divorce trial reported by Walker (1973:45-53), representatives of both the husband's work unit and of the wife's work unit testify about their marraige, details of their problems, and their feelings. In a divorce trial reported by Felix Greene (1962:203) the representative from the wife's place of work begins her testimony by saying, "I have made a thorough study of the case and all its aspects and made many inquiries. Though love was there at the start, there was never any real basis of a good relationship." She continues by analyzing the marriage and particularly the husband's role in the marriage.

Thus, the place of work and one's fellow workers play an intimate role in the life of the worker in China similar to the role that the neighborhood and its leaders play in the lives of housewives and retired persons. This is a society in which one's problems become the community's problems, one in which there are no victimless crimes. When the Chinese are asked about the incidence of child abuse, they have difficulty understanding the question. First, they cannot quite understand the concept of abusing a child, and, second, such an action would never be permitted by friends and neighbors. Perhaps it would be well to note that there is no Chinese character or combination of characters for the word "privacy" as we know it in English. People's lives and behavior are truly considered the responsibility of one's neighbors and co-workers.

IN-PATIENT TREATMENT OF MENTAL ILLNESS

Since the Cultural Revolution there has been increased emphasis in all branches of medicine on combining the techniques of traditional and Western medicine. While the Chinese had been doing so in other branches of medical care since 1949, from the time of Liberation until 1965 the psychiatric sphere seems to have concentrated more on Western methods of treatment and to have neglected traditional techniques. Since the late 1960s, Western-trained doctors have been revamping their psychiatric services to include traditional methods and political techniques adopted by the society at large.

Methods

The methods currently being used to treat mental illness are collective help, self-reliance, drug therapy, acupuncture, "heart-to-heart talks," follow-up care, community ethos, productive labor, the teachings of Chairman Mao Tse-tung, and "revolutionary optimism."

Collective Help. With the participation of members of the People's Liberation Army in the administration of hospitals since the Cultural Revolution, some psychiatric hospitals are using the army model of organization, dividing the patients on the wards into groups so that they can become a "collective fighting group instead of a ward." Within these "fighting groups" the patients who are getting better are paired with newer and sicker patients so that they can help each other with "mutual love and mutual help."

Self-Reliance. The patients themselves are encouraged to investigate their own disease, to examine their symptoms, and to understand their treatment. They are encouraged to study themselves in order to recognize their condition and to prevent a relapse.

Drug Therapy. Seriously ill patients are given "thorazine" (chlorpromazine), though evidently in smaller doses than before the Cultural Revolution. Insulin shock and electric shock therapy have been eliminated since the Cultural Revolution.

Acupuncture. Acupuncture is being used experimentally for certain forms of schizophrenia. Research is being conducted to evaluate acupuncture as a treatment technique.

Heart-to—Heart Talks. A psychiatrist meets with patients individually or in small groups at regular intervals to discuss their problems and to help them understand their illness more completely. The most important form of treatment, according to Chinese psychiatrists, is the relationship between the psychiatrist and the patient.

Follow-Up Care. After the patient is discharged he is followed up, first, every two weeks and then monthly in the out-patient department. Sometimes a doctor or a nurse on the staff of the hospital will make a home visit. Before discharge a doctor will visit the patient's place of work to make sure that he is returning to a job that is best for his mental health. Although the patient's job has been kept for him pending his return, it may be that another task within his work unit would better suit his mental health needs. Often the patient is kept on drug therapy after discharge, but on a smaller dosage.

Community Ethos. The role of the neighborhood committee in looking after the well-being of the residents of the community is considered to be very important in the treatment plan. When a patient is about to be discharged from a mental hospital, he becomes the "special concern" of his neighborhood committee as well as of his family and friends; this community concern plus the assurance of his job and family waiting for him help ease the transition from hospital to community.

Productive Labor. As in the larger society, where all members are encouraged to do productive labor, hospital patients are also encouraged to do what we in the West would call occupational therapy. Patients fold bandages, prepare medications for the out-patient department, and work for a local factory. The factory pays the hospital for the patients' work, and this income is used to provide them with special services.

The Teachings of Mao Tse-tung. Running through this entire gamut of treatment techniques is the philosophy of Chairman Mao. Patients and hospital workers alike study his writings: "On Practice," "On Contradiction," "Where Do Correct Ideas Come From?" and the "Three Constantly Read Articles." Patients are organized into groups to study these writings daily and are encouraged through them to understand "objective reality," rather than function on the basis of "subjective thinking." They "arm their minds with Chairman Mao's Thought during their stay in the hospital in order to fight their disease."

Revolutionary Optimism. A psychiatric patient is encouraged to feel that he is part of a force greater than himself, that of the revolution. He is urged to believe that the revolution will be victorious and that "no matter what the difficulties, he will have a bright future." It is important for the patient to receive treatment and to overcome his disease not only for his own sake, but for the sake of the revolution. Revolutionary optimism gives the patient the "encouragement and the confidence to conquer his disease."

Types of Illnesses

The doctors at the Shanghai Mental Hospital consider schizophrenia to be the most common diagnosis; over 50% of their patients are schizophrenics. Paranoia is believed to be the most common form of schizophrenia; depression, catatonia, and postpartum depression are relatively rare. The suicide rate is said to be quite low.

The hospital also admits a small percentage of patients who have physical illnesses with psychiatric complications, such as disturbed liver function, epilepsy, and heart disease. Both the Shanghai Mental Hospital and the psychiatric ward of the Third Teaching Hospital in Peking reported that the most common age of onset of mental illness is from 20 to 30 years of age. This corroborates findings in the 1930s (Lamson, 1935:411) that revealed that onset of mental illness in 40% of the patients in one study occurred between ages 20 to 30. In a study of a group of 2,000 schizophrenics done in the late 1950s (Cerny, 1965:229-238), it was found that 50% were between the ages of 21 and 30; 1.3% were under 15 years of age; and over 7% were over 40.

The staff of mental hospitals include trained psychiatrists and psychiatric nurses who, after their professional school training, continue their learning in a hospital setting until the senior members of the department feel these individuals are adequately prepared. There is no examination or fixed period of training.

PRINCIPLES OF CHINA'S HUMAN SERVICES

The organization of life in China's communes and neighborhoods can perhaps best be viewed as a total community support system, one fostered and maintained by the residents themselves. It is a society characterized by cohesion and intimacy; people live and work together very closely and know each other well. It is also a society characterized by control. Just as one's personal affairs are a subject of concern for one's associates, so must one's antisocial ideas and deeds be a subject of concern. It was due to just such community concern and the exercise of community control that the Chinese have accomplished what is in the eyes of some Westerners an astonishing feat—the virtual eradication of drug addiction and of venereal disease.

It is a society that is attempting through an ongoing revolution to guarantee the basic necessities to a vast population and to involve people at every organizational level in providing those necessities and the decision-making processes. In the redistribution of wealth and in the provision of human services, the Chinese have employed principles particularly suited to the historical, cultural, geographical, and political conditions of their society.

Stress on the Rural Areas. Since the Cultural Revolution, an attempt has been made to provide services to those who formerly had least—the 80% of the population who live in the rural areas—and to equalize the quality of life in the cities and in the countryside. Large numbers of medical facilities and schools have been built in the countryside, large numbers of indigenous health workers have been trained, and personnel have rotated from neighboring urban areas to the communes.

Decentralization. Services are decentralized to the lowest organizational level in both the cities and the countryside. Local initiative, local funding, and local decision-making are encouraged as part of the larger attempt to involve the general population in the provision of services.

Deprofessionalization. Human services are provided largely by nonprofessionals and paraprofessionals. Local health workers are trained for brief periods of time in the hope of eliminating the alienation that occurs during extended educational experiences and in the hope of decreasing the distance between the helper and the helped. Most social services, marital disputes, interfamilial disputes, welfare problems, and problems of the aged are handled by indigenous leaders in neighborhoods, communes, and places of work. The elderly themselves are used extensively in these roles, thereby drawing on their traditional respected role within the society.

Demystification. People are urged at every level to participate in their own care—their health care, their psychiatric care, the solving of their own and of others' problems. Diagnoses are shared with patients in an attempt to mobilize their own resources and to undermine excessive reliance on authority figures.

Self-Reliance. Concomitant with demystification is the peculiarly Chinese emphasis on self-reliance, a self-reliance that is collective in nature. The focus on the collective relying on its own resources and initiative is clearly due in part to economic conditions, but it is also due to the profound belief that people must be involved in their own destiny, must be active participants in determining that destiny.

Mass Participation. The Chinese public health campaigns against venereal disease, drug addiction, and infectious disease and currently toward lowering the birth rate have been successful in part because of mass health education but also because of an emphasis on the involvement of the entire population. Furthermore, the organization of the society into small groups in which mutual aid is emphasized has led to mass participation in mental health work, both preventive and therapeutic.

Revolutionary Optimism. The feeling of commitment, of working for a cause greater than oneself, is pervasive in China. Recent visitors to China have described the country as one with a "high pitch of collective spirit" (Terrill, 1972:227), a "sense of purpose, self-confidence, and dignity" (Tuchman, 1972:3), and a "deep sense of mission" (Sidel and Sidel, 1972:25-34). The Chinese refer to this spirit as "revolutionary optimism"; its role in the mental health and well-being of the Chinese people, while incalculable, is nevertheless of utmost importance.

An Emphasis on Service. Everywhere in China are the words, *Wei renmin fuwu,* "Serve the People." To the Chinese this phrase seems to be more than an empty cliché; it is apparently intended as the basis for a way of life and for all human services. Clearly the Chinese are attempting to motivate people by altruism rather than by personal gain. To what extent this is a Chinese ideal rather than a Chinese reality is unclear, but it is an attempt which bears close scrutiny by other societies.

REFERENCES

ALLEY, R. (1950). Leaves from a Sandan notebook. Christchurch, New Zealand: Caxton Press.
CERNY, J. (1965). "Chinese psychiatry." International Journal of Psychiatry, 1:229-238.
CHEN PI-CHAO (1975). "Studies in family planning: China, the People's Republic of." The Population Council, 6(August):320-322.
China Reconstructs (1972). "Co-op medical care in Sun Village." 21(November):2-7.
——— (1973a). "Growing up healthy in mind and body." 22(June):7-12.
——— (1973b). "Life at Wenhsing Street School." 22(June):10-11.
——— (1974a). "Factory for the handicapped." 23(December):40-42.
——— (1974b). "Labor insurance and benefits to the workers." 23(May):35.
——— (1974c). "A Tibetan 'barefoot doctor.' " 23(September):9-11.

COHEN, J.A. (1971). "Drafting People's Mediation Rules." In J.W. Lewis (ed.), The city in Communist China. Stanford, Calif.: Stanford University Press.

For the Health of the People (1963). Peking: Foreign Languages Press.

GREENE, F. (1962). China. New York: Ballantine.

GURLEY, J.G. (1975). "Rural development in China 1949-72, and the lessons to be learned from it." World Development, 3(July-August):455-471.

HAN SUYIN (1966). "Reflections on social change." Bulletin of the Atomic Scientists, 22(June):80-83.

HARTH, M. (ed., 1972). New York Times encyclopedic almanac, 1971. New York: New York Times.

HORN, J.S. (1971). Away with all pests: An English surgeon in People's China: 1954-1969. New York: Monthly Review Press.

Hsinhua Weekly Issue (1975). "Peking expands nurseries." 336(July 17):7-8.

KESSEN, W. (ed., 1975). Childhood in China. New Haven, Conn.: Yale University Press.

LAMSON, H.D. (1935). Social pathology in China. Shanghai: Commercial Press.

LI, V.H. (1973). "Law and penology: Systems of reform and correction. Pp. 144-156 in M. Oksenberg (ed.), China's developmental experience. New York: Columbia University, Proceedings of the Academy of Political Science (vol. 31, March).

MAO TSE-TUNG (1966). "On practice." In Four essays on philosophy. Peking: Foreign Languages Press.

MYRDAL, J., and KESSLE' G. (1972). China: The revolution continued. New York: Vintage.

NEEDHAM, J. (1973). "The past in China's present: A cultural, social, and philosophical background for contemporary China." Far East Reporter, (March):1-37.

ORLEANS, L.A. (1960). Professional manpower and education in Communist China (NSF-61-3). Washington, D.C.: U.S. Government Printing Office.

SCHURMANN, F. (1968). Ideology and organization in Communist China (2nd ed.). Berkeley: University of California Press.

Science for the People (1974). China: Science walks on two legs. New York: Avon.

SELDEN, M. (1971). The Yenan way in revolutionary China. Cambridge, Mass.: Harvard University Press.

SIDEL, R. (1973). Women and child care in China: A firsthand report. New York: Penguin.

SIDEL, V.W., and SIDEL, R. (1972). "The human services in China." Social Policy, 2(March-April):25-34.

——— (1974). Serve the people: Observations on medicine in the People's Republic of China. Boston: Beacon Press.

SNOW, E. (1971a). The long revolution. New York: Random House.

——— (1971b). Red China today. New York: Vintage.

SOLOMON, R.H. (1971). Mao's revolution and the Chinese political culture. Berkeley: University of California Press.

SWEEZY, P.M. (1975). "China: Contrasts with capitalism." Monthly Review, 27(July-August):1-11.

TANNEBAUM, G. (1973). Speech delivered at the Forum on Technology and Social Change, Iowa State University, Ames, Iowa, October 4.

TERRILL, R. (1972). 800,000,000: The real China. Boston: Little, Brown.

TUCHMAN, B.W. (1972). Notes from China. New York: Collier Books.

U.S.S.R. Central Statistical Unit (1969). Narodnoe Khoziaistovo SSSR V 1968 Godu (People's Economy: U.S.S.R. 1968). Moscow: Author.

U.S. Bureau of the Census (1971). 1970 census of population (PC(VI)–I). Washington, D.C.: U.S. Government Printing Office.

WALKER, D.B. (1973). "People's court in China: Trial of a divorce case." National Lawyers Guild Practitioner, 30(spring-summer):45-53.

WHITE, T.H., and JACOBY, A. (1946). Thunder out of China. New York: William Sloane.

YU YANG (1974). "An army of new doctors." China Reconstructs, 23(April):6-10.

10

JAPAN: NATIONAL, PREFECTURAL, AND LOCAL SOCIAL SERVICES

SUMIKO NAKAMURA

ADMINISTRATIVE FRAMEWORK OF SOCIAL SERVICE DELIVERY

In Japan, the central governmental organ in charge of social welfare and related services is the Ministry of Health and Welfare. Of its many divisions, the Bureau of Social Affairs and the Bureau of Children and Families take major responsibilities for social services. Other governmental organs, such as the Ministries of Labor and of Justice, the Prime Minister's office, and the Planning Agency of National Economics by and large take charge of social work administration in its broader sense.

On the prefectural level, such sections as the Women's and Children's Division, the Social Affairs Division, the Division of Social Welfare, and the like are responsible for providing for needs in these fields. There are many cities, towns, and villages in each prefecture, and each has a department and/or division similar to those in prefectural government. In addition, each city and each special ward *(tokubetsu-ku)*, which is a special autonomous body in the Tokyo Metropolitan area, as well as each town and village, are provided with a *fukushi-jimusho* (welfare office) and a *hoken-sho* (local health center). Each *fukushi-jimusho* (or welfare office) plays an essential role in providing for welfare needs.

Fukushi-Jimusho (Welfare Offices)

The *fukushi-jimusho* (welfare offices) are organized to handle activities in the local welfare administration districts, and there were 1,108 such offices throughout the country as of June 1, 1972. Due to differences in the size of the different municipalities, the scope and organization of the welfare office also vary. Some 30% render services for areas of under 50,000 population; another

10% serve over 200,000 residents. The average is about 100,000 people. A welfare office consists of a number of welfare field-workers and their supervisor, as well as several professional caseworkers with the name of his or her specialty fixed to his or her title—such as *jido-fukushishi* (professional child welfare worker) or *shintai-shogai-sha-fukushishi* (professional welfare worker for the physically disabled). There are also clerical staff and a director. In addition to these full-time staff and employees, there are many volunteers called *minsei-iin* and *jido-inn,* as well as a number of part-time welfare workers. There were approximately 10,000 welfare field-workers working under 2,000 supervisors, as well as 160,000 volunteers, throughout the country as of June 1972.

The *shakaifukushi-shuji* (welfare field-workers) determine eligibility for benefits and services of those applying for public assistance, in accordance with the six different social welfare laws.[1] They conduct investigative work and give casework services to the recipients of public assistance. (Most of the cases are brought to their attention through the activities of volunteer workers.) In order to qualify as a welfare field-worker, one must be a graduate from a university or a college with 3 credits out of 30 courses related to the field of social welfare. Those who complete special school training for this job can also qualify. The person must be over age twenty, with considerable zeal in promoting social welfare. Of all welfare field-workers, those fully qualified constitute 73.3%. Of their supervisors, 88.3% meet all qualifications required by the law. Throughout the country there are approximately 10,768 *shakaifukushi-shuji,* who work under 2,019 supervisors.

The *jido-fukushishi* (professional child welfare officers) are expected to give professional counseling service to parents and their children. Most are assigned to a child guidance center, while some serve at welfare offices in large communities. They give diagnoses and treatment to their clients. There were 847 child welfare officers in all Japan as of 1973. To qualify for the post, one must be one of the following: (1) either a graduate from an institution designated by the Minister of Health and Welfare as the one for training child welfare officers or a graduate of a special training course; (2) a university graduate who has specialized in psychology, education, sociology, or a course equivalent to these three disciplines; (3) a physician; (4) a welfare field-worker who has engaged in child welfare work for more than two years; or (5) a person who has qualifications equal to those of one of the former categories and who has adequate knowledge and experience necessary for the profession.

The *minsei-inn* (volunteer workers for people's welfare) are lay workers who render voluntary services in close cooperation with welfare field-workers. They give casework services in the community where they are assigned, as well as investigate eligibility for services. Those who would like to get public assistance, those who have problems in their daily life, or those who have any kind of difficulties may come first to *minsei-inn* to seek help. Volunteer workers who assume the post of *minsei-jido-inn* (volunteer workers in child welfare) are expected to cooperate with the professional child welfare officer and the welfare field-workers and also render services for the protection and care of children, pregnant women, and nursing mothers; in doing so, they are expected to cooperate with the welfare office in the field of children's welfare. Mothers who have difficulties in dealing with their children may seek help first from these volunteer workers. The number of cases dealt with by *minsei-jido-inn* in the fiscal year of 1972 was 4,433,540; family problems involved 11.0%, problems of living expenses 11.3%, health problems 16.5%, problems of housing or residence 7.4%, cases related to public assistance 10.9%, problems with pension benefits and social insurance 11.9%, and problems related to employment and work 7.9%. *Minsei-inn* and/or *minsei-jido-inn* are commissioned by the Health and Welfare Minister from among those people who are considered mature, with relevant life experience. They are expected to serve a term of three years. There were approximately 160,000 such volunteer workers throughout the country in 1973. Of all, women volunteers accounted for over 30%. Volunteers are 56.3 years old on the average.

Hoken-Jo (Local Health Centers)

The *hoken-jo* (local health centers) play an important role in promoting public health, rendering services in accordance with the public health policies set forth by the central Ministry of Health and Welfare. The main services given by the *hoken-jo* are preventive work against various illnesses, including contagious diseases; X-ray examinations; health consultations; periodic examination of expectant mothers, as well as new babies, children up to 3 years old, and aged people over 65; a diversity of visiting services by public health nurses; nutrition consultation; health education; and inspection as well as supervision of environmental and food sanitation. The centers also conduct tests and collect statistics in the field of public health. The health centers are staffed with a number of medical doctors and public health nurses and a variety of technicians. The professional staff assigned to the health centers throughout the country totaled approximately 31,000, as of July 1973. In April 1973, there were 839 health centers, 708 of which were under direct control of prefectural governments and 131 of which were established by cities.

Jido-Sodan-Sho (Child Guidance Centers)

The *jido-sodan-sho* (child guidance centers) are the agencies playing the leading role in the field of child welfare in each locality. Established as well as financed by prefectural governments, most are also under their direct control. Major cities such as Osaka, Kobe, Yokohama, Nagoya, and Kyoto, as well as the Tokyo metropolis, operate their own guidance centers financed by their own municipal budgets. As of August 1973, there were 149 child guidance centers throughout the country with staffs and employees assigned them totaling over 3,500. They offer counseling services to parents, teachers, and other people concerning the children under their care, as well as give therapy and treatment directly to children with behavior problems. In the conduct of their various services, they administer many different diagnostic tests, examinations, and investigations. The total cases handled by the 149 child guidance centers in the fiscal year of 1973 were 243,403. The nature of the cases is shown in Table 1.

It should be pointed out that recently the cases involving the protection and care of children without parents or guardians have shown a trend of gradual increase. Over 20% of these cases resulted because the mother or guardian deserted or otherwise left the family. Over half the number of the children in this category are under 3 years of age. On the other hand, the total number of cases handled by the child guidance centers in the country have declined since 1964, when it reached a peak of 276,000 cases.

A *jido-sodan-sho* contains a variety of staffers and workers, including medical doctors, psychiatrists, psychologists, and caseworkers who are called *jido-fukushishi* (professional child welfare officers). A director of a *jido-sodan-sho*, according to the law, should be a person who is either (1) a physician with knowledge or experience in mental health, (2) a university or college graduate who has completed a course in psychology or a related field, (3) a person who has served as a *jido-fukushishi* (professional welfare officer) for over two years, or (4) a person who has qualifications corresponding to those of the categories above.

At child guidance centers, each accepted case is treated in accordance with results of diagnosis tests (both psychological and medical) and the judgment of the professional staff. Specific treatments are shown in Table 2. One-third of the cases involve more than six interviews, and the number of cases is gradually increasing.

Table 1: Classification of Cases in Japanese Child Guidance Centers,
         April 1973-March 1974

	Number	Percent
Behavior problems in general	50,798	18.6
Truancy and other similar misbehavior	32,593	12.0
Mental retardation, multiple physical-mental handicaps	49,457	18.1
Physical handicaps, including audiovisual handicaps and difficulties in speech	31,124	11.4
Cases of protection and care for those without parents or guardians due to death, desertion, family breakup, etc.; those with environmental problems; those neglected, mistreated, or abused	33,829	12.4
Delinquency:	30,011	11.0
Law violation cases such as stealing, inflicting harm or injury on others, arson, etc.	18,675	6.8
Cases involving antisocial or other serious behavior, such as vagrancy, emotional disturbance, sex-related delinquency	11,336	4.1
Other cases, including general health consultations	15,591	5.7
TOTAL	273,414	100.0

Table 2: Kinds of Specific Treatments or Actions Performed at Japanese
Child Guidance Centers, April 1972-March 1973

	Number	Percent
Advice and guidance through interview (one interview)	137,307	57.0
Treatment by counseling and/or psychotherapy (more than two interviews)	26,091	10.8
Placement for institutional care at child-care facilities, including those for the mentally-retarded	27,057	11.2
Guidance or treatment by child welfare officers and other caseworkers	6,683	2.8
Placement with foster parents or other proper guardians	1,030	0.4
Scoldings or oath-taking	8,985	3.7
Other actions or treatment	33,645	14.0
TOTAL	240,798	100.0

SOURCE: Report by Ministry of Health and Welfare (April 1972-March 1973).

Each child guidance center has shelter facilities for children who are brought into the center because they have been deserted, their families have broken up, or they have run away. Often under such provisional care, the children's behavior is observed and diagnosed for treatment. Approximately 20,000 children are given shelter care at child guidance centers each year.

CHILD WELFARE

Social service systems and programs in the field of child welfare in Japan are geared to follow the principles of the Child Welfare Law enacted in 1947, as well as the Children's Charter proclaimed in 1951. Since the law became effective, the programs in this field have developed considerably. The number of children under 18 years of age covered by the Child Welfare Law were (according to the census, October 1970) approximately 29,870,000. It is anticipated, however, that the children's population in Japan will gradually decrease proportionately in relation to the gorwing number of the aged.

On the national level, the Children and Families Bureau of the Ministry of Health and Welfare, is responsible for enforcing the Child Welfare Law. Also on the national level there is the Central Child Welfare Council, whose purpose is to evaluate and study the current needs of children and expectant and nursing mothers. Each prefecture also has a council designed after the central council and serving as a consultative body. Cities and towns may have similar organizations, as needed. In general, on the local levels, there are three types of public agencies for those people needing help in the field of child welfare: the welfare office, the child guidance center, and the local health center. Instead of seeking help directly with any of these agencies, people may visit a volunteer worker in their community. They may then be referred to a public agency.

The cost of administering services for children's welfare amounts to over half—and sometimes over 60%—of the total cost of supporting all social welfare programs. Thus, it is obvious that the child welfare programs share the major part of the field of social work in Japan.

Voluntary Agencies for Family Counseling

Voluntary counseling services are provided by the Councils of Social Welfare in major cities. The counseling staff consists of volunteer careworkers. Some of these voluntary counseling facilities are partially financed by a national government subsidy.

Services to advance the sound growth of infants and very young children include services for expectant mothers, visiting-nurse services for the newborn, a variety of preventive measures, and family planning.

Significant among the various voluntary groups are the parents' organizations designed to promote wholesome leisure-time activities for children as well as to increase parents' knowledge about child-rearing. There are approximately 4,300,000 parents participating in such adult activities groups, totaling about 100,000 organizations in 1973.

Most day-care centers and other voluntary agencies for children's groups grow out of neighborhood efforts. Some, however, have not yet been accredited by the government, due to inadequate adherence to the standards required by law. Voluntary day nurseries operating under substandard conditions numbered 2,407 in 1969, according to a survey by the Ministry of Health and Welfare, and they cared for some 110,000 infants. In recent years, a considerable number of day-care facilities for preschool children have been established by companies on the premises of their buildings and factories. As of February 1973, 3.2% of all the plants or firms with over 30 employees operated such a service, financed by their own expenditures. This system is presently promoted by the Women's and Minors' Bureau of the Ministry of Labor to help fill the urgent need for day-care services as well as for better welfare of working mothers.

Families' Consultation Room for Their Children

A special Families' Consultation Room for Their Children, established in local welfare offices in 1964, specializes in parent's needs regarding their children's welfare and in behavior problems. As of March 1974, there were 875 such consultation rooms throughout the country. Staffed by welfare field-workers and two family counselors, they offer counseling services to help parents or relatives in bringing up children. It is a matter of the degree of seriousness of a case whether it is taken up in the guidance center or the consultation room—the consultation room being reserved for minor cases. From the consultation room, however, a case may be referred to a child guidance center for further study and treatment.

After-School Care for Children

With the marked increase of working mothers there has been a great need for programs in the area of after-school care for children, especially for the lower grades. However, unfortunately, this area is left out by the child welfare administration and by education authorities as well. Thus programs have been developed by working mothers themselves, with the cooperation of professional people engaged in children's care. Working mothers' activities have developed gradually into a nationwide organization for liaison and debate and have strengthened the after-school care programs for their children.

As of September 1972, there were 620 day nurseries for school-age children and 500 smaller places in the country designed to care for children while parents work. Such arrangements are referred to by the nickname *kagikko kyoshitsu* (a classroom for children carrying their house keys). The children cared for by these programs total approximately 40,000 in the country. Up until 1970, the Bureau of Social Education of the Ministry of Education helped finance these programs. (Public financing ended, however, when the government turned to new measures of juvenile delinquency prevention, i.e., in opening all the public school athletic fields and facilities for children's leisure-time activities after school and on weekends.) Providing after-school care for children of working mothers is very essential, to give them a "home-substitute" where they may feel a sense of security and comfort during their parents' absence. The service should also relieve the working mothers' sense of concern about their children. It must be emphasized that this is an area which urgently needs improvement by the government in Japan today.

Institutional Care

Children who need protective care, due to physical or mental handicaps, unfavorable environmental conditions, absence of parents, antisocial behavior, etc., are generally served through institutional care. Table 3 shows the overall picture of current institutional programs providing care for these and other children and their mothers.

Foster Home Care

It is supposed to be more desirable for a child to be placed with foster parents when he or she lacks natural parental care for one reason or another. However, in Japan the foster home system is rather underdeveloped. In 1972, there were only 4,366 children under foster home care, while the number of children placed in children's or infants' institutions totaled 34,539. The reasons for the deficiency derive from the particular social conditions in the country. First, housing is very constricted in the urban areas. Second, more housewives are now working outside the home and thus lack time to serve as foster mothers for

Table 3: Number and Types of Child Welfare Institutions in Japan,
         December 1971

Kind of Institution	Total Number	Number of Public	Number of Private	Percentage Public	Capacity
Infant homes	127	27	100	21.2	4,126
Day nurseries	14,806	9,142	5,664	61.7	1,276,967
Children's homes	520	64	456	12.3	34,181
Mentally retarded children's homes	328	95	233	29.0	24,587
Mentally retarded children's day-care centers	103	79	24	76.7	4,135
Homes for blind children	32	15	17	47.0	1,781
Homes for deaf and dumb children	35	16	19	45.7	2,512
Homes for invalid children	33	7	26	21.2	2,059
Day-care centers for crippled children	20	17	3	85.0	830
Homes for crippled children	76	37	39	48.7	8,888
Hospital-homes for seriously disabled handicapped children	26	3	23	11.5	3,309
Short-term treatment centers for emotionally disturbed children	6	5	1	83.8	300
Homes for juvenile training and education	58	55	2	94.8	5,211
Children centers	1,552	1,266	286	79.0	
Children playgrounds	2,356	2,346	10	99.6	
Maternity homes	1,010	607	403	60.1	
Homes for mothers and children	501	363	138	72.4	
Mother and child welfare centers	34	25	91	73.5	
Weekend homes for fatherless families	16	4	12	25.0	
TOTALS	21,639	14,173	7,547	65.5	

additional children. Finally, rural families find it almost impossible to serve as foster parents because most farm work is now done by the aged and women since the heads of households are away from home seeking employment in factories. As of December 1972, the number of homes registered as potential foster homes was 13,260, but the number actually containing foster children was only 3,643.

Services for Single Mothers with Dependent Children

According to a survey conducted by the Ministry of Health and Welfare in October 1969, there were about 352,000 female-headed families with dependent children under 18 years of age. The percentage of such families that contained working mothers was 86.7% (as compared to 47.8% of mothers in other households); 12.3% were welfare recipients; only 25.8% paid taxes. Obviously the income level of these families is considerably lower than that of two-parent households (only 1% of whom are on welfare).

Family counseling services are available to the mothers and children in this group, and there is a program providing them with a consultant ("consultant for single mother with dependent children"), who is assigned to a local welfare office. Single mothers are helped with vocational training, employment, and special loans.

The welfare services for fatherless families are as follows:

Financial Assistance

(1) Public assistance: Aid for the support and education of dependent children and aid for housing.

(2) Mother's welfare fund loans: Special low-interest loans for single mothers. These are available for financing small businesses, for purchasing clothing or other needs, for vocational training, for children's schooling, etc.

(3) Widows' welfare fund loans: Low-interest loans to widows over 40 years of age.

(4) Child rearing allowances: In 1961, as a means of improving the financial condition of female headed households, the Child Rearing Allowance Law was enacted. However, the sum of the allowance is too small to enable single mothers to support their young children.

Tax Reductions: A variety of special provisions grant the tax reductions to widows.

Vocational Guidance and Employment Services: Various vocational training programs have been designed for the women of this group, and the local offices of the Women's and Minors' Bureau of the Ministry of Labor provide special consultants for their employment needs.

Special Institutions and Facilities

(1) Dormitories for single mothers and their children: Facilities for women without a spouse and having dependent children are provided by the prefectural level. There are 467 places for 6,503 families.

(2) Welfare centers for widowed mothers and their children: There are 40 of these centers.

(3) Recreation homes for single mothers and their children: There are 23 accommodations providing low-cost or free vacations.

(4) Low-cost housing for fatherless families: There are 1,295 units in this category.

WELFARE OF THE PHYSICALLY HANDICAPPED

According to a national survey of October 1970, there were 1,314,000 persons over 18 years of age with some kind of physical handicap.

The welfare administration for the physically handicapped was neglected until about 1949, when the Law for the Welfare of the Physically Handicapped was enacted. Prior to that time, the emphasis was largely on granting financial aid, though there were comprehensive programs for the war-wounded. The Division of Rehabilitation of the Social Affairs Bureau of the Ministry of Health and Welfare is the national agency in charge of welfare for the disabled. The Advisory Council on Welfare of the Physically Handicapped, a consultative organ for the Ministry of Health and Welfare, evaluates and studies the administration and policy making in this field. Welfare administration for the disabled greatly improved with the enactment of recommendations offered in 1966 by the Advisory Council.

In addition to the welfare office, physically handicapped persons may get service through other agencies and persons: (a) consultation centers for the physically handicapped; (b) welfare officers specially designated for the physically handicapped; (c) lay volunteer workers who offer physical aid, give advice, and lead community efforts in improving environmental conditions for the handicapped; and (d) volunteer workers for people's welfare.

The national government issues handbooks to persons who have physical handicaps and who have been diagnosed by an authorized agency. The handbooks qualify the bearers to receive a variety of governmental services.

Institutions for Rehabilitation of the Physically Handicapped

There are three kinds of facilities for the rehabilitation of the physically handicapped: those giving institutional treatment and training for the recovery of physical functions; those providing hospital care for the severely handicapped; and those providing outpatient care. In December 1972, there were 1,233 establishments giving professional medical services for treating the physically handicapped toward rehabilitation, in both a vocational and a social sense. Such services are either free (as a part of public assistance), partially charged, or fully charged, according to the client's financial condition.

As of 1972, there were several types of institutions for rehabilitation of the physically handicapped:

> *Rehabilitation centers for those with disabled limbs:* These provide medical care and treatment, vocational training, and counseling. There are 3 national centers (350 patients), 57 prefectural (2,912 patients), and 12 private (755 patients).

> *Rehabilitation centers for the blind:* These provide training and vocational guidance. There are 5 national centers (1,080 patients), 3 prefectural (122 patients), and 5 private (290 patients).

Rehabilitation centers for the deaf and mute: These provide medical treatment, auditory training, speech training, and other measures necessary for rehabilitation. There are 1 national center (100 patients), 2 prefectural (37 patients), and 1 private (30 patients).

Rehabilitation centers for those with handicaps resulting from impaired internal organs: These provide accommodations, counseling service, and training for rehabilitation under medical doctors' supervision. There are 18 prefectural centers (950 patients) and 8 private (570 patients).

Sheltered workshops: These accommodate those physically handicapped who are somewhat self-supporting, giving them vocational training as needed and helping them with finding a job. There are 19 prefectural workshops (810 patients) and 68 private (4,047 patients).

Braille libraries: These circulate books free of charge or for a small fee and also provide service by mail. There are 31 prefectural or local libraries and 20 private.

Homes for the blind: These rehabilitation facilities provide a variety of services for persons without sight or with visual defects. There are 5 prefectural or local homes and 28 private.

Sheltered factories for the welfare of the physically handicapped: To furnish severely handicapped people with gainful work there are a total of 7 sheltered plants in Japan. These have been established by prefectural governments and major cities and are administered by social welfare foundations with the cooperation of certain industrial firms.

Protective or Aiding Devices or Appliances for the Handicapped

Welfare services include issuing protective devices and appliances to patients upon request, as well as providing repair services. Appliances include artificial legs, wheelchairs, hearing aids, safety canes, etc. These devices are dispensed at the welfare office in accordance with diagnoses made by the staff of the Consultation Centers for the Physically Handicapped.

A National Research Institute for Protective Aid Equipment for the Handicapped was founded in 1970 to invent and improve appliances and equipment for the handicapped (until now, Japan has lagged behind Western countries in this area). With the new devices, seriously handicapped people can return to their own homes to live with their families, since they can be taken care of at home with aid of the devices. The service is available to those with severe disabilities of the lower limbs or of body-trunk functions, if the persons are diagnosed at an authorized agency. There were 3,400 recipients of this service in 1973.

Home Aid

There is also the "homemaker," who functions as a consultant to the home-bound and who is sponsored by local government. There were 967 homemakers in the country in 1973. In addition, home visits by teams consisting of a medical doctor, nurse, and welfare worker may be provided to those in need of medical services. Such services are sponsored by the prefectural and local governments via the welfare offices.

Services for the Blind and Partially Sighted

In addition to institutional programs there are specific programs for the blind, as follows:

Services to offer various goods and appliances at low cost: These include such things as watches, thermometers, and appliances for braille printing.

Research and study to develop occupations for people without sight or little sight: Efforts to develop new vocational possibilities as well as new divices and methods to help blind people in their daily life are now in progress, with the National Tokyo Research Center for Eyesight Disabilities at the center of such activities. Training programs are given through the Japan Lighthouse, a social welfare foundation, with a grant of government subsidies.

Training and trainers for the blind: This program was newly started in 1972 and provides personnel to train the blind in mobility. It is conducted by the Japan Lighthouse at the request of the national government.

Seeing-eye dog services: This service is still rather uncommon, but is gradually growing. There are six training agencies for dogs throughout the country, but only about 100 blind persons now have seeing-eye dogs.

Other programs: There are a variety of other programs for aiding the blind financially. In addition to grants of pensions and allowances, there are benefits such as long-term loans, various tax deductions, discounts on the National Railway, and free postage for braille-written mail.

THE MENTALLY RETARDED

As of 1971 there were 356,300 mentally retarded in Japan, including 312,600 who lived in their own homes and 43,700 who were institutionalized. The age group of 10 to 14 years old had the highest ratio of mentally handicapped (8.3 per 1,000 normal population, as opposed to 3.4 per 1,000 for all age groups).

Until 1960, when the Law for the Welfare of the Mentally Retarded was enacted, there were few special welfare measures for the mentally retarded, except for financial aid. Since 1967, the central governmental organ in charge of administering the law, for both children and adults, has been the Children and Families Bureau. Other agencies and officials that render services on the prefectural and local levels are the Consultation Centers for the Mentally

Handicapped, the Welfare Offices, the Child Guidance Centers, the Health Centers, the Welfare Officers for the Mentally Retarded, and the Child Welfare Officers. Local welfare offices served a total of 72,315 mentally retarded clients from April 1972 to March 1973. Child Guidance Centers throughout the country treated 41,327 children (5,414 of whom were institutionalized). The number of mentally handicapped adults served by the Consultation Centers for the Mentally Handicapped between April 1972 and March 1973 was 31,281.

In recent years, a number of private voluntary organizations and groups have been set up by parents of the handicapped for the purpose of helping each other as well as sharing one another's feelings and hardships in this particularly unfortunate situation. Their activities or programs include consultation and guidance via such means as radio programs, pamphlets, and magazines.

In view of the importance of discovering mental handicaps as early as possible in a child's life, various efforts are being made by the authorities concerned. Three-year-old children, for example, are given physical and psychological examinations. Babies diagnosed as mentally defective are given detailed examinations accompanied by a series of follow-up treatments and guidance at the Child Guidance Centers.

Treatment and Care for Those at Home

For children with IQs of from 25 to 50, whose physical condition is adequate for daily travel, day-care services are available. They are guided toward learning certain skills which may be useful for them in eventually attaining self-supporting status. As of March 1973, there were 126 day-care centers, caring for 5,056 such children. The national government grants subsidies to local municipalities toward small-scale programs of special day-care.

Summer camp programs are held each year for children with serious handicaps. There are also parent education programs. These programs are sponsored by the National Foundation for the Welfare of Mentally and Physically Handicapped Children, assisted by government subsidy initiated in 1972.

In order to relieve parents of the burden of caring for a child with a serious handicap, a homemaker's service is available. The system was started in 1970 and aims at promoting a better home environment for the mentally handicapped. Although it is still far from fully meeting the needs of the whole population of this group, in 1972 there were 1,193 personnel in the program.

Institutional Care

For retarded children under 18 years of age, who are without parents or a guardian or whose home situation does not allow them to stay at home, there are various institutions providing care as well as education and training. In 1973, there were a total of 337 institutions providing care for 24,722 children. There are two kinds of institutions for those over 18 years old: (1) facilities for protective care and rehabilitation (as of 1973, there were 226 such institutions, with a total capacity of 16,296) and (2) facilities which provide shelter and care as well as vocational training and jobs (as of 1973 there were 59 such institutions with a total capacity of 3,259 adults).

For those whose IQ is about 35 or who have a physical as well as a mental disability, institutionalized care at the National Colony began in 1971. This large facility is designed to provide programs for 550 severely retarded. It is administered by the Welfare Society for the Physically and Mentally Handicapped, Special Foundation, and financed by the national government.

The Vocational Guidance Parent

The retarded person over 18 years of age whose IQ is approximately 40 may be assigned a vocational guidance parent, who is an employer. This person gives vocational guidance as well as protective shelter and food for the purpose of helping the mentally retarded person become self-supporting. The government pays the vocational guidance parent for his effort. A total of 2,384 employers are registered in the system; but, as of 1973, only 457 were actually entrusted with a total of 714 mentally retarded persons.

THE AGED

Until the enactment of the 1963 Welfare Law for the Aged, little was done to meet the social needs of older people. Until then, services for the aged were largely financial, under the Public Assistance Law, Health and Welfare Pension-Insurance Law, etc., or consisted of placement in an old-age home. The introduction of the new law for the welfare of the aged may mean the onset of a new era in this area in Japan. The Division for the Welfare of the Aged and the Division for the Health of the Aged, both in the Social Affairs Bureau of the Ministry of Health and Welfare, are responsible for promoting the welfare of old people on the national level. On the prefectural and the local levels, there are governmental sections bearing similar names. Also, an old person or a person caring for an old person may visit any of the following agencies or persons: the Welfare Office, the Local Health Center, the Welfare Volunteer Worker, or the Welfare Field-Worker for the Aged.

Japan's older population has been growing, as it has been among the Western European countries, starting in the mid-fifties following the postwar "baby boom." The trend is shown in Table 4.

Special Employment Services for the Aged

With the recognition of the significance of older people having a sense of being wanted and contributing to society, a free employment service to serve

Table 4: Aged Population Trends and Future Estimations in Japan

	Total Population (in thousands)	Those Over 60 Years of Age		Those Over 65 Years of Age	
		Number (in thousands)	Percentage of Total Population	Number (in thousands)	Percentage of Total Population
1935	68,662	5,099	7.4	3,189	4.6
1950	83,200	6,414	7.7	4,109	4.9
1960	93,419	8,290	8.9	5,350	5.7
1970	103,356	11,038	10.7	7,335	7.1
1980	115,972	14,646	12.6	10,279	8.9
1990	124,744	19,620	15.7	13,080	10.5
2000	131,838	24,925	18.9	17,692	13.4
2015	138,614	31,356	22.6	23,477	16.9

SOURCES: Figures for the years of 1935, 1950, 1960, and 1970 are from the National Census. Those after 1980 are estimations of the Research Institute of Population Problems.

aged job seekers has been started by the Social Welfare Councils in certain prefectures and some major cities. With the aid of national governmental subsidies, these employment agencies for the aged are usually run by the welfare foundations. In 1973, there were 94 such agencies.

Group Activities for the Aged

For the purpose of sharing recreational opportunities there are neighborhood organizations or clubs organized by old people. There were at least 35,873 such groups throughout the country in 1963, when the government started to encourage their activities by giving financial aid. In 1973, there were 91,416 such clubs. In order to qualify for government aid, an old persons' club must have at least 50 members, of whom 30 must attend programs regularly year-round.

Welfare for the Home-Bound Aged

Homemaker service is provided to low-income families with a bed-ridden member over 65 years of age. The homemaker may feed the aged patient, wash or mend clothes, clean the house and shop, as well as give minor consultations in meeting the aged person's daily needs. The program is operated by the municipal or local governments, with the national and prefectural governments contributing one-third of the total expenses. In 1973, there were 7,060 such homemakers serving approximately 49,000 low-income elderly.

There has also been set up a system of dispatching a helper to an invalid old person who has nobody to take care of him and who is suffering from illness or accident. The program is administered by local governments and uses the services of volunteers who live in the neighborhood of the clients. These helpers prepare meals, clean house, and shop for the patient. Because the program is recent, there were only 8,025 helpers registered to serve in this project in 1973.

Welfare Centers for the Aged provide various consultation services in health, employment, recreation and entertainment, and other areas. The centers are generally equipped with a counseling room, a health clinic, a library, swimming facilities, and rooms for physical activities, meetings, and recreational activities.

A telephone counseling service for the aged was initiated in 1971 when centers for this purpose were established in two cities. It aims at promoting the welfare of solitary aged people by phoning them daily at certain regular times in order to check on their safety and give counseling as needed. For those without telephones, city authorities lend them free of charge. As a general rule, those eligible for the lease service are solitary old persons over 65 years of age and of low income. In 1973 the phone consultation system was in operation in nine major cities, and it is expected to expand gradually throughout the country.

Another service for isolated old persons is an arrangement for those living in the neighborhood of an old-age home to take meals at the institution. In cases of those who are unable to make trips to the dining room of the institution, delivery services are also available. The program, begun in 1973, is operated either by the local government or by the welfare organization in charge of such institutions.

Low-interest loans are available for building an additional room for families with an elderly member.

Homes for the Aged

There are three types of homes for the aged provided by law: nursing homes, special nursing homes, and people's homes.

Nursing homes are for persons over 65 years of age who cannot be cared for at their own homes, due to physical, psychosocial, or financial reasons. Fees are charged on a sliding scale. The homes are operated by either prefectural or local governments; 80% of the costs are financed by national government subsidies.

Special nursing homes are for the bed-bound aged patients whose care in their own homes is quite difficult because of emotional problems or similar reasons. In 1973, there were some 350,000 old people in this category throughout the country. Any aged person, regardless of financial condition, is eligible for this type of home.

People's homes provide care for old persons who have no relatives or come from low-income families. Fees are charged according to a sliding scale, ranging (in 1973) from 28,900 to 31,400 yen ($98-$106) per month. The homes are operated either by national or local governments or by welfare foundations. Some homes furnish one private room for each resident, often equipped with kitchens and toilet facilities. Residents must necessarily be healthy enough to utilize such facilities.

Homes for the aged run by voluntary agencies furnish room and board as well as other conveniences in return for certain fees. In 1973, there were 66 such establishments, with a total capacity of 2,667. The prefectural governors are responsible for seeing that these establishments meet the requirements of the law.

A foster family care service was established in 1963. Under this program, an old person may be placed with a private family so that he or she may enjoy family life and companionship. The family receives a fee from public funds and also receives professional guidance and supervision by the local welfare office.

In order to enable old people to take vacations at a moderate expense, a program of building lodgings has been in progress and is encouraged by the government. Such accommodations are built at scenic spots or hot springs. There were approximately 50, as of 1973, throughout the country. Persons over 60 years of age and those accompanying them may utilize such facilities. The old persons' recreational accommodations are built by the Welfare Pension Fund and operated by the local governments. In some cases they are sponsored by a welfare foundation approved by the Health and Welfare Minister.

Annual Physical Examinations for the Aged

As a means of preventing disease, cities and towns provide a free annual physical checkup for those over 65 years of age. In case any abnormalities are indicated, a further examination is conducted in order to give individual guidance and treatment. Home-visit service was made available for the bedridden in 1969. The number of medical examinees has been increasing annually; in 1972 it totaled 1,756,000 persons or 22.2% of the total aged population. The expense of the program is shared equally by three levels of government. In 1973, all medical services for those over 70 became free of charge.

MENTAL HEALTH PROGRAMS

Mental health programs are carried out through the provisions of the Mental Health Law enacted in 1950 and revised in 1965. It provides not only for treatment and protection of the mentally ill but also for preventive measures. Until the law was enacted, the mentally ill person was dealt with as a public nuisance. In prewar days, the only way to deal with the insane was confinement or isolation; that is, the patient was put under police control. In fact, the mental health administration still depends largely on the isolation method, i.e., hospitalization through enforcement of the law. On the other hand, efforts have been made to put more emphasis on prevention through public education rather than depending merely on hospitalization of the patients. Hospitals and asylums have switched from mere "locking in" to the use of more medication, occupational therapy, and other more scientific treatments for rehabilitation of the patients, although psychotherapy is still not commonly practiced.

The central agency in charge of mental health administration is the Ministry of Health and Welfare, with the Bureau of Public Health taking the main responsibility. More precisely, the Mental Health Division of the bureau carries out most of the administration on the national level. The administrative organization on the prefectural and the local levels is similar to that on the national level. *Hokensho*, the local welfare centers which play important roles in hospitalizing the mentally ill under the Mental Health Law, are under direct control of the prefectural governors.

According to a national survey on the mentally ill in 1963, there were some 1,240,000 persons with mental disturbances: 30.1% of this number were under psychiatric treatment; 5.2% were receiving some kind of guidance or consultation; and 64.7% stayed home with their relatives without any treatment or guidance.

Local Health Centers

The primary facilities for carrying out the Mental Health Law are the local health centers. First, they are the intake agencies for hospitalizing those "who are likely to injure themselves or others." They also administer a variety of programs geared to the better mental health of the people in the community —e.g., conducting studies of behavior and of the emotionally disturbed in the community, offering psychiatric consultations, making home visits to homebound cases, guiding the group activities of ex-psychiatric hosptial patients, enlightening the community with regard to emotional health.

Procedures for Hospitalizing Psychiatric Patients

By law, a mentally ill person can be hospitalized only at a mental hospital or other establishment authorized by the law. Accordingly, admission to the psychiatric hospital in Japan is a somewhat different procedure from that for general medical or surgical cases. There are five procedures for sending a mentally ill person into a psychiatric hospital. They are as follows:

Admission through enforcement of the law: A person who is considered "likely to injure him/herself or others" shall be hospitalized following due procedure.

Emergency hospitalization by law: This hospitalization is that above but includes more drastic procedures for more serious cases. (These first two procedures are carried out under the authority of the prefectural governor in order to isolate the person in question from society and put him or her under psychiatric treatment and care at public expense.)

Admission by law with consent of the relative or the person responsible for safeguarding the patient: Hospitalization in this case aims at putting the person under psychiatric treatment and care at his or her own expense. Nevertheless, this procedure results in similar treatment for the patient, in that freedom of movement becomes greatly restricted.

Temporary hospitalization: This procedure allows for the admission of a person who has been diagnosed as likely to have a mental disturbance by a superintendent of a mental hospital; the person is subjected to a period no longer than three weeks with the approval of his or her spouse, close relative, or guardian.

Hospitalization at one's own will: Hospitalization may take place in accord with the person's own decision. (This procedure is not regulated by law.)

Mental Hospitals and Clinics

The law requires that every prefecture have at least one mental hospital, as well as one designated for admission of emergency cases. In 1972, there were approximately 259,000 beds in psychiatric hospitals throughout the country —that is, 24.4 beds per 10,000 population. This proportion is almost equal to that in European and North American countries; however, in terms of quality, there is yet much to be done.

Outpatient care is also provided. Under such programs, one-half the total costs are paid by the national and prefectural governments, each sharing half the sum. The system aims at early discovery and treatment and better psychiatric treatment, including adequate after-care for ex-mental hospital patients. The number of the outpatients who have benefited from this program since its inception in 1965 is about 78,000 (as of the end of June 1974).

The cost of psychiatric treatment has shown a steady increase and totaled some 1,863 billion yen for the 1971 fiscal year, equivalent to 6.7% of the nation's total budget for medical costs. Only about 10% of these expenses were paid by the patients themselves.

The law prescribes that each prefecture establish a mental health center. These centers provide technical guidance and help; education and training programs for the staff and employees of various related agencies, including the local health centers; activities toward enlightening residents in the whole prefectural area with regard to their emotional problems; and research aimed at promoting mental hygiene. The mental health centers also deal with psychiatric cases on referral from local health centers and other agencies. In addition, some of the centers conduct rehabilitation training programs for those who have been discharged from mental hospitals. At the end of the 1972 fiscal year, 33 prefectures and provinces had mental health centers.

PROBATION AND PAROLE

Only comparatively recently has a rehabilitation system for criminal offenders been established by law in Japan. The following five laws establish the basic probation and parole structure: (1) the Amnesty Law of 1947, (2) the Offenders Rehabilitation Law of 1949, (3) the Law for After-care of Discharged

Offenders of 1950, (4) the Volunteer Probation Officer Law of 1950, and (5) the Law for Probationary Supervision of Persons under Suspension of Execution of Sentence of 1954. The central organ responsible for implementation of these laws is the Rehabilitation Bureau, which is one of the six major departments of the Ministry of Justice and consists of four divisions—the General Affairs Division, the Investigation and Liaison Division, the Supervision Division, and the Amnesty Division.

Actual rehabilitation is administered by the regional parole boards and the probation offices.

The Regional Parole Board

There are eight regional parole boards, located in eight major cities, one each at the site of a high court. With three to 12 members, each conducts such duties as the following:

(a) It makes the decision on release for parole from training schools, prisons, women's guidance homes, and workhouses.

(b) It can revoke paroles under certain conditions established by law.

(c) It can terminate sentences. It may terminate the indeterminate sentence of persons convicted as juveniles or persons in training schools.

(d) It can extend the parole period.

In Japan there are 84 probation and parole officers, attached to the secretariat of the parole boards to work with the board members.

The Probation Office

There are 50 probation offices in the country—one in each prefecture and four on Hokkaido. In addition, there are three branch offices and 18 minor local agencies. Their functions briefly are: (1) supervision of probationers and parolees on all age levels; (2) adjustment of inmates' relations to their families and society prior to release from correctional institutions; (3) aftercare of offenders who have been discharged from prisons or detention houses without supervision; (4) investigation and application for pardons; and (5) promotion of crime prevention activities in the community. These functions are all carried out by probation officers in close collaboration with volunteer probation officers who are enlisted from the local community. In cases where shelter care is required, halfway houses run by voluntary organizations are utilized.

In addition to the probation-parole officers attached to the parole boards, there are 785 probation officers whose main duties are supervision and aftercare of offenders and who are employed by the Ministry of Justice on the basis of a merit system. They are required to have certain degrees of competence in the area of medicine, sociology, psychology, education, and other disciplines relevant to behavioral science. In practice, probation officers are recruited from the list of candidates who have passed the national civil service examination specializing in psychology, education, sociology, social work, law, or public administration. The field probation officer belongs to one of the 50 main probation offices or 21 local branch offices and functions as the essential force of the rehabilitation services. It is hard to estimate the average caseload because the total number of 785 includes not only those in administrative and supervisory posts but also those engaged in a variety of duties other than probation or parole, such as aftercare, liaison, and public education. However, in 1967 a survey of 100 allegedly typical probation officers disclosed that their caseload averaged 273 offenders and that they were assisted by some 90 volunteer workers.

When the noninstitutional treatment system was reorganized around 1949, it was argued that probation and parole services should be professionalized, as they are in many other countries. However, the services still include both professionals and volunteers, because the authorities placed great trust in the potential of volunteer workers. In brief, their roles are to help offenders rehabilitate themselves in society and to influence public attitudes for the promotion of crime prevention. More specifically, their most important function is to supervise and assist probationers and parolees assigned to them. Their activities also include visiting an inmate's home to advise the family and make reports to the probation office as a part of prerelease preparations, locating a probationer or parolee who has moved in from another area, making preliminary investigations of candidates for pardons, and assisting an offender's family. Volunteers carry out many community activities, including collaborating with public and private organizations to explore and mobilize social resources in the community, interpreting the philosophy of rehabilitation to individual neighbors or the public as a whole, and eradicating environmental conditions that generate crime, working in cooperation with community residents. Legally, the volunteer probation officer is defined as a nonpermanent official of the national government, but he is not paid any salary for his services; he receives only sums to cover expenses incurred in discharging his duty. Voluntary probation officers are selected through a careful screening process that involves the directors of probation offices, advisory committees, and the Minister of Justice. To help in their training, the Japan Rehabilitation Aid Association offers a monthly publication, parole boards and probation offices regularly offer various training courses, and local associations of volunteer probation officers hold conferences and workshops under the leadership of professional probation officers.

Procedure in the Probation-Parole System

Probation and parole supervision is conducted by the probation office. The following five categories of offenders are specified by law:

Juvenile probationer: A juvenile who has been placed on probation by the Family Court. The maximum period of supervision for this category is generally up to 20 years of age.

Adult probationer: An offender who has been placed on probation by the Criminal Court when sentence is suspended. The term of supervision ranges from one to five years, in accord with the sentence specified by the sentencing court.

Training school parolee: A juvenile offender who has been conditionally released on parole from the training school at the discretion of the parole board. As in the first category above, the term of supervision is usually up to age 20.

Prison parolee: An offender who has been released from prison on parole by the parole board. The period of parole supervision is for the remaining term of his or her sentence (for a life-termer it is the rest of his life).

Guidance home parolee: A woman whom the parole board conditionally released on parole from the Women's Guidance Home, a nonpunitive correctional institution for ex-prostitutes, governed by the Criminal Court. The period of supervision is up to six months, which the antiprostitution law specifies as the maximum period of confinement for any inmate of the home.

There are two kinds of probation: one is generally applied to juveniles and the other to adults. The former is a noncriminal disposition of the Family Court and is based on the Juvenile Law, whereas the latter is a form of suspended sentence rendered in the Criminal Court in accordance with the penal code. When the panel of three board members finds not only that an inmate is formally eligible for parole in the light of the requirements, but also that parole will better serve the goal of correctional efforts, it determines a definite date of parole, the place where the parolee should return, and the conditions that the parolee should abide by during the period of supervision. Parole aims at releasing at an optimal time an inmate who has proved to be capable of leading a law-abiding life in the community, if adequate supervision and assistance are provided.

Certain conditions are imposed on every offender who is placed under supervision of the probation officer. In carrying out supervision, the officer tries to help the offender comply with the terms of probation or parole. Many offenders under probation or parole supervision face financial difficulties. The probation officer often has to help the offender in finding a satisfactory job or adjust his or her relations with his or her family. For offenders in certain categories, the term of supervision is fixed by the law automatically; for others it depends on the discretion of the court. Probation or parole is revoked when there has been a serious violation of conditions or a repetition of crime.

Halfway Houses

Since 1880 there have existed many halfway houses for helping discharged prisoners. Juvenile institutions having the dual role of offering training and supervising probation are also operated by voluntary associations. In 1974 there were 112 halfway houses for adult and juvenile offenders, run by voluntary organizations or the Rehabilitation Aid Association, under the authorization of the Justice Minister. The halfway houses provide room and board as well as guidance for juvenile and/or adult probationers and parolees as well as other discharged offenders.

NOTE

1. The six different social welfare laws are the Daily Life Security Law, 1942 (entirely revised, 1950); the Child Welfare Law, 1947; the Law for the Welfare of Physically Handicapped Persons, 1949; the Law for the Welfare of Mentally Retarded Persons, 1960; the Law for the Welfare of the Aged, 1963; and the Law for Maternal and Children's Welfare, 1964.

11

COLOMBIAN ELITES AND THE UNDERDEVELOPMENT OF THE SOCIAL WELFARE SYSTEM

JOSEFINA   ACOSTA   C.

The description of the Colombian social service system will be presented first from the historical perspective of how government interest and concern for social welfare developed, and second in the context of the social problems of an underdeveloped country, analyzing how the human and material resources are organized in order to face such problems. Colombia, an underdeveloped country, has an underdeveloped social service delivery system which is characterized by lack of coordination and available information and by inadequate means to meet the basic needs of the great majority of a population that lives in conditions of poverty and misery. Colombia is a country where the national income distribution is one of the most unjust in the world: 5% of the population, the richest group, receives more than 40% of the total income, while 60%, the poorest group, receives only 16% (Adelman and Morris, 1973:19). The concentration of land ownership by a small minority is another drawback to the Colombian economy. In the countryside the *latifundio*, with 1.3% of the farm units, holds 49.5% of the land and employs 4% of the agricultural workers, while the *munifundio*, with 64% of the farm units, holds 4.9% of the land and occupies 58% of the agricultural workers (CIDA, 1965:14). After 10 years of official agrarian reform, only 1% of the land to be affected had been expropriated. The supposed expropriation has been a commercial negotiation with the landowners (A. Garcia, 1973:51). These figures explain what keeps naturally rich countries, like Colombia, in a perpetual state of underdevelopment and backwardness.

A social service system is a means to reach a greater objective: human welfare, especially for the poor and needy. Its exact conception will depend on the values that inspire and guide the development of a country, understanding that there can be no economic development without social development and vice versa.

History proves that this objective cannot be reached when the gap between the rich and the poor becomes greater each day.

Having this in mind, the author will try to give an adequate perspective of the social service system in Colombia showing it as the product of a traditional and closed society that has to face changes in order to survive.

HISTORICAL BACKGROUND:
A TRADITIONAL SOCIAL ORDER FACES CHANGE

The present legislation on social matters has its roots in the period after World War I and in the thirties, when important economic, social, and political changes took place. The social legislation of the period was more abundant than ever before. In 1921, private sector workers were given the right of collective insurance, and laws designed to bring decent health and hygiene conditions to the mining and oil industries were passed. In 1923 public workers were given the right to subsidies for illness. Since child labor was common practice, different laws were passed in 1923, 1924, and 1927 to protect the child. Since 1926 the Sunday rest has been obligatory. By 1929 the idea of social security began to be discussed in Congress.

The deep changes that were taking place in the old order are the explanation of the development of this social legislation. The strongest groups in the Colombian oligarchy based their power on their land holdings or *latifundios*. [1] For them the possession of land was a factor of production. The old landowning classes did not conceive of land as a modern productive industry or enterprise. Except for the coffee and banana plantations, agriculture was at a primitive level. The country was sharply divided into two groups: a few families with great power and privilege, and the great mass of the population with all the responsibilities and poverty. According to Colombian tradition, these few families had a *natural right* to rule the country, and they are still considered the "natural chiefs." The rights of education, decent housing, and health care were the privileges of the few, keeping the masses in ignorance and subhuman conditions that were at the same time taken as proof of their inability to participate in the decision-making of the country. The privileged groups managed commerce, industry, and government according to family ties and private interests.[2] Yet during this period of history they could not escape the changes taking place in the world, changes which were to clash with the old order, sometimes obliging them to give up privileges or to retreat strategically.

The influx of foreign investment after World War I induced the growth of large cities, the beginning of industry, and the spread of a proletariat class organized in labor unions or syndicates, often under the influence of the socialistic doctrines that had spread all over the world. The mining industry, the banana plantations, the exploiters of the wood and rubber resources, together with the exporters of oil and coffee were to challenge the old concept of land tenure. Although these exploitations, except for that of coffee, were in the hands of foreign companies that left no direct benefits to the Colombian economy, they contributed to changes in other respects. The changes meant the beginning of a working class and the increased building of modern means of communication needed to bring the products to the external market and also to an incipient internal one. It also meant the building of the modern cities that were to become the center of the economic and political world. Consequently it meant the abandonment of the fields by the peasants seeking better living conditions in the cities, since the agrarian structure did not offer them adequate means of subsistence. The foreign inversion of credits, together with the influx of the $25 million paid by the United States for the separation of Panama, were the cause of an inflationary process that aggravated social and economic conditions at that time. The government had invested in the building of public works, employing peasant workers taken from the fields, thus lessening agricultural production. The increasing demand for consumer goods, resulting from this migration, could not be coped with, since the government had no agricultural policy. Exports, which in 1923 amounted to 56 million Colombian pesos, rose to 132.5 million pesos in 1928, but it must be noted that a great part of this sum did not return to the country: the oil, banana, and platinum exploitation managed by North American companies did not have to return the value of the exports to Colombia. Coffee was, as a matter of fact, the basis of Colombia exports, which meant that the whole economy rested on one product. This is a situation that prevails to date. To the economic chaos was added the social discontent manifested by strikes and riots. The Banana Zone strike, in 1928, suppressed by force and bloodshed, was to leave a lasting impression on the country.

The 1929 Depression was to deeply influence the Colombian economy. It signified the beginning of a process of industrialization in which national products began to replace imports. The period coincided with political changes in the administrative order. After 40 years of conservative party government, the liberals won the presidential elections. The liberal party appeared to be a revolutionary one imbued with the socialistic doctrines that gave the new classes a sense of their social and political rights to fight for better living conditions. The year 1936 is a landmark in Colombian history because of a constitutional amendment passed after 40 years of conservative legislation. The changes and social reform of President Lopez Pumarejo were the basis for modern social legislation. The influence of the New Deal reforms was also felt in Colombia. Yet the liberal party was two different things: a revolutionary movement of the people influenced by the new proletarian doctrines and an elite republican circle (A. Garcia, 1972:118).

The growing unrest of the people, especially the peasants and the working class, had to be faced, and reform was needed. The first liberal president was elected because of his moderate line. But this was not sufficient to answer the expectations of the people. The man who was able to open the reformist line,

[224]

ACOSTA C.

and who was considered very revolutionary, was President Lopez Pumarejo (1934-1938). No other government has left such a lasting impression on the nation. Lopez called his administration "the revolution on the march." Although his policy was a gradual and planned revolution, he had to face the opposition of the most conservative oligarchical groups. His liberal reforms signified the polarization of classes that was to explode a few years later and provoke a counterrevolution inspired by fascist doctrines.

For the purpose of this article we shall consider the social reforms, making it clear that Lopez was not a revolutionary but a member of the oligarchy, who understood the need of "cleaning the house" in order to preserve the structure. In order to be able to fulfill his programs, Lopez amended the Constitution in 1936. The amendment and the laws passed were the boldest acts of reform ever enacted by a Colombian government. The reform stated that "labor is a social obligation and it shall enjoy the special protection of the State." It gave legitimacy to the organization of labor syndicates under the name of Confederacion Nacional de Trabajadores de Colombia (CTC). For the first time the labor unions were recognized as legal, and the right to strike was guaranteed except for public service workers. The law also regulated labor contracts, established a minimum wage, imposed a minimum social security, required paid holidays and retirement benefits, and set the 8-hour day and the 40-hour week. It created the Judicial Jurisdiction for Labor, a special tribunal to provide arbitration and conciliation. An Agrarian Reform Law, however, did not satisfy the hunger for land by the dispossessed peasants. It recognized titles and improvements and the colonization of marginal lands as a substitute for a much needed agrarian reform. One of the most important amendments was Article 19 of the Constitution, which says:

Public assistance is a function of the State. It shall be given to persons who, being physically incapable of working, lack means of self-support or the right to demand the same of other persons. The law will determine in what form assistance shall be given and the cases in which the state should give it directly.

For conservatives and liberals this law meant the beginning of a welfare state that was contrary to their liberal principles, since Colombian political parties, in practice, hold both liberal economic ideas and politically conservative ones. But the important fact was that it broke with the traditional concept of charity for the poor or the fatalistic explanation of poverty and misery as a necessary condition. Lopez went even further and stated in Article 20 that "property is a social function which implies obligations" and in Article 32 that "the State may intervene in the exploitation of public and private business and industry, for the purpose of rationalizing products to which it has a right." For the first time there was an income tax law. Before that no one in Colombia paid income taxes. Different projects concerning social security were presented to Congress, but only in 1946 was the law passed. These and other achievements explain the great popularity of the Lopez' presidency, even if later on the counterrevolution paralyzed this movement.

Post-World War II was a time in which political power became more concentrated, and the Colombian economy faced critical conditions. These resulted in a concentration of economic power in the hands of the few with concomitant impoverishment of the lower classes. The subsequent discontent manifested itself in a movement of the people that, under the leadership of Gaitan, became a revolutionary threat. The liberal and conservative oligarchy united to demobilize the popular movement through political violence, which in the 1950s cost the country 200,000 lives (Guzman et al., 1964). At the same time, the guerrilla movement, with 40,000 men in arms, became such a threat to the system that the only solution for the power groups was a military takeover, which was engineered under the leadership of General Rojas Pinilla (Fluharty, 1957:118-142). One of the results of this political violence was the flight of the peasants to the cities, causing the chaotic growth of the large cities that were unable to provide basic services for these immigrants.

In matters of social legislation the 1950s were poor, which is understandable in a period of institutionalized political violence. In 1957 a law concerning family subsidy was enacted, and in 1958 the "acción communal" was organized under the leadership of the Ministry of Government. In the 1960s, the decade of the Alliance for Progress, the issue of agrarian reform was discussed again because of the clear recommendations of the Punta del Este charter. Yet the law has been as ineffective as can be expected of an agrarian reform that was put into effect by the great landowners. After 10 years, 90% of the so-called agrarian reform has been the legalization of titles to land that was untilled state property, but had been spontaneously colonized. According to one estimate, in 1960 more than one million peasant families were in need of land. Only 0.5%—about 5,300 families—from 1962 to 1969 had benefited, while the number of peasant families increased at a rate of 40,000 a year (A. Garcia, 1973:52). In other words, agrarian reform, considered the basic need for development, has been enacted by the government only in order to receive the benefits of the Alliance for Progress, which demanded a condition: "The effective transformation of unjust structures and systems of land tenure and use through peaceful and legal means to avoid that it be achieved by revolution, as in Cuba and many other countries throughout the world" (Feder, 1970:206).

The most important law of recent years has been Law 75 of 1968, special legislation adopted to protect the family, through which the Colombian Institute of Family Welfare was created. After 30 years of social reforms, the conditions of the larger dispossessed masses has become worse—a situation that is aggravated more and more by the high level of expectations of the people generated by modern means of communication. At the same time, the Colombian economic system has become dependent on the great multinational corporations that contribute to a widening of the gap between the great modern enterprises and the small national industries. In Colombia, 16 great corporations have control of 82% of the total capital, and in the "Anonymous" societies, 0.6% of the shareholders own 56% of the total. According to estimates of the Federal Reserve Bank of New York, about 140 million dollars of funds owned by persons living in Colombia are in North American banks (Musgrave, 1969:141).

ASPECTS OF COLOMBIA'S SOCIAL PROBLEMS

A report presenting the economic and social conditions of the country and written by a French commission under the direction of Father L. Lebret, was published in 1958. The importance of this report is that it has been used as the basis for many governmental social policies and economic programs. According to this report "the great majority of the rural population is still living at a level slightly higher than primitive life." In describing the urban population, it said that

> the popular urban classes are characteristically subproletariat. Their way of living, in spite of being in the city, is very near the primitive level. . . . The popular "barrios" (slums) are anarchic, that is to say, there is no organization, there are no commercial zones, cultural, health or adminis- trative installations that allow for a community living that will benefit all. These are producing a subproletariat and marginal population that could easily be induced to riot. . . . These series of conclusions should impress the public power and move it to immediate and long range action. [Lebret, 1958:106]

As we shall see, the condition of the poor has changed very little since the report was published.

Demographic Aspects. [3] Colombia has a territory of 440,000 square miles with a population of 24 million. The urban population is about 52% of the total. Fifty-one percent of Colombians are less than 15 years old, and the annual birth rate is about 3%, the highest in Latin America.

Economy. In 1970 the gross national income was $6,609 million with a per capita income of $310. More recent information shows that 70% of the population has a family annual income of about $440, far below what is supposed to be the minimum to satisfy the basic needs of a family. In general the economic structure is characterized by the concentration of wealth in the minority and by a low capacity of acquisition of the great majority of the population.

Health. In 1970 the average life span was 54 years, and the rate of mortality was 9.8 per 1,000. About 47% of deaths occur to children under 5 years old. The cause of one-third of these deaths is malnutrition. There is an average of 2.5 hospital beds per 1,000 people, taking into account that most of the hospitals are in the big cities. More than 23% of the population has no access to hospitals, and in the rural zones the figure is 87.5%. The proportion of physicians is 4.5 for 10,000 inhabitants (1 for 2,200); 74% of them live in the larger cities, and 47.3% of the physicians dedicate half their time to tasks other than medical practice. A very serious situation is the trend of the Colombian physician to migrate to other countries, especially to the United States. According to statistics, about 25% of graduates each year leave the country. The proportion of dentists is about 2 per 10,000 population, and nurses 8 per 100,000.

Nutrition. Colombia's nutritional problem is one of the worst. The intake of proteins per habitant is 78% of the normal requirements and 85% of the basic caloric needs. In the urban areas the upper class intake of proteins is 126%, while for the lower class it is 67% of basic needs.

Education. About 27% of the total population is illiterate, and in the rural areas the figure is 42%. Of every 1,000 children of school age, 230 never go to school. Of the 770 that start school, only 216 finish elementary school. Of these, only 37 finish high school; and of the 25 that begin university studies, only 11 can finish.

Housing. In 1970 it was calculated that 3.6 million people, about 600,000 families, did not have any housing, and 300,000 lived in subhuman conditions. In the urban areas, 24% of the population do not have a municipal water system, and 46% do not have any sewage system. The situation is worse in the rural areas, where 72% of the population do not have any water system, a fact very serious in a tropical climate.

This brief description of the principal problems that weigh over the majority of the population has been aggravated in the last several years by the growth rate of 5% to 7% of the large cities, one of the biggest growth rates in the world, and by the inflationary process that is manifested in the high degree of social insecurity and elevated crime rates. According to official statistics in 1974, there were 339,359 criminal acts reported, which represent an increase of 183% from the year before. Bogota has the highest index, with 71% of the total (*El Tiempo,* November 17, 1974, p. 1).

THE SOCIAL SERVICE DELIVERY SYSTEM

In order to cope with numerous and frequent social problems, the Colombian government has gradually assumed the responsibility of welfare programs. Many of these functions were formerly carried out by private individuals or the Church. In general, these services are inadequate and insufficient and fail to cover or reach the population most in need. The political system is one of the obstacles to the development of social services. "Where programs of public works or social welfare have existed, individual and regional interest have tended to dilute them, or their execution, to the point that truly national programs become difficult to carry out" (Dix, 1967:178). In spite of the many efforts and laws to guarantee different types of welfare and social security benefits, the rapid rate of urbanization and demographic growth are producing quantitative and qualitative changes in the population that demand more services than the state is able to provide. Private social services are few, handle problems in small quantity, and function more under the inspiration of charity concepts. The description of social services will be made considering the three major aspects of the state system: social security, family welfare, and public assistance.

The Social Security System

The Colombian social security system was institutionalized in 1946 after many years of discussion in Congress. There are two different institutions that render services: the Colombian Institute of Social Security (Instituto Colombiano de Seguros Sociales, or ICSS), organized to give services to private enterprises, and the Office of Social Security (Cajas de Prevision Social), which serves government employees.

The Colombian Institute of Social Security is in charge of organizing and administering the social security programs for all employees of the private sector. It depends upon the Ministry of Labor and Social Security, but the executive director is appointed directly by the President of the Republic. The Board of Directors is composed of the Ministers of Labor and Health, a representative of the workers, and a representative of the private sector. The services and benefits cover all workers employed under contract by a private organization. It does not cover domestic workers or most agricultural workers, foreigners working in the country for less than a year, or persons transferred to another country. The system is compulsory and it is financed on a share basis: one-half is donated by the private organization, one-quarter by the worker, and one-quarter by the state. There is a monthly 3% salary deduction and a deduction of one-third of the first salary.

The benefits are medical assistance, surgical care, hospitalization, and odontological and pharmaceutical services. The woman worker or the wife or companion of the employee has a right to maternity, prenatal, and postnatal services, plus a two-month leave after delivery. The social insurance covers work accidents and professional illness; the pension is paid according to the wage, and in case of death, the insurance is paid to the widow and/or dependents; the risks of incapacity, old age, and death are covered, as is nonprofessional illness. There is also unemployment compensation consisting of a month's salary for every year worked, and rights are retained when the worker moves from one job to another. The retirement age is 55 years after 20 years of work. If the worker is not married, the dependent's parents are the beneficiaries. Since September 1975, medical services have been extended to the worker's family, but only in the city of Barranguilla. The services do not cover the whole country, and have been developing gradually, starting in the most industrialized cities.

According to the 1974 report published by the ICSS there were in that year a total of 101,892 private sector organizations in Colombia with 1,126,208 affiliated workers. The data offered by this official report is very important in order to understand the qualitative aspects of the area covered by social insurance. Of the total number of private industries affiliated, 91% employ from 1 to 19 workers and these represent 31% of all workers. Another 8% of these industries employ from 20 to 99 workers, representing 27% of all workers, while 1% of the industries employ more than 100 workers, representing 42% of all those affiliated. These figures show the polarization between the large, modern industries, most of foreign origin, and the innumerable small industries that scarcely provide a level of subsistence to their employees. Seventy-four percent of the affiliated workers live in the four largest cities, showing once more how the economy and industry are concentrated in a small area of the country.

Social security for agricultural workers is compulsory in only three districts of Colombia, covering a total of 103,864 peasants in 1974. Considering that about 48% of the population is peasant and that the economically active peasant population is about 2,800,000, the social insurance would cover less than 0.04% of the peasant population. The Indian population, about 300,000, has no social security services at all, and most of them have no access to any type of social services.

The report also classifies the workers according to salaries (see Table 1). Adding up items 1 and 2 of the table will show that 70% of the workers earn less than 2,040 Colombian pesos a month (less than $80) to support an average family of six members, that is to say, about $2.50 per day. Nine percent of the workers belong to the primary sector and 44% to the secondary, while 47% are in the tertiary sector. The distribution of salaries according to sectors shows that 78% of the workers in the primary sector earn less than 1,500 Colombian pesos a month (about $50); 50% earn the same salary in the secondary sector and 53% in the tertiary. Women's wages are inferior, by 748 pesos a month, to those of men and, by $390, to those of the total average, showing a discrimination against women, despite a law that guarantees equal salary for all. Only 1% of the women affiliated earn a monthly salary of more than 6,530 pesos, while 80% hardly earn 2,040 pesos. The workers' economic condition is aggravated by inflationary devaluation as shown in Table 2. According to this information, the amount needed to meet the daily requirements of a middle-class family has

Table 1: Affiliated Workers' Salaries, 1974

Monthly Salary*	% of Workers
Up to 1,500	54.0
Up to 2,039	16.0
Up to 6,500	25.0
Up to 10,500	3.0
More than 10,560	2.0

*In Colombian pesos (the exchange rate was about 28 pesos per U.S. dollar).
SOURCE: Instituto Colombiano de Seguros Sociales, Informe Estadístico, Bogotá, 1975, page 11.

Table 2: Acquisitive Power of Salaries, 1970-1974

Year	White-Collar Workers	Blue-Collar Workers
1970	100.0	100.0
1971	110.9	111.8
1972	125.5	127.3
1973	150.2	155.3
1974	185.1	194.4

1970 = 100

SOURCE: Instituto Colombiano de Seguros Sociales, Resumen y Comentarios del Informe Estadístico, Bogotá, 1975, page 20.

increased over 85% within the last 5 years, and for the blue-collar class it has increased over 94%. Over the same period, purchasing power has declined almost 49% for the blue-collar worker and 46$ for white-collar workers (see Table 3).

Administration of the ICSS. The total budget for 1974 was 4,475,535,693 Colombian pesos. Of this amount, 178,661,422 pesos was financed by the government; 34.4% of the budget was paid in salaries distributed in the manner shown in Table 4. For the proportion of personnel classifications in relation to distribution of salaries, see Table 5.

Health services are provided through 159 hospitals and clinics; of these, 24 are the property of the institute, and the rest are under contract. The total number of hospital beds is 5,355. Of these, 66% or 3,524 beds are in the three major zones, while in regions like Choco, where gold and platinum are mined, there are only 2 beds. Data on birth rates are important indicators of the public health of Colombians. In 1970, 180 of every 1,000 women gave birth, while in 1974 the number was 96, representing a decrease of 47%. Abortions have increased 5% in 10 years.

The Social Security System for Government Employees. Public employees receive their social security services through a special administration called Cajas de Prevision Social. The benefits are similar to the ones already described, but in some instances they have greater coverage. For example, some public institutions give social and medical services to the employee's children up to 16 years of age. The main official institution is the Caja Nacional de Prevision Social, which covers about 60 official departments with a total of 168,000 recipients and

Table 3: Indices of the Acquisitive Power of the Colombian Peso, 1970-1974

Year	White-Collar Workers	Blue-Collar Workers
1970	100.0	100.0
1971	90.2	89.4
1972	79.7	78.6
1973	66.6	64.4
1974	54.0	51.4

SOURCE: Instituto Colombiano de Seguros Sociales, Resumen y Comentarios del Informe Estadístico, Bogotá, 1975, page 20.

COLOMBIA   [231]

Table 4: Distribution of Personnel and Salaries (Instituto Colombiano de
          Seguros Sociales), 1974

Type of Personnel	Total	Percentage Personnel	Total Salaries*	Percentage Salaries
Executives	805	5.0	6,108,263	8.0
Professionals and Assistants	9,366	53.0	51,145,411	66.0
Office clerks	4,207	24.0	12,198,789	16.0
Transportation	502	3.0	1,336,435	2.0
General services	2,715	15.0	6,494,340	8.0
TOTAL	17,595	100.0	77,283,238	100.0

*In Colombian pesos
SOURCE: Instituto Colombiano de Seguros Sociales, Resumen y Comentarios del Informe
Estadístico, Bogotá, 1975, page 22.

12,000 receiving old-age or retirement pensions. There are 26 branches to cover
social security services in the country. There is one hospital in Bogota with 219
beds. The financing of social security is through a 3% monthly deduction for
white-collar workers and 2% for blue-collar workers, plus one-third of the first
salary. The state's contribution is supposed to be 3% of the national budget (C.
Garcia, 1975:16-17).

The rest of the 800,000 public employees are covered by many other "Cajas"
that are organized independently by the public institutions. In this way the
Ministry of Communication, the Military Institution, the Police, etc. have their
own social security administrations. In most of them the medical and hospital
services are given through contracts with private institutions.

Adding up the employees covered by the social security system, about 2
million people, and considering the economically active population to be about
7.5 million persons, we can conclude that about one-fourth of the working
population is covered by some type of social security.

Table 5: Classification of Professionals (Instituto Colombiano de Seguros
          Sociales), 1974

Type of Professional	Total	Percentage
Physicians	3,651	39.0
Dentists	855	9.0
Nurses	386	4.0
Nurses aides and auxiliaries	3,358	35.0
Social workers	15	0.1
Other medical assistants	1,101	12.0
TOTAL	9,366	99.1

SOURCE: Instituto Colombiano de Seguros Sociales, Resumen y Comentarios del Informe
Estadístico, Bogotá, 1975, page 53.

FAMILY WELFARE PROGRAMS:
THE INSTITUTE OF FAMILY WELFARE

In 1968 the Colombian government created an important official agency to protect children, especially those of the low-income classes, and to guarantee and preserve the stability of the family. The philosophy that inspired this social legislation was the importance of children and the unity of the family for the development of the country. The agencies that up to then had been taking care of some aspects of these problems were integrated into a new Institute of Family Welfare. The main objectives of this institute were (a) the protection of children, especially those under 7 years of age, and of the family, (b) the provision of nutritional programs, and (c) the treatment of the social pathology of youth.

Child Care

According to estimates, more than 5 million children and 1.5 million families are potential clients of the institute's services. A great majority of these families, spread all over the country, have little or no access to any type of service. At the moment there are not enough human and material resources to reach the needy.

Preschool Child-Care Centers. By a law passed December 21, 1974, preschool child-care centers are to be established for working persons, especially to assist low-income families. The service is compulsory for both private and public organizations, and eventually it will cover the unemployed. The financing will derive from a 2% payroll deduction laid on all public and private organizations. The beneficiaries will pay a fee according to their income. Other financial resources will be made available for nutritional programs for mothers and children. The institute will regulate and administer all the centers. Up to now it has taken care of preschool children through direct contracts with existing child-care centers. In this way it covered a total of 8,000 children in 1973 and 13,500 in 1974, representing 0.27% of the needy children (which, according to an institute report, could be as many as 5 million). The cost of this program for 1974 was 17,280,000 pesos, and the most important action has been the distribution of nutritional complements to cover 30% of children's basic nutritional needs. This aspect of the program has been extended to the rural areas, covering 2% of the needy families. The service is also given to pregnant women and to the newborn and involves distributing milk, vitamin A, and iron sulfate. This program is conducted through the Public Health Centers, distributing a total of 47 million pounds of food at a cost of 240 million pesos.

Care of Elementary School Children. This population (about 28 million) shows very high rates of malnutrition, which has resulted in retarded physical and mental growth and has also been the cause of a high rate of primary school dropouts. In 1973, 47% of the elementary school children were benefited by a food supplement given in school. A total of 42 million pounds of food was distributed. Part of this program will be the establishment of school restaurants and nutritional education programs for both children and mothers. In the rural areas, promotion of the production of food at a family level is done through financial credit and distributing meat products.

Family Care. According to the Economic Commission for Latin America, 78% of Colombian families have a monthly income under 1,000 pesos (about $40). This low income is aggravated by an unemployment rate that reaches 20% in the cities and by a population growth that annually adds 250,000 persons to the labor market. These problems, together with the rapid demographic growth and the rising social decomposition manifested by high rates of prostitution, juvenile delinquency, drug-taking, etc., have made family care an objective of high priority. The programs are intended to strengthen the family structure, to better the economic, social, and cultural level of low-income families. Educational programs are the basis of this action, seeking to help parents to recognize their responsibilities and to assist them in legal matters and in family planning. In 1973 about 20,000 families were covered by these services at a cost of 6 million pesos. The eradication of slums is part of the objective of the family care program. In order to carry it out, the institute works in coordination with other official housing institutions. The family is also reached through modern communication media to guarantee the diffusion of information about programs.

Of all the criminal acts reported in Colombia, 3.3% were against the family. Of these, 50% were for desertion of the breadwinner; the rest were for bigamy, incest, rape, etc. To take care of these situations, the institute has established six Family Counseling Centers. In 1974, of a total of 14,100 known cases, only 4,230 were served. The lack of trained personnel has limited the service.

In 1968 the law gave special protection to the family, making the parents legally responsible for the children even in the case of abandonment. In order to enforce the law, the institute offers family legal services for those who are unable to meet the cost of a private attorney. In 1974, services of this type were given to 179,250 persons in 92 centers. In Colombia, 30% of the parents are united without a civil or religious act. The situation of illegitimate children has been very precarious in a strongly traditional society like that of Colombia. Up to 1968, these children were totally unprotected by law, a fact that was aggravated by the irresponsibility of the father. In many instances, in order to prove paternity, special scientific tests are necessary. The only genetic laboratory functions in Bogotá, where, in 1974, 1,200 cases were examined.

Care of Neglected Children. In Colombia, neglect and abandonment of children are among the worst problems. The street child, called *gamin*, is a universal phenomena. These children live in the streets 24 hours a day, subsisting by stealing, moving in groups called *galladas*, and sleeping on the sidewalks, covered with old newspapers. Police estimates give a number of about 9,200 children living under these conditions. They are the product of the severe deprivation that affects low-income families. Many programs have been started to solve this problem, but the number of *gamines* seems to increase each day, especially in the streets of Bogotá. Besides this population, there are about 400,000 abandoned children in the whole country. There are 402 institutions taking care of 56,000 of these children, or 14% of the total. The Institute of Family Welfare has tried to supervise these institutions and to elaborate a "Guide" to guarantee the quality of the services given. In 1974, 18% of these children were under supervision of the institute, which employed 170 social workers.

A new law, passed in January 1975, provides protection for the adopted child, by specifying adoption procedures and stating the rights of an adopted child. The law establishes that only agencies or persons authorized by the Institute of Family Welfare can offer children for adoption. In 1974, 784 children received services for adoption through the institute. Yet there are no official figures on the children adopted, especially through private agencies, by foreigners who take them out of the country.

Juvenile Delinquency. According to statistics, the number of delinquent children under 12 years of age is growing at an alarming rate. The institute has special programs to protect children. Up to now, it has taken care of 46,339 cases including neglect of all types, such as drug addiction, dishonesty, and prostitution. Legal assistance is provided through Youth Defenders, having an objective to reeducate and integrate delinquents into a healthy family environment. Foster home care is being planned for these children, but this is very difficult to carry out in Colombia.

Children with Behavior Problems. There are 61,264 children between 7 and 18 years of age in 550 institutions for rehabilitation, reeducation, and protection. The Institute of Family Welfare takes care of 10,000 of them through contracts and 2,200 in its own institutions. Only 1% of these youths receive any type of job training, and very few of them are able to find employment afterwards. The institute has been studying different forms of rehabilitation, starting with a group of 500 children. It also encourages the training of specialized personnel, and changes of societal attitudes.

The outdoor treatment program for children leaving the rehabilitation institutions served about 1,200 children in 1974 out of 3,000 that annually need this service. A total of 26 social workers are engaged in this program. There are 83 rehabilitation institutions in the country serving 8,708 juvenile delinquents. The treatment they receive is very inadequate. The reasons are lack of interest from the regional governments (which, according to the law, are responsible for services to delinquents), lack of coordination among the different institutions, lack of policies and supervision, lack of educational programs, and lack of trained personnel. In 1974, 5,960 of these problem children under 16 years of age received some type of care through the institute.

Legal Assistance to Juvenile Delinquents. In Bogotá the institute has built a special "Comisaría de Menores" or police station for minors, where juvenile delinquents under 16 are taken and kept separate from common criminals. Similar institutions will be built in other cities. In 1974, 1,521 youths were covered by this service in Bogotá. Juvenile delinquents between 16 and 18 years of age are brought to the common jails, placing them in situations of learning from all types of criminals. In the future, the institute plans to build special rehabilitation facilities for this age group. Juvenile courts for delinquents 12 to 16 years of age are in charge of specialized personnel, who in 1974 gave legal assistance to 13,298 young people.

Handicapped Children. There are 32 institutions in the country taking care of 1,505 children with problems of communication. The Institute of Family Welfare gives a monthly subsidy of 600 pesos (about $20) to 732 of them. To some of these rehabilitation institutions it also gives a subsidy of 3.6 million pesos a year. Only 0.1% of the children in need are covered by the service.

Mentally Retarded Children. Three percent of the population up to 18 years of age suffers from mental retardation with the potential of rehabilitation. In 42 private institutions, 3,763 children are taken care of. They belong to families with incomes high enough to pay for the services. The children belonging to low-income classes, about 200,000, receive no attention at all.

Nutritional Programs. It is estimated that 66.6% of the children under 7 years of age suffer from malnutrition. Of these, about 100,000 (17%) suffer from third-degree malnutrition. The National Nutrition Program has been given priority in 1976, calling for related measures in agriculture, industry, health, and rural development. These programs are carried out in cooperation with different international organizations, such as CARE, OMS, AID.

Old-Age Assistance. There are 24,000 old-age, low-income people who are in a situation of total or partial abandonment. Most of the rest homes belong to charity or religious organizations, but there are a few private institutions for the higher income levels. Of 125,450 referrals in 1974, the Institute of Family Welfare was able to give care to 6,699 cases through contracts with 180 institutions. The cost of the program was 10 million pesos.

Research. There are different research projects which provide the basis for new types of programs and treatment. In the nutritional field, where more advances have been made, the production of "Bienestarina," a chemical substance that replaces meat, has been developed.

Administrative Organization. The Institute of Family Welfare functions under the Ministry of Public Health. According to the law, the president of the institute is the Colombian President's wife. The executive director is appointed directly by the President of the Republic. The central offices are in Bogotá, and there are 18 branches in the whole country. In 1973 the institute had 2,240 employees distributed in the following ways: more than 1% were executives, 30% professionals, 23% auxiliaries, 26% in administration, and 19% in services. About 77.5% of the personnel worked in the branches. The budget for the institute was 464 million pesos in 1972 (about $18 million). It is financed by the Ministry of Health by a five cent tax per pound on salt, by special bonds issued by the Bank of the Republic, and through the aid of international organizations.

PUBLIC WELFARE INSTITUTIONS

La Beneficencia de Cundinamarca

This public welfare organization was created by a legislative act in 1869 to supervise and direct all the charity and welfare organizations then in existence. Today, 22 institutions are a part of this program, among them the San Juan de Dios Hospital, a university hospital that is the most important of the country. It has 1,400 beds and takes care of 200,000 daily consultations. The outpatient program serves the entire region. There is a fee charged according to the patient's income. One of the university hospital's divisions is the Institute for Mother and Child, where mothers-to-be with no income are taken care of. This organization also takes care of the aged and mentally insane indigents, in two homes with a total of 2,700 beds. The program for children, in total or partial abandonment, includes 2,200 beds. The mental health hospital with inpatient, outpatient, and community services has a total of 1,200 beds (*El Tiempo*, August 11, 1975, p. 11C). This welfare organization depends on taxes from lotteries and beer sales, horse races, football bets, or any other kind of game. It is also financed from the rents on all the Beneficencia's properties that have been donated or acquired.

The Municipal Public Assistance Department, Bogotá

This institution has been functioning since 1960. Its objectives are the protection of children and the family. The department has 14 neighborhood centers offering casework, group work, and community organization services. There is one employment service office that tries to find some solution to the thousands of unemployed in Bogotá. There are 32 child-care centers, for 30 children each, which receive the children of working mothers in the barrios of Bogotá. The youths with behavior problems receive treatment in a clinic through an outpatient program. Abandoned children, who are daily left in the streets, are received in special centers and then placed under family group, foster family, or institutional care. The older children, from 12 on with more serious problems, are placed in rehabilitation institutions that the department has in the outskirts of Bogotá. This department is financed with income from the city lottery, taxes on games, and the municipal budget. Most large cities in Colombia have some type of public assistance program similar to the one described. These institutions have to cope with an insufficient budget and with the daily increase of social problems and needy people.

Public Health Assistance

The problem of health assistance is taken care of through governmental institutions that comprise 88% of the total of 735 hospitals and 1,120 public health centers. These hospitals, most of them totally financed through public funds, have 76% of the total of 47,175 beds. The fees charged are computed according to the income of the patient, but the majority of those who go to public hospitals cannot even pay the minimum. The hospitals are financed in part through the national budget and the 8% tax on beer and by contracts with the social security institutes. In 1971 the total budget was 459 million pesos, which was not sufficient to cover the services for growing numbers of people who, because of low nutritional levels, demand more hospital services than they can afford. Preventive actions in public health have aimed at eradicating epidemic diseases and acute diseases of early childhood. Some hospitals are employing social workers to organize community health programs in an effort to better the sanitary conditions of the population. Sanitation and environmental control programs have received more attention from the government in recent years, yet still a great part of the population has no filtered water services or sewage systems. In Colombia, more than 90% of the population suffers from amoebic or intestinal diseases. In 1967, 4% of the population was suffering from some kind of mental disorder. One of every 6 beds is occupied by a mentally sick person, and 2% of the medical consultations are for mental cases.

CONCLUSION

The need for more and better social services is an urgent task for a country that has to develop simultaneously in three sectors: the economic, the political, and the social. This is precisely the basic problem that the social services as an institution have to face. Under the present structures the job seems impossible since it will demand a radical change in the social and political system and in the distribution of income. In spite of the many services given by the different social institutions, only a small percentage of the needy population is covered by any type of welfare benefits. Another serious problem is the fact that the state, as well as the political parties and the ruling elites, give first priority to the economic aspect of development, thinking that social development will result from it.

A welfare state—considered as the product of a developed society—cannot exist, as history is showing, in underdeveloped countries, since human welfare and situations of political backwardness and social injustice are incompatible. No economic development can exist if the enormous and countless material and human resources of a country like Colombia are not fully used or if they are used for the benefit of the few. There can be no social development if education is the privilege of a traditional, closed-in, and elitist minority that believes that the poor are so because they are ignorant and that they are ignorant because they are poor.

The nation has to realize that *development* is a total concept; in other words, it is impossible to have a growing level of economic development without a social one (involving better income distribution, a better salary system, better social and welfare services). At the same time there can be no social welfare if there are no better conditions for the full employment of existing resources.

In recent years the problem has become worse in Colombia, because the concentration of economic power has resulted in a greater social polarization and consequently in a great concentration of political power. These circumstances explain why social welfare programs have failed to reach the vast poor majority and why income distribution has become more and more inequitable. Underdevelopment is not only economic; it is also social and political and there can be no successful development policies or programs if they are not comprehensive and total. This article has insisted on this point because otherwise the trends and limitations of the Colombian social service delivery system cannot be understood.

NOTES

1. The concept of *latifundio* not only means a great expanse of land owned by a person, but also implies the type of economic, social, and political relations that landholding by a few can bring about. See A. Garcia, 1973; Barraclough and Collarte, 1971; Stavenhagen, 1970.
2. For a good analysis of the Colombian social and political system, see Fluharty, 1957.
3. Statistics and data in the following paragraphs on Colombian social problems are taken from the following sources: Informe del Banco Murdial, 1972; ICBF, 1973a, 1973b.

REFERENCES

ADELMAN, A., and MORRIS, G. (1973). "An anatomy of income distribution patterns in developing countries." Development Digest, 10(October).
BARRACLOUGH, S., and COLLARTE, J.C. (1971). El hombre y la tierra en America Latina. Santiago de Chile: Editorial Universitaria.
CIDA (1965). Evolución y reforma de la estructura agraria en América Latina. Santiago de Chile: ICRA.
DIX, R. (1967). Colombia: The political dimensions of change. New Haven, Conn.: Yale University Press.
FEDER, E. (1970). "Counterreform." In R. Stavenhagen (ed.), Agrarian problems and peasant movements in Latin America. New York: Doubleday.
FLUHARTY, V.L. (1957). Dance of the millions. Pittsburgh: University of Pittsburgh Press.
GARCIA, A. (1972). Dialéctica de la democracia. Bogotá: Ediciones Cruz del Sur.
––– (1973). Sociología de la reforma agraria en América Latina. Buenos Aires: Amorrorto.
GARCIA, C. (1975). "La seguridad social en la sector público." Revista del ICSS-Seguridad Social (January-February).
GUZMAN, G., FALS, O., and UMANA, E. (1964). La violencia en Colombia. Bogotá: Ediciones Tercer Mundo.
ICBF (1973a). Estrategia para desarrollar el sector: Bienestar familiar en Colombia. Bogotá: Author.
––– (1973b). Plan nacional de bienestar familiar, Colombia, 1974-1977 (Tomo 1). Bogotá: Oficina de Planeacion.
Informe del Banco Murdial (1972). Desarrollo económico de Colombia. Bogotá: Ediciones Banco Popular.

Instituto Colombiano de Seguros Sociales (1974). Rusimen y comentarios del informe estadístico. Bogotá: ICSS.
LEBRET, L. (1958). Estudio sobre las condiciones del desarrollo en Colombia. Bogotá: Aedita.
MUSGRAVE, I. (1969). Bases para una reforma tributaria en Colombia. Bogotá: Ediciones Banco Popular.
STAVENHAGEN, R. (ed., 1970). Agrarian problems and peasant movements in Latin America. New York: Doubleday.

12

BRAZIL:
SYSTEMATIZING SOCIAL SERVICES

BALBINA OTTONI VIEIRA

Brazil, a federal republic of 23 states, is a large country of more than 8 million square kilometers with 100 million inhabitants. The economic, social, and cultural development of the country has been uneven; the southern states are more developed than the northern ones. This is due to the temperate climate which appeals to emigrants from Europe and to the natural resources which provide material for industry. The northern states have a warm climate with periodical floods and droughts. While the South is densely populated, the North and Northeast have a sparingly distributed population. The government has been very attentive to foster equal development opportunities in all regions, and therefore most of the financial and technical assistance of the federal government has been given to the northern states.

Harmonious development of the country being the aim of the federal government, national development plans have been issued periodically. The II° Plano Nacional de Desensolvimento (the II PND—or 2nd National Development Plan) covers the period between 1975 and 1979 (Planejamento e Desenvolvimento, 1975). It is an economic plan to "reduce the distance between the country and the developed world by the control of inflation and balance of trade."

The often reiterated goal of Brazilian society is economic development. Our country chooses economic development with a better income distribution and equality of opportunities, so as to build a truly open and democratic society. To fulfill these goals, we shall need a set of policies capable of bringing order to the growth process under way. [Vaz da Costa, 1971:8]

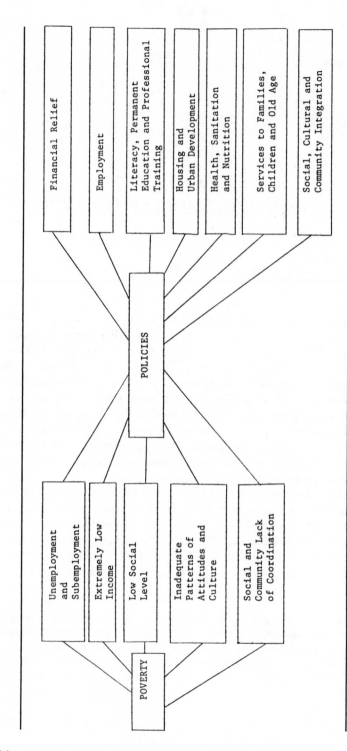

Figure 1: STRATEGY FOR THE STRUGGLE AGAINST POVERTY

The II PND recognizes that economic objectives alone do not help to reach a higher rate of development. Therefore emphasis is put on social policy which is expressed in the "valuation of human resources and social integration" (Planejamento e Desenvolvimento, 1974).

To reach these goals, the objectives of the II PND are as follows: (1) to raise the family income of all classes by a combination of employment and salary policies offering more jobs with better pay, (2) to improve human resources by offering better opportunities for education, professional training, health and medical care, hygiene and nutrition, (3) to integrate the social system by raising and complementing income through saving, by providing home ownership for the working class, by offering social security to all classes of the population, and by better application of labor laws, (4) to protect consumers and encourage lower prices for basic consumer products.

The attention of the government focuses on the "struggle against poverty." Poverty is a concept applied to individuals and families who have no access to basic means of subsistence. It is caused not only by low income or lack of it, but by social, cultural, and psychological dependency. Although poverty exists in many communities, it tends to concentrate in definite areas, such as the valley of the Jequitinhenga (state of Minas Gerais), and in the rural areas of the state of Rio de Janeiro, which were rich and developed in the last century and have degenerated since then. Policies must be established and put into practice to fight poverty through adequate legislation and services. The strategy of this struggle can be illustrated by Figure 1.

A system of social services is therefore necessary to put into operation this part of the II PND. Social services in Brazil refer to all agencies, public or private, whose objectives are to provide relief, education, medical care, etc. to those individuals and families of the lower-income bracket or who have few means of subsistence. There are three systems of social services in Brazil: public, semiprivate, and private. The public and semipublic systems are divided into national, state, and municipal systems. The private system is less well articulated, being mostly local. The three systems are integrated through identity of interests and through the financial aid given by federal or state agencies to local and private agencies.

PUBLIC SYSTEM

Federal System

A consultive body to the presidency is the Planning Bureau, whose functions are to coordinate (1) planning, budgeting, and modernization of public administration, (2) economic, social, and scientific and technological development policies, (3) common aspects and interests which involve more than one ministry. The Planning Bureau does not decide or implement; it plans and coordinates action. The ministries propose legislation to the President, who, after hearing the Planning Bureau, sends the project to the Congress to be discussed and approved or rejected. The President proposes, the Congress decides, and the ministries execute.

There are two councils to help the Bureau: the Council for Economic Development (CDE) and the Council for National Development (CDN), whose members are the ministries dealing with economic or special subjects. The Council for Social Development (CDS) focuses its attention on the social goals of the II PND—the struggle against poverty and for social integration. Integration means integration of individuals and families who do not ordinarily participate in the process of development because of illiterarcy, poor health, and lack of basic education or training. In order to evaluate the needs of the population and results obtained by programs and projects, the CDS has organized a system of "social indicators" These indicators refer to monthly indices of salaries; annual distribution of manpower by age, salaries, field of activities, and place of work; statistics of medical care; and benefits of social security. These indices help the government to rationalize their operations and establish priorities by a clearer notion of the situation. According to consultants of the Ministry of Social Security and Social Assistance, an autonomous system of social data collection will maintain a closer relationship between economic and social planning. In the struggle against poverty, the CDS has proposed a "Program of Community Centers."

> The rapid urbanization and metropolitanization of the country . . . has had a strong influence on the II PND and led the planners to emphasize the social aspects of development. Recent studies of several government agencies led to the recommendation to implement integrating direct services and promotional activities units, as a complement to housing, water and sewage, transportation, pollution and control systems, etc. already under was in many Brazilian cities. The objective of the urban community centers is to give the urban population, in an integrated and multisectorial form, a set of activities or services considered of importance: education, culture, sports, health, nutrition, professional training, social security, social assistance and recreation. [CBCISS, 1975:6]

Six ministries are concerned with the implementation of the social aspects of the II PND and are members of the CDS. They are the following:

—The Ministry of Education is responsible for planning the programs of primary schools (known as 1st level), high schools and colleges (2nd level), and universities with both graduate and postgraduate courses (3rd level). It also plans for the education of physically disabled or mentally deficient children.

—The Ministry of Health plans medical care, hygiene, and prevention of all kinds of diseases and organizes campaigns against polio, meningitis, and measles through early vaccination and treatment.

—The Ministry of Labor plans the application of the labor laws, seeks solutions to problems related to employment, including professional training, and supervises trade unions.

—The Ministry of Interior in 1970 established the Coordinacao de Programas de Desenvolvimento Comunitario (the CPDC—or Coordination of the Community Development Programs) "to link at national, regional and local levels the undertakings which are carried out by the poeple and by the Government and which are aimed at overcoming the obstacles that hinder the development of the country." It has also the task of converting the plans into a permanent flow of information, taking the program and aims of the government to the local communities and forwarding the suggestions made by local communities to the planning bodies of the government. The philosophy of the CPDC rests on two themes: first, economic growth becomes true (economic and social) development only through integration and articulation; second, a long-term development plan can achieve its fullness only when it reflects the aspirations of the people, who must participate and consciously see to it that development goals are reached. Of course this presupposes the institutionalization of a dialogue and the incorporation of different sectors of the population within the adopted economic development model. The CPDC is complementary to other participating agencies, such as political parties (CBCISS, 1974).

—The Ministry of Justice is concerned with applying the Civil Code of Laws, combating crime and delinquency, and supervising the courts and police forces.

—The Ministry of Social Security and Social Assistance, the most recent of the ministries, was created in 1974 and took over part of the responsibilities of the Ministry of Labor. It assumed the function of the former National Institute of Social Security.

Social Security, as an insurance system, has been gradually covering all classes of workers. In the last two years it has finally included rural workers and domestic servants. Social security provides retirement benefits to workers aged 65 years or over or having 35 years of active service, pensions to widows and children of deceased workers, marriage grants, family allowances, and funeral expenses and covers risks of disease, accident, and death. The National Medical Plan provides medicines for those who are unable to pay for them. In urban and developed areas, social security covers almost all the workers, but, in rural areas and underdeveloped small communities, many do not contribute, either because they do not know about the benefits provided or because they assume that they have no means to pay. For many years, a large percentage of the population thought that it was just another way to make poor people pay for the government's expenses. It was only when the number of retirement benefits, pensions, and other social benefits began to be paid out and when medical care was extended, that the population realized that this was a real benefit to everybody. Social security is financed by the workers, the employers, and the government through an 8% contribution on salaries.

Social Assistance was formerly considered as material and financial relief and direct services to the needy. As a new concept, it means modern administration and control of direct services to the population and systematic implementation through modern professional techniques. Social assistance is now provided by the government and/or private agencies. It now includes a new kind of clientele: individuals and families in emergency situations. Everybody recognizes that relief agencies are still needed in view of cataclysms affecting some parts of the country periodically: floods, droughts, and heavy frosts, which destroy agriculture and leave families without shelter. In every community there are also a number of individuals and families who have no means of solving their financial problems. However, efforts are made to lead social relief agencies, particularly private ones, to launch programs that will foster the "social promotion" of their clients.

Social Promotion is understood as a "set of actions to unchain the human and social development process and provide lower classes of the population with the opportunity to satisfy their basic economic, social and cultural needs as well as to rouse conscious and responsible participation of all classes in the development process." The Ministry of Social Security and Social Assistance provides funds and technical assistance to local public and private agencies, fosters research on problems, and evaluates results.

State System

In each state of the republic, there are a certain number of state departments corresponding to the federal ministries. The wealthier states, like Rio de Janeiro, São Paulo, and Rio Grande do Sul, have state departments for each area covered by the ministries. Other states combine two or three of those areas in one state department—for example, Education and Health, or Labor and Social Security. Their function is to apply federal legislation by issuing special state laws and to plan and organize adequate services for their specific situations. Therefore, states have different views concerning their various situations. The programs planned depend a great deal on the financial and technical potentialities of each state and also on the mentality, traditions, and customs of the population.

Municipal System

Municipal systems offer a great variety of plans and organizations. Large cities, like Rio de Janeiro, São Paulo, Belo Horizonte, Recife, or Porto Alegre, have an elaborate government with municipal departments corresponding to the federal ministries or state departments, although these might not have the same name or the same position in the whole system. For instance, the state of Rio de Janeiro, recently created by the merger of the state of Guanabara and the state of Rio de Janeiro, has a special committee attached to the mayor's office which is responsible for welfare; social assistance, however, is handled by the Health and Education City Department. Some large cities, like São Paulo, have a special department for each field of social welfare and assistance. In smaller cities, there are no funds for such an elaborate government. There might be only two or three city departments: Finance and Administration, Labor and Social Security, Education and Health and Welfare. In rural areas there might be only one department for tax collection.

PRIVATE WELFARE SYSTEM

Private agencies, mainly church agencies, have been a long tradition in Brazil, since the days of the Portuguese colonization. These agencies can be divided into three categories: (1) direct service agencies, (2) coordinating agencies, and (3) fund-raising agencies.

Direct Service Agencies

These agencies have the following characteristics: (1) they are generally local or church agencies, (2) their objectives are financial or material relief, (3) they offer care to children, old people, and disabled persons, and (4) they are financed through donations, bazaars, shows, charity teas, and other forms of fund raising. They depend a great deal on government financial aid.

Specialized agencies for the blind, hard of hearing, mentally deficient, and physically disabled are, in general, well staffed with doctors, nurses, psychiatrists, psychologists, teachers, and social workers. According to the number of clients and available resources, the staff works part- or full-time. Salaries are usually lower than those of public and semipublic agencies. Some agencies ask for a small fee, according to the financial possibilities of their clients. They are located in large cities—Rio de Janeiro, São Paulo, etc.—which offer better facilities for recruitment of staff, fund raising, and help from the community. To receive subsidies from public funds, specialized agencies must have an organized social service department staffed with graduated social workers. Relief agencies are seldom staffed with social workers and rely on volunteers and religious personnel. Applied social work consists of casework and group work with clients and their families. If large cities are relatively well equipped with private agencies, this is not the case in small cities and in rural areas. Public, semipublic, and private agencies do not exist and the only resource is the "Santa Casa" (Holy House) with its tradition of hospital care, relief, and asylum for children, old people, and insane persons.

However, Caritas Brasileira (a national church agency that distributes relief in kind donated by the people of the United States through the Catholic Relief Service) has stimulated dioceses to organize multiple service agencies for fundamental education, homemaking training, recreation, etc., staffed with volunteers and using graduate social workers from the diocesan and regional offices of Caritas to organize and supervise local services. Many previously existing social centers joined Caritas in order to benefit from its technical assistance program. There are actually about 500 centers allied with Caritas throughout the country. Through its regional and diocesan offices Caritas has helped private agencies to organize promotional services, to participate in community development programs, to train their personnel, as well as to conduct their traditional relief activities.

Some private agencies work in the field of community development and organization. For example, the Acao Comunitaria do Brazil (Brazilian Community Action) has been fostered by an American agency Community Action. In Rio de Janeiro, this agency works in *favelas* (slums) and housing projects to stimulate better relations in the community and help to solve problems through active participation of the population. ACB is financed by industrial concerns who elect a council and is staffed with full-time workers from different professions: social workers, sociologists, educators, engineers, etc.

Coordinating Agencies

Coordinating agencies are found in larger cities. Their objective is the study of community needs and problems, the study of methods and techniques to improve services, and the coordination of programs of different agencies of the community to avoid duplication of services, to cover unmet needs, and to foster joint fund raising. Such agencies are limited to local and municipal areas and include all kinds of private welfare agencies. One of them is the Federacao das Instituicoes Beneficientes (the FIBE—or Federation of Welfare Agencies) in Rio de Janeiro. The Catholic Church has made a great effort to coordinate its welfare agencies and to improve its services. The Confederacao dos Bispos do Brazil (the CNBB—or National Conference of Bishops of Brazil) has a special plan for the welfare field, based on Catholic philosophy and gives consultation to dioceses for carrying out their programs. The Conferencia dos Religiosos do Brazil (the CRB—or Conference of Religious Orders of Brazil) has a department for giving technical assistance to religious agencies and for introducing modern techniques and equipment. Through their regional offices, both men and women are encouraged to graduate in nursing, teaching, and social service and to work in that capacity in their agencies.

Fund-Raising Agencies

Fund raising for charity purposes has always been very difficult. It is always the same group of wealthy people who contribute—those in the higher income brackets. Private agencies have to rely on donations and other forms of fund raising or on subsidies from public funds. The Banco da Providencia of Rio de Janeiro (Bank of Providence), a private relief church agency, is an example of a private fund-raising agency. Every year this agency organizes a four-day sale, which is quite a social event with the participation of high society members and representatives of banks, industry, and the diplomatic corps. The product of this sale supports services during the entire following year. Some foreign agencies have sponsored the organization of Brazilian fund-raising agencies. For example, the Fundo Communitario (Community Fund) is sponsored by an American agency and raises and distributes donations from American firms to Brazilian welfare agencies. The Fundo began its activities in Brazil in 1965; it has now expanded to include Brazilian concerns as donors. Grants are given after a careful study of an agency and its possiblities; supervision is given to help toward the good application of the money, and the agency must report on the use of the resources given by the Fundo. According to last year's report, 70% of the donations were for education and for community and self-help projects, 20% for relief, and 10% for emergencies.

SEMIPUBLIC SYSTEM

The semipublic system includes government foundations and tax-supported agencies. They are usually national, sometimes state, and seldom municipal or local agencies. Foundations are agencies that have obtained substantial grants from the government or from private resources, grants that constitute capital for their services. Tax-supported agencies are financed through taxes created by law. Both kinds of agencies are autonomous and registered as private enterprises. A council of representatives of social agencies is the legislative body for foundations. Tax-supported agencies have sometimes a council of leaders of the communities. These agencies usually work in specialized fields. The main foundations are the Fundacoa para o Bem Estar do Menor (the FUNABEM—or Foundation for the Welfare of Children), the Movimento Brasileiro de Alfabetizacao (the MOBRAL—or Brazilian Movement for Literacy), the Banco Nacional de Habitacao (the BNH—or National Housing Bank), and the Legiao Brasileira de Assistencia (the LBA—or Brazilian Legion of Assistance). Tax-supported agencies are the Service Social da Industria (the SESI—or Social Service for Industrial Workers), the Servico Nacional de Aorentizagem Industrial (the SENAI—of National Service for Industrial Training), the Servico Social do Comercio (the SESC—or Social Service for White-Collar Workers), and the Servico Nacional de Aprendizagem Comercial (the SENAC—or National Service for Commercial Training).

Brazil has organized semipublic welfare systems to meet special needs identified by the II PND. The principal systems involve urban development and housing, anti-illiteracy, children services, family and maternal and infant care, and rural development.

Urban Development and Housing System

There is no doubt that Brazilian cities grow very rapidly. Migration to towns and cities has been the result of changes in agricultural methods requiring less unskilled manpower, the attraction of higher wages, and the attraction of basic services not existing in rural areas. All these factors brought about a demographic explosion in many cities, the concentration of poor families and unskilled workers in slums and other types of subhuman dwellings, the frustrations of inadequate welfare services to attend such a large number of incoming people, lack of drinking water and sewage services, schools, clinics, and transportation. The slums have a tendency to grow on the outskirts of cities on surrounding hills. All these factors cause unemployment or underemployment, lack of training, low incomes, inadequate housing, and lack of social integration with all its worst consequences. Nevertheless, according to modern economic and social theories, urbanization is necessary for a developing country; cities are creative centers through markets, universities, research facilities, and industries. "Man developed when he began to live in groups, away from the isolation of rural life (Vaz da Costa, 1971:8).

According to the II PND, the government has therefore organized an "Urban Development Housing System" composed of the Banco Nacional de Habitacao (the BNH–or National Housing Bank), the Companhias de Hanitacao Popular (the COHAPS–or State Housing Companies), and private financial and saving concerns. The system works within the Plano Nacional de Habitacao Popular (the PLANAP–or National Housing Plan), whose objective is "to help towards the social raising of low-income families, in order to cover in 10 years the deficit of housing, to provide dwelling for all families, to improve existent buildings, to stimulate and extend community development programs and projects" (PLANAP, 1973:38). PLANAP gives priority to the following: (1) cities over 50,000 inhabitants, (2) metropolitan areas, or centers of development, (3) rapidly growing cities under 50,000 inhabitants, and (4) areas where isolated units are considered convenient. The social objectives of PLANAP are to provide dwellings for families whose heads have regular jobs with minimum wages, and to offer greater security, comfort, and welfare. With these objectives in view, PLANAP hopes to contribute to a better income distribution, to reduce the regional disparities in the country, to create employment for unskilled workers (for example in the building industry), and to stimulate professional training.

The BNH is the principal agency of the system (BNH, 1974). Its functions are (1) the supervision and control of the whole system, (2) the stimulation of savings, (3) the financing of state and local programs, (4) the supervision and control of all agencies working in the area of housing, and (5) the training of staffs and the provision of technical assistance to local agencies. the BNH stimulates the organization of special state housing, funds which are used by the COHAPS. These local companies study their respective areas and plan and finance the overall housing programs in their areas. Projects might be executed by private concerns, in accordance with the local COHAP standards, or by the would-be owners on a mutual-aid system. (Private concerns build housing projects in large cities; mutual-aid systems are used in smaller cities or in rural areas.)

The whole system is financed by federal, state, and municipal governments. Those concerns or persons applying for funds are subject to specific rules according to the type of project: there are special funds for housing projects, for community equipment, for organization of local COHAPs, for technical assistance, and for training of staffs for COHAPs and local firms.

Local agencies are responsible for community development programs. Priority is given to short-term projects operating with the participation of the people and agencies of the local community.

The BNH and the Ministry of Health are working together on a very ambitious program called the Plano Nacional de Saneamento (the PLANASA—or National Sanitation Plan) to provide urban communities with good quality drinking water and with sewage treatment stations to control water pollution. Such programs are important not only for the modern convenience of old and new houses and industries but also for fighting diseases transmitted through water, waste, and garbage. Installation of state services has been slow, because in many cities the local government has contracted private companies—even foreign ones—which are reluctant to transfer their assets to the state or to the municipality.

Anti-Illiteracy System

Public and private schools provide elementary education for children from 6 to 12 years old. Unfortunately all children cannot go to school for various reasons: lack of schools, distance in rural areas, children helping mothers in domestic services, etc. Many adolescents do not know how to read or write properly, and lack of cultural opportunities lead them to forget the little they have learned in school. Many attempts have been made by Government as well as by private agencies to fight illiteracy; even local efforts have been made in rural areas. However, they all have produced poor results.

The latest is the Movimento Brazileiro de Alfabetizacao (the MOBRAL—or Brazilian Movement for Literacy). MOBRAL, created by federal law on December 13, 1967, is a foundation under the Ministry of Education and, like all federal agencies, has national, state, and municipal offices. The national office is the normative body. It gives technical assistance and allocates funds for local teachers' salaries. State offices plan and coordinate programs in the states, but municipal offices are the real executors of the MOBRAL program. The aim of MOBRAL is to fight illiteracy and to stimulate continuing education for adolescents and adults. Up to the last decade a large percentage of the population and the most needy classes were stigmatized by lack of opportunity in education, because they had no regular school facilities. In 1970, there were 18 million illiterates in the country—33% of the adult population. MOBRAL's plan established priorities: (1) the *urban illiterates* were considered the neediest part of the population because of the complexity of urban life and the high degree of competition in modern society, and they were also considered the people who could be most rapidly and easily recruited; (2) *adolescents and adults between 15 and 35 years old,* who constitute the largest percentage of the active population, were considered the persons least resistant to change and most likely to have a chance to develop productive lives.

The characteristic aspects of the MOBRAL program are (1) *community participation,* through a committee of local voluntary leaders; (2) *decentralized implementation,* whereby the national office gives financial help and technical assistance, but state and municipal offices plan their own programs and adapt national norms to their particular needs; (3) *incentive to private initiative,* through contacts with various private educational agencies for carrying out literacy programs, through cooperation with publishing houses for the printing of teaching materials and through cooperation with schools, churches, clubs, trade unions, and associations which can offer quarters for MOBRAL activities and which can recruit and train volunteers to help in various capacities. Financial resources come from public funds through the Ministry of Education, with the addition of 24% of the proceeds of the Football Pool and 1% or 2% from the income taxes paid by all industrial and commercial firms.

MOBRAL has three types of programs. The *Functional Literacy Program* is by far the most important; its objective is to teach basic reading and other skills in order to help individuals secure better working and living conditions.

It is called "functional" because it helps the student to discover his function, his role in society today. It aims to transform man into an agency and beneficiary of the development process. The program hopes to create opportunity for the semiqualified worker to develop his capacities to provide for his family. [MOBRAL, 1973:9]

The program helps the adult to acquire a large vocabulary, develop rational thinking, adopt better working habits, develop creativity, acquire knowledge of his rights and duties, take interest in the improvement of health and hygiene, maintain and improve community services, and thereby discover better ways of living. The course covers five months and is given in areas where there is a concentration of would-be students. Although a specific teaching method has not been adopted, the teaching does not consist merely in teaching basic skills but also in teaching students "to be responsible, to be free, and to become integrated into society" (MOBRAL, 1973:20). The work done by the municipal office is the most important:

It is a form of participation in the development of the community and of the country. The success of the work is the result of the capacity of the municipal office to stimulate the community to participate in the program by mobilizing human, material and financial resources and using them in an adequate and creative way. [MOBRAL, 1973:25]

The municipal office must be registered as a local private agency. It must have a community council of local leaders from various groups, who evaluate the program and help in any way they can. It also has an executive office with the necessary professionals (teachers and supervisors). Groups of volunteers work in different capacities to further the program.

The second MOBRAL program is the *Program of Continuing Education.* To learn to read is not enough in a complex society. The adult can easily forget what he has learned if he has no opportunity for reading. Moreover, radio and TV facilities have accustomed a large part of the population "to hear" and not "to read." The adult who has learned his ABC's is still living in an "oral culture," whereas urban man lives in a "typographical culture." An illiterate is not perforce an ignorant person, but his schooling is limited and he has difficulty in reaching a more sophisticated level of knowledge. MOBRAL has therefore launched a program of continuing or permanent education to give people an opportunity (1) to learn about different areas of knowledge corresponding to the subjects of the first four years of grammar school, (2) to acquire vocational training which does not require knowledge beyond these first grades, (3) to develop gradual autonomy and responsibility so as to become integrated in society as producers and consumers. This course covers 720 hours, approximately one academic year. The subject matter is related to the facts of industrial and social life that can stimulate debates on the personal experiences of the trainees. The technique used is small-group discussion to exchange experiences, criticize and analyze problems, participate actively, and develop creativity. Individual and diversified work techniques are also used to attend to individual differences, interests, and rhythms of learning. Evaluation of these programs includes not only what the students have learned and absorbed but also their changes of attitude.

The *Cultural Program* (or *MOBRAL CULTURAL*) is a program that is complementary to the first two programs above. Its objective is to enlarge the cultural universe of former students and other interested persons through the principles of continuing or permanent education. Therefore, its aims are to prevent regression to illiteracy and dropping out of school and to reduce the number of failures by inciting adults to learn, stimulating the community to foster a spirit of association, and providing opportunity for self-development. MOBRAL CULTURAL works through two types of units: the Cultural Center and the Mobralteca. The Cultural Center functions in communities where there are a large number of former MOBRAL students and no other cultural agency in the area. If this is the case, MOBRAL makes a contract with a private agency to help carry out the MOBRAL program. The Cultural Center also encourages the community to organize other types of agencies needed to attain objectives other than those of MOBRAL. The Mobralteca is a traveling unit, a truck equipped with a small library, TV, radio, and movie. It serves communities where there are only a small number of former MOBRAL students and helps to promote interchange and cooperation between small communities. It also serves communities where a Cultural Center can be organized in the future. It stimulates municipal offices and communities to plan and implement MOBRAL CUL-TURAL programs. The MOBRAL national office maintains training programs for students from foreign countries interested in the Brazilian anti-illiteracy system; several African countries have sent teachers and technicians to be trained to adapt the MOBRAL system to the needs of their own countries.

Children's Services

Traditionally services for children have been provided through institutions. New forms of services are being gradually introduced, such as adoption and day-care principally for working mothers. Although the law on adoption has been recently modified and offers more facilities to families who wish to adopt children, as well as to agencies dealing with this kind of service, the greatest obstacle is the diversity of ethnics which makes adoption difficult when children are of one race and future parents are of another.

Foster care is even more difficult, due to a great number of socioeconomic factors. The middle classes prefer to adopt children instead of receiving payment to look after them and be obliged to give them up later on. The lower classes, who gladly accept payment for the care of children, are seldom able to give them adequate housing, physical comforts, and maternal care. Adoption and foster care services are rendered, in general, by private agencies.

Children's courts are the highest authority in deciding about the care of children. They exist in every municipality and decide what has to be done with orphans, abandoned children, and delinquents; they also grant unaccompanied children and adolescents permission to travel and supervise theaters and recreational places used by children and adolescents.

The coordinating agency which applies national policy governing the welfare of children is the Fundacao Nacional do Bem Estar do Menor (the FUNABEM —or National Foundation for the Welfare of Children). FUNABEM was created by federal law on December 13, 1964, as a public foundation with the characteristics of a private agency, and it is based on the Declaration of the Rights of Children accepted by the United Nations Assembly on November 20, 1959. Its objective is the formulation and implementation of a national policy for the welfare of children. This policy is based on the following principles: (1) development of programs that foster integration of children into the community through services to families or agencies of adoption or foster care, (2) organization or reorganization of public and private institutions to accord with optimum family life, and (3) stimulation of private initiative for the organization of services according to the needs and peculiarities of each area of the country. FUNABEM has a council composed of representatives of large private and semiprivate agencies which is designed to formulate policies and plans; an executive secretary puts the plans into operation. At the state level, a regional agency aids state and private agencies to execute the national policies.

The field of FUNABEM is "that part of the population whose children might be victims of a marginalization process." "Marginalization" of children is "a progressive withdrawal from the development process and human promotion leading to neglect, dependency, abuse and anti-social conduct" (FUNABEM, 1975:16). Priority is given to marginalized children in dependency situations, child victims of abuse, children exhibiting anti-social conduct, and children of the lower classes suffering from poverty and lack of education. FUNABEM tries to expose the problems and convince the government and the public of the importance of the problems. To promote its cause, it has advocated the following system: (1) treatment and prevention programs should be the responsibility of local agencies, at municipal, intermunicipal, or state levels; (2) programs must gradually cover all needs and problems of a specific geographical area; (3) state or municipal plans should integrate all agencies' programs in an area in order to avoid duplication of services or, conversely, to avoid having specific problems remain undiscovered; (4) private agencies should be contracted to improve or enlarge their services for meeting children's needs in their geographic areas; and (5) agency plans and programs should take into consideration the policies of FUNABEM. FUNABEM does not itself implement any program but offers technical assistance, training to personnel (both lay and professional), supervision, and evaluation of programs and activities. FUNABEM has biven a lot of attention to delinquency, mainly in cities where lack of schools and inadequate services leave a great number of children and adolescents without shelter, work, or recreational facilities.

Special attention has been given to the old reform schools. They are now organized to provide direct observation of the delinquents, to plan adequate treatment through the cottage plan or other programs similar to family life, and to lead the youth into reintegration into the community. These institutions are usually public agencies, except for the well-known Good Shepard, a church agency for delinquent and promiscuous girls. Specialized institutions for physically disabled and mentally deficient children, subsidized by FUNABEM, are also usually private agencies. Orphans and abandoned children are generally cared for by professional agencies. FUNABEM has done much to encourage these institutions to adopt the modern system of family or cottage life, as well as modern educational methods and equipment.

Maternal and Infant Care System

Maternal and infant care is provided by public and private agencies (Ministerio da Saude, 1974). In the II PND, high priority has been given to these services, due to the fact that children constitute a large percentage of the population (69.5%) and infant mortality below 2 years old is still very high (108 per 1,000). Causes of maternal death can be easily removed, because they are due mostly to lack of hygiene and health education, illiteracy, malnutrition, folk medicine, and witch practices in rural areas and in city slums. Another important factor is the multiplication of public and private agencies working alone without coordination, wasting resources and efforts, resulting in high cost of services and duplication of activities.

The objective of the II PND in maternal and infant care is a reduction of 40% in infant mortality below one year of age, of 60% in infant mortality between one and four years of age, and of 40% in the maternal death rates. To attain these objectives, the Ministry of Health has transformed the former Children's Bureau into a Coordination of Maternal and Infant Care Services, which is responsible for the planning and supervision of public and private agency programs. The principles established for these programs are as follows: (1) adequate distribution of services according to the needs of the area, (2) staff training at all levels, including midwives in rural areas, (3) taking the family as a whole as the target of services, (4) participation of the community, and (5) coordination of agencies. The program emphasizes prenatal treatment as early as possible, birth in hospitals and clinics, infant follow-up during the first two years, and vaccination at birth and periodically thereafter. Overall planning is the function of the Coordination of Maternal and Infant Care Services; regional planning comes under the state departments of health through a specialized service; and execution of the program is the responsibility of the municipality.

At the municipal level, services must be distributed evenly so that all the population can have access to them. In rural areas of scattered population, some universities (such as the University of Brasilia) have organized mobile units staffed with interdisciplinary teams—doctors, nurses, and social workers operating under supervision of the central units. Local agencies are stimulated to have day-care centers for children of working mothers, but these projects cannot be isolated from others and must be integrated with other programs in the community. Health education is necessary in the continuing education program of the community and is not a separate item. Mothers' clubs are organized in many clinics and are quite popular in rural areas where other recreational facilities are nonexistent. Mothers have an opportunity to go out, meet other mothers, talk about their interests and problems, and learn homemaking techniques and handicrafts. Other kinds of groups, such as Parent-Teacher Associations, serve the same purpose. Volunteers organize and orient groups of mothers or work in vaccination and health campaigns. Such programs stimulate the organization of health councils, not as isolated units, but as integrated parts of the community councils or committees. Where such a council does not exist, the program starts with a health committee project which will gradually include other welfare aspects. These councils are composed either of social agencies or of leaders of the community.

A large private agency has been working in the field of maternal and infant care for the last 30 years: Legiao Brasileira de Assistencia (the LBA—or Brazilian Legion of Assistance). Founded during World War II by the wife of President Getulio Vargas as a family service for the soldiers of the Brazilian army fighting in Europe, it was transformed after the war into a maternal and infant care agency. The LBA organizes regional maternal community centers to give prenatal and infant services through clinics and promotes social activities such as mothers' clubs, home economics courses, and health education campaigns. The function of the LBA's regional centers are (1) the study of the socioeconomic reality of the community, (2) the interpretation of LBA's policies and plans, (3) the stimulation and technical orientation of local programs, (4) participation in community programs, (5) the recruitment and training of volunteers, (6) collaboration with regional development programs, (7) the garnering of information for the LBA national office for the evaluation of plans, and (8) the coordination and supervision of local agencies with which LBA maintains agreements. According to the needs of the community in the field of maternal and infant care, the regional center plans and implements special projects for mothers, babies, and small children. Most of these projects focus on nutrition, recreation, orientation of mothers, home vegetable gardening, and home poultry-raising. The centers are administered by a committee of representatives and leaders of the community; technical services are directed by professionals such as doctors and social workers; technical and financial assistance are given by the LBA national office.

Family Welfare Services Systems

Under this heading are included private and tax-supported agencies that offer general family services and social services for workers. Private family services are usually provided by local agencies, which offer relief, casework services, sometimes group-work services, and referrals to community resources. Reference to these agencies has been made in various parts of this article. Social services for workers are of two kinds: social services operating inside the work place and social services provided by national tax-supported agencies. Inside the work place the employer is responsible for the general welfare of the workers during worker hours and for the administration of welfare services in such places as restaurants, canteens, recreation rooms, libraries, day-care centers for babies of working mothers; there are also referrals to community agencies which can help the worker and/or his family with their personal problems. Only large concerns are able to maintain such services. National tax-supported agencies are the Servico Social da Industria (the SESI—or Social Services for Industrial Workers) and the Servico Social do Comercio (the SESC—or Social Service for White-Collar Workers). Both were created in 1946 by federal law and are financed by taxes levied on industry and commerce. They are connected respectively to the Confederation of Industry and the Confederation of Commerce, which are large economic associations of businessmen. Both have national offices to establish policies and overall planning and regional offices to adapt national plans to regional needs and put programs into operation. They are very similar in programs and activities. Their main difference is their clientele: the SESI serving industrial workers and the SESC white-collar employees.

Furthermore, both must follow as closely as possible the policy of the II PND. Emphasis is put on development (education and integration of all classes of the population in the development process), through programs and projects to make the community conscious of its problems and take an active part in their solutions.

Explaining its social policy, the SESI has asserted that "as an organization created to perform welfare services, SESI will act as a channel for redistribution of national income and improvement of standards of living. The multiplied effect of such action will contribute to the acceleration of the national development process" (SESI, 1974b). SESI believes that welfare services to workers and their families will lead to a better performance of their duties as heads of a family, improve efficiency in their work, and contribute to the development of the country. SESI focuses on better conditions for education, health, nutrition, housing, social companionship, work hygiene, and leisure. Its activities are articulated with government programs at national, regional, and local levels "taking into consideration the needs and resources of each community."

In working with industrial plants, SESI (1974c) presents two different approaches: (1) with industrial plants, it offers systematic or occasional consultation regarding welfare aspects of the plants and stimulates the organization of social work departments in the plants, (2) with workers and their families, it offers direct services through social centers. In these latter, social clubs are organized and administered by their own members under supervision of SESI social workers. The object of these centers is to foster initiative and cooperation among members. Activities are organized according to the interests of the clientele: sports, recreation, homemaking and handicraft classes, health education and preventive medicine. Some local centers have developed social projects such as campaigns for vegetable gardens (Rio Grande do Norte), sports competitions and theatricals (São Paulo), education for trade unions (Rio Grande do Sul), nutrition for school children (Brasilia), etc.

SESC's objective is to improve the welfare and standards of living of white-collar employees and their families. SESC takes into consideration growing urbanization and the increasing number of men and women working in commercial activities. This population is, in general, young, single or newly married, with small children, and the great majority do not have more than an elementary education. Because of this, they earn low salaries, even though they are obliged to be presentably dressed and socially educated. SESC has adopted "permanent education" as its basic method of making good use of their leisure time (SESC, 1974a). Through its regional offices, SESC has established Activities Centers which offer adult education, homemaking, recreation, and sports, according to the interests of the clientele. Each center is quite different from the others. One of the SESC publications says that Activity Centers must be *umuaramos* (places where friends meet), and not just places for activities. SESC has been quite efficient in launching a large vacation camp program for low-income white-collar employees.

Unfortunately, because white-collar workers exist only in cities of some importance, SESC services have been largely limited to state capitals and other large cities—except in the state of São Paulo, where mobile units equipped with a library, radio, TV and a movie regularly visit small cities of the interior.

SESC and SESI have a large homemaking and family education program. Education for home and family life is considered part of a complete education, and raising home standards also contributes to the development process. In a special guideline leaflet, SESI (1974a) writes that the objective of this program consists in the "training of youth and adults to assume a role in the family, to acquire a capacity for good management of the home," and to develop other values, attitudes, and habits that will lead them to participate in the life of the family and the community. The program is very popular among women and girls, but courses in home repairs, painting, electricity, plumbing, and upholstery also attract men and adolescent boys. Both SESI and SESC national offices maintain a staff or professional social workers, home economists, teachers, librarians, and sports instructors to supervise regional offices and activities centers. This type of sophisticated staffing is more difficult for municipal agencies to acquire; the regional office has to train and supervise auxiliary workers.

Rural Development System

Brazil is still an agricultural country, and more than half of the population live in rural areas, some of them sparingly populated. For many years the land has been owned by rich farmers, who produce only one type of crop—coffee, sugar cane, or cocoa—or raise cattle. Through internal migration families have established themselves on lands without formalizing either the occupation or the sale. In the southern states, foreign immigrants of good quality have fostered medium-sized farms and modern know-how; in the northern states, however, a large rural population lives at a subsistence level on small rented parcels. After many attempts at agrarian reform, the federal government finally created the Instituto Nacional de Reforma Agraria (the INCRA—or National Institute for Agrarian Reform).

INCRA's objectives are a better and balanced distribution of lands, stimulation of land ownership duly legalized, colonization of unoccupied lands, substantial aid to farmers through subsidies, and organization of welfare services necessary for a normal life. INCRA works through local projects administered by local offices. The local office stimulates the community to cooperate in the execution and administration of the project. This is a way of training leaders (individuals or agencies) to take over the responsibility of the project when INCRA withdraws.

INCRA's projects are of two kinds: programs executed by INCRA itself and promotional or integrational programs executed in cooperation with other agencies and the community. Programs under INCRA's responsibility are predominantly economic, except for community development, the main objective of which is the integration of newcomers into the community or the fostering of better relations among all the families living in an area. INCRA also promotes projects covering the following subjects: education, health and social security, housing, cooperatives, rural credit, and commercialization of agricultural products.

INCRA does not work alone; planning, implementation, and evaluation are done with the participation of public and private agencies, whether national, regional, or local. State and municipal departments of education and MOBRAL help in educational programs; state departments and the Coordination of Maternal and Infant Care cooperate in preventive medicine and health education; BNH helps in building and remodeling of rural dwellings; FUNABEM aids in the welfare of children and adolescents; SESI and SESC work in small communities, and the Church in its traditional agencies. Rural credit is given by the Bank of Brazil through its local branches. Technical assistance to farmers who obtain supervised credit is given by the Associacao de Credito e Assistencia Rural (the ACAR—or Association for Rural Credit and Assistance). ACAR has a large home economics program with home economists and social workers to educate families by improving homemaking practices, hygiene, gardening, and child education. INCRA is certainly the best example of cooperation between private and public agencies and the community. It is a living demonstration of a complete system working toward a definite objective: the welfare of rural communities.

STAFF TRAINING FOR WELFARE WORKERS

Since World War II universities have been established in many cities in Brazil. Large universities have medical schools and usually also teacher's colleges and departments of sociology and psychology. (There are also many independent teachers' colleges.) There are 47 schools of social work, most of them belonging to a university. Some universities offer large postgraduate programs leading to master's and doctorate degrees in several disciplines, including social work. In graduate courses, students of education, psychology and social work have to do fieldwork under the supervision of local agencies. Supervision for social work is far superior to that of other professions; there is a careful selection of fieldwork agencies, and there is training of supervisors.

The welfare professions also have national associations which organize advanced courses, seminars, and national and regional conferences. The work is enhanced by the publication of several technical magazines. A large number of publications in Portuguese and other languages are available.

The professions of medical doctors, nurses, psychologists, teachers, and social workers are recognized by law. Professionals have to register their diplomas with the Ministry of Education and be members of the councils of their own professions if they want to practice their careers.

The government has tried to encourage welfare personnel to work in the interior of the country and in rural areas. Many universities have an "advanced campus" where students perform fieldwork. Such a campus may be established in a small community or underdeveloped area where the university maintains projects in health, education, sanitation, research, etc., to foster development of both the community and the students.

Another project, which has won the ever-increasing enthusiasm of students, is Projeto Rondon. This project operates during the vacation months—July and January-February. Small municipal or local projects are planned and implemented by a team of the students of medicine, nursing, social work, agriculture, sociology, administration, economics, and engineering. The projects organized by Projeto Rondon have two objectives: to train professionals in the various fields and to stimulate communities to work for their own welfare. Because they operate only during vacation months, the Rondon projects are time-limited. In the area of health, they concentrate on health education, hygiene and vaccination campaigns, training of rural midwives, and first aid; in administration, they focus on the organization of municipal services; in engineering, they emphasize the building and repair of local roads and bridges and the building of schools and small hospitals, sewage systems, markets, etc.; in welfare services, they organize community centers, recreation, sports, mutual aid projects, etc. The Projeto Rondon has concentrated on special areas selected according to their importance for regional development and for solving problems detected in the communities. All projects must be accomplished with the participation of the community in order to enable the people to take over when the Projeto Rondon withdraws from the area.

SOCIAL WORK METHODS IN WELFARE AGENCIES

Social work methods were introduced to Brazil in 1936 by European social workers. The first two schools of social work were founded in São Paulo in 1936 and Rio de Janeiro in 1937. Graduates from these schools organized the new schools established in the subsequent 15 years.

At the beginning, social work in Brazil was greatly influenced by European methods. Scholarships from the United States introduced what Latin Americans called the "American methods and processes." Social work development in Brazil has a long story of adaptation. During the first 20 years, casework, group-work and community organization were applied by various agencies having various objectives and clientele. Group-work soon complemented casework in family and health agencies and was the principle process applied to rural projects, slum clearance, and housing projects. However, the application of these methods varied, and social work schools had different methods for different problems. Gradually all the processes merged into one; it was impossible for small agencies to have different social workers for each problem.

In rural communities, the interprofessional programs have only one social worker, who must know and apply the three processes. Social work is now viewed as a unified method.

Early on, social workers realized that direct services to clientele were insufficient as a contribution to the development of the country. Efforts were made to have graduate social workers administer social services departments and small agencies. Gradually, experienced social workers were appointed to planning and evaluation projects, both in rural and urban development programs in national, regional, public, and private agencies.

CONCLUSION

The main characteristics of the system of social services in Brazil are (1) the integration of public and private agencies at all levels, (2) the coordination of planning and evaluation to aid less resourceful agencies to work in the community and reach their objectives, and (3) the coordination of agencies with the objectives of the II PND.

Difficulties arise everywhere. The successful road is a strenuous one. Much has still to be done, but progress has begun and can no longer stop. Social workers in Brazil are conscious that a new age is slowly but surely coming to crown their efforts with success.

REFERENCES

Acao Comunitaria do Brasil (1974). Metodologia da acao comunitaria no Brasil. Rio de Janeiro: Author.
BNH (1974a). "Alternativa da politica assistencial Brasileira" (Serie Verde, Ano VIII). Rio de Janeiro: Author.
——— (1974b). Legislacao basica. Rio de Janeiro: Author.
CBCISS (1974). Report presented to the 17th International Conference of Social Welfare, Nairobi.
——— (1975). Boletin Informativo (Ano XII, no. 2).
FUNABEM (1975). Politica nacional do bem estar do menor. Rio de Janeiro: Author.
INCRA (1971). Metodologia e pragramacao operacional dos projetos de assentamento de agricultores. Rio de Janeiro: Author.
——— (n.d.). Atos normativos (Documento de Trabalho no 13). Rio de Janeiro: Author.
Ministerio da Saude, Coordenacao Materno-Infantil (1974). Programa de saude materno-infantil. Brasilia: Author.
MOBRAL (1973). Documento basico. Brasilia: Author.
PLANAP (1973). Plano nacional de habitacai popular: Objetivos e normas de execucao. Rio de Janeiro: Author.
Planasa (1974). Solucao Brasileira de problemas Brasileiros: Objectivos e normas de execucao. Rio de Janeiro: Author.
Planejamento e Desenvolvimento (1974). "A nova estrategia que ampara o homem Brasileiro." Numero especial (Outubro).
——— (1975). "A tarefa a ser conquistada." April.

SESC (1974a). "Diretrizes Gerais de acao." D.N.
——— (1974b). "Normas Gerais apra aplicacao das diretrizes Gerais de acao do SESC." D.N.
SESI (1974a). "Educacao familiar no SESI."
——— (1974b). "General action guide."
——— (1974c). "Servico social do brabalho no SESI."
VAZ da COSTA, R. (1971). Urban growth: Foundation of economic development. Rio de Janeiro: BNH.

13

PANAMA: SOCIAL SERVICES, PUBLIC AND PRIVATE

LUZ E. RODRIGUEZ S.

Although there are elements in Panama's political constitution and in the objectives of the main governmental institutions to formulate a national social welfare policy, the nation lacks such a policy. Due to that fact and for the purpose of writing this paper, I have intended to elaborate on the concept of social welfare services as follows: social welfare services are programs directly contributing to a rise in the standard of living of the majority of the population, to an increase in civic participation, and to a better satisfaction of basic needs. Such programs aim to help people in both and individual and a cooperative way to eliminate the causes of social inequality and injustice and to strengthen or change basic structures. These programs are related to such other fields as health, education, land reform, and labor and include services in the areas of human development, prevention, treatment, and rehabilitation. They should be based on knowledge of the country's realities and implemented with the participation of the population during the whole process and at all levels.

Benefits and Services

The country offers the following social welfare services to different groups of the population:

Community: Counseling on organization, informal education, health, community councils and government, health committees, farming settlements, agrarian councils; political education, citizen participation, infrastructural needs such as roads, schools, etc. financed by matching funds; training of volunteers and leaders for community work; community orchards and vegetable gardens; training in health, education, and mental health; studies, investigations, and surveys; health programming, supervision and evaluation; helping the community to implement the sectorial goals on production, consumption, capital formation; recreation; community pharmacies; housing commissions.

Preschool Children: Nurseries; psychosocial orientation centers; services for personal and family problems; clinics; mental health recuperation services; kindergarten.

Children: School lunches; advice on personal problems; institutional care; physical and vocational rehabilitation; recreation, correctional services (probation, parole, institutional care, home vigilance with either weekend or night stays at institutions); public libraries; postinstitutional care; folklore, art, and sports; scholarships; organized recreation; promotional health services; outpatient and hospital services.

Youth: Extracurricular training (vocational training, civic education, training for summer volunteers); institutional care; correctional services (adoption, probation and parole, home vigilance); training as voluntary health educators and leaders; orientation and guidance for scholarships; recreation; public libraries; counseling on personal problems; services for rural youth (civic education, farming, poultry).

Adults (both sexes): Consumer education; civic and political education; social aspects of health; in-service training; building rural latrines; building and maintenance of rural roads; modification of nutritional habits; improving rural housing; handicrafts; counseling on personal problems, small industries.

Public and private employees and their families: Administrative orientation, housing; counseling on family and personal problems; recreation; political, nutritional, and health education; cooperatives; physical and vocational rehabilitation; promotion of health; in-service training.

Women (rural, housewives, pregnant women, special groups): Family life education; cooperatives, improving of housing conditions; nutrition; health education; services for interfamily problems; family budgeting; rearing of children; counseling on personal problems; corrections; handicrafts; cooking.

Rural men: Cooperatives; participation in local government; housing projects; political and civic education; changing of mental attitudes that interfere with the process of development; learning modern ways of production and farming.

Industrial workers: Health and social security education; counseling on personal problems; planning with labor unions; cooperatives; recreation; housing; scholarships for workers' children; registration into social security services for families of insured workers.

Occasionally employed adults: Vocational training; cooperatives; housing; nutrition.

Indians: Nutrition; cooperatives; health education.

Delinquents: Correctional institutions; vocational rehabilitation; counseling on personal problems.

Aged: Union for retirees; institutional care; counseling on personal problems; ambulatory social services.

Families: Family life education; services for interfamily relations; housing; nutrition; rearing of children; health education; family economic enterprises; family recreation; family psychotherapy; family allowances; family orchards.

Eligibility for the Programs

Generally speaking, the whole population is entitled to access to the programs listed above. Major limitations for accomplishing this would be the lack of financial and human resources; the lack of a national planning system in the social welfare area; and the geographical inaccessibility of certain populations (groups in the bigger cities are more likely to have access to social welfare programs). On the other hand, although some programs such as health charge a certain amount for providing services, no one is excluded because of inability to pay; and the social security system is designed to cover such concerns as sickness, maternity, disability, old age, death, professional disability, and family allowances for the wife and children (up to 18 years of age) of retired and disabled insured persons. According to the social security law all employees are insured—both public and private, national, provincial, and local; those self-employed or working part-time or occasionally; domestics; and pensioners. Health care under social security covers the wife or concubine, children up to 18 years of age (25 years, if still a student), invalids, the mother of the insured person if she is living with him and the father if he is over 60 years of age (Panama, Goceta Oficial, 1975). Eligibility is determined through policies established at national, regional, or local levels by the government, the provinces, the municipalities, the counties, private enterprise, and church and civic groups. More and more the opinion of the people at the grass-roots level is taken into consideration for determining eligibility through the county representatives, the local councils, and various organized groups.

Population Groups Served by the Various Programs

In general, most services are delivered to communities and population groups in the middle- and the lower-income brackets; however, there is no uniform collection of data among social welfare agencies to show the number and characteristics of the population that they serve, and there is little coordination among programs. The programs are intended to cover the majority of the population, and some emphasis has been given to the rural areas. A study exists which identifies the different levels of poverty in Panama according to four social indicators, but as yet no policy has been formulated to act accordingly.

There are no studies at the national level determining the several social welfare services needed by the majority of the population; there is nevertheless a trend toward decentralization (in terms of administration, planning, and services) which could contribute to the formulation of a more accurate diagnosis of the situation, to the establishment of more services, and to the coordination of programs. (The Constitution created Provincial Councils for coordination—their functions being to promote and coordinate all official activities at the provincial level and to serve as consultation bodies; such councils have planners from the national planning office among their personnel.) Some of the facts that give an idea of the amount of the population covered by social welfare services are as follows:

By 1973 the social security system covered 32.7% of the civil population; 16.1% of the women and 41.9% of the economically active population (Panama, Contraloría General de la República, 1974).

By 1972 approximately 67% of the population was covered by health programs (Panama, Ministerio de Planificación y Política Económica, 1974:9).

The ratio between social workers and inhabitants in the health field is one to 24,234. In the province where the capital city is located, it is one to 8,009 (Primer Seminario Regional de Trabajo Social en Salud, 1974:10).

The Community Development Program in 1973 was working in 1,400 communities (out of a total of 9,313 communities); in the same year there existed 828 health committees at the community level (Panama, Consejo de Bienestar Social y Desarrollo Comunal, 1974:43-47).

Administrative Organization of the Programs

The programs are governmental (national and regional level), municipal (local level), and private (business enterprises, churches, civic groups). There are matching programs, and, in such cases, whoever provides funds has some administrative responsibility for the program (supervision, consultation, budget control, etc.). More and more there is a tendency to decentralize the administration of some governmental programs (health, for instance) so as to delegate major responsibilities to local authorities. In general, the administration and the supervision of programs can be handled by the same person or by different persons with different degrees of communication among them. In the health programs there are national and local teams which administer and supervise the program (a team may be composed of a social worker, a health educator, a nutritionist, an agronomist, a nurse, a sanitarian inspector, and a community helper; a physician may attend meetings, but he is not considered a part of the team). The Social Welfare Council offers consultation to members upon request; it is a private organization whose purpose is to help public and private organizations working in the social welfare field, mainly by planning, coordinating, and training personnel in the social welfare field.

Financing the Programs

There are different sources of funding for the social welfare programs; they can be public or private or both. The public programs are financed by the national and municipal governments; private programs are funded by business enterprises, churches, and civic organizations. Matching funds can be provided by the government at the national and local level, by the Social Welfare Council at the local level, and by international or foreign organizations both public and private, which can give financial help to either governmental or private programs. The social security system is funded with contributions from employees and employers both public and private; the Catholic Church and other civic organizations can organize fund-raising campaigns to finance programs. The Social Welfare Council organizes an annual fund-raising with purposes of financing the council as such and of giving financial help to some of its members.

Staffing and Manpower Patterns

In general only those on a professional level—social workers—receive a formal education through the Department of Social Work, University of Panama. These social workers receive a five-year generic course, at the end of which the students receive a "Licenciatura" degree. This education prepares social workers for direct service by providing them with some basic knowledge and field instruction in administration. Most of the social workers are working in the metropolitan area, and 74% of them are employed in the health field. The heads of social work programs are, in general, graduate social workers with postgraduate training (MSW) and with in-service training or formal accelerated courses in administration and supervision. The professional practice of social work is regulated by an official decree, which prescribes the following requirements: An "administrator" must have a license to practice social work and a minimum of three years experience as a supervisor; he preferably should have a postgraduate degree, knowledge of social planning and policy, and experience in the administration of social work at the national level. A "supervisor" must have a license to practice social work, at least three years of field work experience, courses in the supervision of social workers, and experience in administration and personnel management (Panama, Gaceta Oficial, 1963:1). The social work programs within the Ministry of Health require a minimum of five years of experience and/or postgraduate training for their administrators and supervisors.

At the middle personnel level are the community workers, extension agents, social work auxiliaries, etc. The social work auxiliaries are students in social work. The community workers are persons with a high school education and in-service training; since 1973 the United Nations Development Program (UNDP) has participated in training such personnel and has offered three formal courses. The extension agents have a complete high school education, which may include specialized training in the subject. The School of Home Economics within the

Agricultural College offers courses of nine semesters' duration, and graduates obtain a degree as home economics educators; the majority of such graduates are already working in home economics education programs at the high school level. Administrators and supervisors of personnel working in the community may have a university degree in such diverse disciplines as law, administration, or sociology. The supervisors of the extension agents within the Ministry of Health are nutritionists; the supervisors for the extension agents in the Ministry of Agriculture may be graduates from the School of Home Economics.

Formal training programs are not available for volunteers. However, some voluntary organizations give initial orientation to new members, and at the community level, occasional courses are offered to volunteers. The Social Welfare Council has offered periodic seminars and in-service training courses to members in the areas of direct service and administration and also in such special areas as budgeting or characteristics of population groups. In 1973, the Community Development Program offered 38 seminars to 1,638 leaders at the national level and 4 seminars to 238 persons (including elected officials) at the county level. University and high school students from public and private institutions work in rural communities as volunteers during their vacation time. They receive some training before going to the communities. The University of Panama and public school students are trained by the Ministries of Education and Health, which, at the same time, administer the programs. The students from one Catholic school, for whom this community work is compulsory, receive more thorough training; the director of the school administers the program, and the school teachers supervise the students.

Assessment of Outcome

In the programs staffed by graduate social workers, there are several devices to evaluate the direct service rendered, among them formal data-gathering sheets and periodic staff or team meetings. In the local health centers there are several kinds of evaluation: the team meets periodically and the national team meets with the local team every three months to evaluate the program; the seminars offered at the community level are evaluated with the participation of the population served. In some other programs we find that periodic diagnosis of communities is done in order to update information and plan accordingly, that verbal or written reports are presented in order to evaluate a program, that periodic meetings are held by a staff with the people it serves, that teams meet weekly to evaluate and plan according to their findings, and, finally, that some programs do not carry out any kind of evaluation. The students from the Catholic high school evaluated their programs, and the findings were published.

With regard to research, the Health Programs have carried out several investigations—for instance, the evaluation of 3,094 families living in communities where health committees exist, and the summary of seminars held at the community level. The Social Service Department in the social security system has carried out the following investigations: a survey of the more relevant socioeconomic characteristics of 100 families living in an agricultural settlement incorporated into the social security system, and an evaluation of the Health Education Program. The Community Development Program has performed several social investigations to understand the national reality. Some students of the Department of Social Work, University of Panama, have written their theses on subjects related to social welfare services in the country.

REFERENCES

CALVO SUCRE, A.E. (1974). "Las droyecciones de cambio en la atención médica integral por la Caja de Seguro Social al asumir la responsabilidad de la integración de los subsectores gubernamentales de salud" (Curso nacional sobre teoría y práctica de la seguridad social, Panamá). Unpublished paper.

Editora Renovación S.A. y Caja de Seguro Social (1970). Legislación vigente: Art. 39, 43, 45, 50 y 55. Panama City: Impresora Panamá S.A.

Panama, Consejo de Bienestar Social y Desarrollo Comunal, Comité Nacional para Asuntos Internacionales de Bienestar Social (1974). Desarrollo y Participación: Implicaciones operacionales para el bienestar social (Informe del Comité Nacional a la XVII Conferencia Internacional de Bienestar Social). Panama City: Editora de la Nación.

Panama, Contraloría General de la República, Dirección de Estadística y Censo (1970). Censos nacionales: Características de la vivienda (vol. 2). Panama City: Author.

––– (1974). Panamá en cifras, 1969-1973. Panama City: Author.

––– (1975). Censos nacionales de 1970: Compendio general de población (vol. 3). Panama City: Author.

Panama, Gaceta Oficial (1963). "Decreto-ley No. 25 de 25 de Septiembre de 1963, por el cual se reglamenta el ejercicio de la profesión de trabajo social en todo el territorio de la República." No. 14, 978 (October 8).

––– (1975). "Ley No. 15 (Marzo) por la cual se modifica la Ley Orgánica de la Caja de Seguro Social: Art. 2, 41, 53-B." No. 17, 830 (April 30).

Panama, Ministerio de Planificación y Política Económica (1974). "Radiografía de la pobreza: Resumen." Unpublished paper.

Primer Seminario Regional de Trabajo Social en Salud (1974). "Informe de Panamá." Unpublished paper.

Veraguas, Jefatura Provincial de (1973). "Programa de trabajo social para la provincia de Veraguas (Junio)." Unpublished paper.

INTERVIEWS

Matilde Gómez, Master en Trabajo Social, Jefe del Departamento de Trabajo Social, Ministerio de Salud

María de González Licenciada, Sub-jefe del Departamento de Trabajo Social de la Caja de Seguro Social

Digna Quintero, Licenciada, Jefe del Departamento Téenico de Trabajo Social, Alcaldía del Distrito de Panamá

María Luisa de Quintero, Trabajadora Social, Jefe del Departamento de Trabajo Social del Tribunal Tutelar de Menores

Elvia Quinzada, Licenciada, Encargada de la Dirección General de Bienestar Social, Ministerio de Trabajo y Bienestar Social

Nivia de Vargas, Licenciada, Jefe del Departamento de Trabajo Social de la Cervecería Nacional

María Villarreal, Profesora, y Directora, Escuela de Educación para el Hogar, Facultad de Agronomía, Universidad de Panamá

14

CURRENT SOCIAL SERVICE ARCHITECTURE:
A RETROSPECTIVE APPRAISAL

DANIEL THURSZ
JOSEPH L. VIGILANTE

Our goal for the first two volumes of this series was to bring together the experience of more than 20 diverse countries throughout the globe and to make available a fairly comprehensive view of the social service architecture of these lands. Assembling and analyzing the reports, often written by colleagues overseas, was a difficult task. The comparison of these experiences remains a difficult if not impossible goal. Language differences, for example, make it difficult for American editors to comprehend essential elements and important nuances that are often hidden in translation. The variables that affect the development of structures in different parts of the world, however, are endless. Each country presents a special set of circumstances, and the structure of its delivery system is inevitably affected by its history, economic ability, political ideology, cultural heritage, religious traditions, degree of ethnic heterogeneity, military needs, whether imaginary or real, and so on.

Perhaps one of the most rewarding results deriving from the investment of time and energy in this project has been the opportunity for an intensive overview of what social welfare systems are like in these many places. A part of this reward is the recognition that there is a commonality of understanding among social workers about what is meant by human needs and some of the necessary tools—institutional and individual—required to provide a structured response to need. We have found similarities in programs where we did not expect that they would exist. We have uncovered commonalities in need recognition as well as commonalities of omission in response to need in many countries. Our review of the materials in these two volumes suggests to us that there are important identifiable differences and similarities in the varied approaches, new and old, to the development of social service systems throughout the world. Our reading suggests to us that these similarities and differences have significant implications not only for the organization, administration, and manpower development for the social services but also for the possible transferability of services from one country to another.

Predominant among the reports from almost every country is the *importance of human values* in the organization and development of social services systems. Values have been variously described—from those concerned with the dignity and worth of the individual and those concerned with social change to those which emphasize the importance of "solidarity and mutuality" in the development of services. This term "solidarity and mutuality" is identified in the report from Yugoslavia, but, although an emphasis on mutuality tends to be more typical of socialist countries, it was also identified in nonsocialist countries as an important aspect of delivery systems. In the Western countries it is the emphasis of the "social" component of social welfare that illuminates the mutuality connotation. However, it is not without some significance, we believe, that socialist countries like Yugoslavia also refer to the importance of individual "personal" needs. We would suggest some evidence, therefore, of an effort in the development of social welfare delivery systems to bring together individualized services with social responsibility.

All countries further report *relatively wide gaps between needs and services.* This phenomenon apparently is as true of pre-industrialized countries as it is of post-industrialized countries. Nowhere, apparently, have nations on this planet as yet achieved a state of grace whereby the personal social needs of the citizenry are adequately met. To make the observation may only beg the question as to whether such a state of nirvana is possible. Be that as it may, the gaps remain quite clear.

In many countries there is a common *trend toward decentralized social services systems.* The move to the neighborhood level as the operational nexus for social service delivery systems is an example. It appears that there is a search for some way to build in services at "a caring scale," and it is strongly suggested by the information we have obtained that large public bureaucratic systems (with some rare exceptions, which will be discussed later) seem not to achieve the goal of delivering massive services "at caring scale." The evidence is to be found in such widely different national cultures as that of the United Kingdom and that of the People's Republic of China. It is not our purpose to illuminate or enunciate all the areas in which we see similarities in the approach to social service systems development but only to illustrate representative cases where they do indeed exist.

There is an enormous wealth of material in these two volumes that should help reduce the complacency or rigidity that seems to characterize the design of service delivery systems. More accurately, perhaps, is the problem that the *systems have not been consciously designed.* Social services systems are not the result of long-range policy planning; rather, they spring up haphazardly in response to crisis and urgent need. Many programs, established in response to crisis as temporary measures, endure and resist change.

Our study leads us to a deepened awareness that throughout the world there is agreement among social workers and others concerned with the issues of social services about what is meant by human needs and some of the tools—both institutional and individual—required to provide a structure of response to such common needs. At the same time, it becomes abundantly clear that in most countries—regardless of political ideology—*there are divisions among policy makers as to the role of government and the extent to which such needs can be met or should be met on a universal basis.* Even in communist countries, one finds continued concern for the "deserving" and "undeserving" members of the society, as illustrated by the following quotation from the action program of the Czechoslavakian Communist Party adopted in 1968:

The pursuit of equality has developed in an unprecedented manner, and this fact has become one of the most important obstacles to intensive economic development and higher living standards. The negative aspects of equality are that lazy people, passive individuals and irresponsible employees profit at the expense of dedicated and diligent employees, unskilled workers profit at the expense of skilled ones and those who are backward from the point of view of technology profit at the expense of those with initiative and talent.

The debates which characterize the conflicts in ideology in the United States are reflected in almost every part of the world, including Great Britain and the Scandinavian countries, which have been defined as models to be imitated and emulated by the United States. The worldwide debate can easily be summarized in a phrase taken from remarks made by Margaret Thatcher, leader of the Conservative party of Great Britain, in a recent lecture given for the Institute for Economic Studies: "Government must temper what may be socially desirable with what is economically reasonable."

The dream of universal services within nations—desirable as it may seem to most students of social policy and service delivery structure—must also be contrasted with the fact that in most parts of the world those in greatest pain are not served. No review of the articles appearing in these two volumes can leave the reader with the sense that we are close to being a world in which all personal social needs are met. On the contrary, one is forced by the evidence to ponder means for establishing priorities on a worldwide basis if we are to ever achieve a sense of peace on this planet. The inequality of services throughout the world parallels or exceeds the lack of equitable distribution of resources within countries.

Another fascinating aspect of the review of the material assembled in the two volumes is the degree to which large delivery systems are defined as inadequate, leading to a search in most countries for decentralized social service systems. However, the decentralization of services without adequate decentralization of decision making creates enormous problems. This was acknowledged in the United States by one of the study committees created by the Office of

Management and Budget, within the Executive Office of the President. The report states: "Taken together, the pressure on the political leaders of State and local government represent a formidable management challenge. What they are being asked to do with limited authority and generally brief tenures is to provide—from a highly complex and non-harmonious mix of programs, fiscal sources and administrative entities—an integrated package of services tailored to the special needs of their jurisdictions." On the other hand, the assignment of both responsibility and authority to a series of decentralized bodies brings with it the danger of a lack of coherence in the country's overall policy, lack of accountability, and, in some cases, the vagaries of individual choices and prejudices with the concomitant result of lack of equity for all who need services. In some of the countries reporting within these two volumes, the hope of millions depends on a nationally directed and administered thrust. Here again, it is clear that there are enormous differences in the current reality of these countries and the options available to them.

The desire for a "caring system" has led many countries to explore the communal rather than the institutional route for meeting the needs of some of the population, especially those accused of crimes or delinquent behavior or those who have suffered from mental illness. For instance, those responsible for the organization and structure of social services in the United States and Scotland are equally concerned with the lack of available halfway houses for adults and youth who are between the institution and the community in rehabilitative systems. However, the concern for reducing alienation and alleviating the impact of bureaucracy goes far beyond the establishment of halfway houses. The report from Yugoslavia emphasizes the importance of "solidarity and mutuality." Volunteers play a crucial role in the delivery of social services in Poland. In the People's Republic of China the small group, in which primary relationships are developed, serves as the basis for most social services—meeting the need for individualized and potentially tailor-made services within the context of an immense country with a population of equal dimension.

If most countries share the same ideals and are aghast at the difficulties in reaching such goals—regardless of the level of their economic and social development—it is fascinating to discover how their more immediate concerns tend also to be similar.

Throughout all the reports received, there is ample evidence of an articulated concern with intrafamily problems characterized by tension in family relationships. Yet those who have had even a brief experience with the education at American professional schools of social workers from countries outside the United States have been chastising each other for years that social workers returning to their home countries had little use for family counseling techniques and other interventive methodologies designed to assist individuals or groups with their personal relationship problems.

Another problem area that seems to have reached universal importance is the care of the aged in both pre-industrial as well as industrialized countries. For some countries, the aged constitutes a new population at risk—notably Israel, where the founding generation is becoming older, creating essentially novel issues for such innovative institutions as the kibbutz. As health maintenance efforts meet with some success, death, which essentially has reduced the problem of aging, has been pushed back, creating both a greater population and a vulnerable and needing sector. Coupled with little if any reduction in the birth rate, the population problem puts new pressures on the working population in the middle years to support an ever-widening youth and aging segment.

Services to youth generally—and specifically to that portion of the youth population that is deviant, with problems ranging from truancy, vagrancy, and delinquency to drug and alcohol abuse—represent one more area in which there seems to be almost universal concern. To this list must be added care for orphans and for abandoned, neglected, or abused children.

Finally, we must add to this list of common issues that seem to transcend national boundaries an increasing challenge involving minority or so-called native populations. No country seems to be immune to the peculiar problems of meshing various national or ethnic groups, of differentiating services according to the particular needs and folkways of such groups, and of meeting the accusations of having neglected such populations in the development of national policies. There are few long-lasting homogeneous nations these days. In Israel, the issue centers on both the Sephardic Jewish and Arab populations. In the United States, it is the black, Spanish-speaking Americans, and Indians. In South Africa, the conflict centers on blacks and those of mixed blood. In Great Britain, the focus is on the immigrants from the Commonwealth countries that often inhabit the slums of the large industrial cities. In many European countries, the migrant industrial and farm workers are pointed to as suffering from neglect in social services, and so on.

Another major area in which one can find a great deal of similarity among the nations is that involving the organization and administration of social services. Almost all countries report the *relative haphazard nature of the organization of social services*. Social welfare experts in the Western countries should not be surprised at this, since this continues to be a major problem for the more advanced countries despite major efforts over the past two decades to reduce the overlapping services of multiple agencies and to clarify the relationship between voluntary and tax-supported agencies. Coordinated planning systems for attacking major social problems remain an elusive goal for most countries. It should be noted that in this regard Sweden and the United Kingdom are perhaps exceptions to the rule. In addition to these two countries, there is evidence that in Australia, the People's Republic of China, and Poland a great deal of concern is being directed toward developing national systems for administering human services. The efforts of these countries—despite their contrasting ideologies—may reveal, upon subsequent evaluations, some desirable directions for other countries to follow. It must be stressed that, in all the countries listed above, the social services do become instruments of national policy. This, in turn, raises questions about the political power and influence of social welfare as an institution and the potential use of that power in future socioeconomic political planning.

The dilemma which we noted in an earlier section of this appraisal of the current state of social service development has a particular significance in the discussion of planning to avoid or reduce fragmentation of services. In most countries, the social welfare responsibility is already spread in a variety of administrative departments at the national and subnational levels. Where social welfare planning does exist, it is usually because the overall responsibility lies clearly in one top governmental system such as a ministry for social and health affairs. At issue is the desirability of organizing social services in a single central department which acts as a service organization for other departments or governments in contrast to an alternate scheme which calls for establishing social service units in discrete state or federal agencies or ministries such as housing, labor, and the like.

The degree to which income-maintenance programs should be fused with social services continues to perplex most of the architects of such systems. Even United States proponents of a sharp separation are now having second thoughts as they realize the need to provide additional support to families receiving cash benefits. In too many instances, the real needs of a family are ignored because they are "handled" by personnel trained to deal with cash benefits only. On the other hand, many who are seeking social service support also require financial assistance—without the long bureaucratic process of referral to a totally separate agency.

Furthermore, in some countries the availability of both income support and social services is tied to being identified as part of the working force. Once that status has been lost—or if indeed it has never been gained—the individual may not be eligible for any assistance and must depend on the historic but limited charitable efforts of the church and volunteer groups, if not on begging.

Not all countries make an equal commitment to income-maintenance programs as well as social services programs. In some, one or the other may lag considerably behind. In Australia and Canada, for instance, there is considerable recognition of the need for social services; yet the major emphasis is on income-maintenance programs. Neither of these countries has the long tradition of voluntary social services which the United Kingdom possesses. It is possible to hypothesize that without a history of voluntary services, moving social services into the public sector may be unusually difficult. Furthermore, we find that among all nations, regardless of their level of industrialization, there is considerable confusion as to the relative role of government and the voluntary sector in the delivery of social services. There is little movement toward solving that issue. Whereas the move toward public and government-financed social services has been the trend since World War II, the accomplishments of this trend are being challenged. Alvin Schorr, in delivering the Titmus Memorial Lecture in

Coventry, England, in 1974, questioned whether public responsibility for social services had produced the kinds of humane services that are needed. Although voluntary agencies continue to play a major role in most countries included in these volumes, we observe increasing efforts by governments to purchase services from voluntary agencies, if not to provide them with outright subsidies. As with all government support, the private sectors lose a degree of independence and the freedom to innovate. The paradox is that the concept of voluntarism seems to be enjoying a renaissance in many parts of the world, again without regard to the political or economic system of the countries involved. Several of the reports highlight the importance of "self-helpers" or "volunteers." The reliance, for example, on informal, family, and local community groups for the delivery of social services typically in the Soviet Union and the People's Republic of China is being considered by other nations, including the United States and Great Britain. The concept of a service corps such as the Peace Corps or VISTA in the United States is being copied in other lands, notably in Iran and Israel. Volunteers, small self-help groups, ethnically oriented and differentiated services, and neighborhood social service shopping centers are among the innovations that are piercing national and political ideological boundaries throughout the world. At the same time, the trend toward national income-maintenance programs administered centrally or under specific national dictates is continuing.

The training of personnel to conduct the many functions grouped under social services varies considerably from country to country. In some, like the People's Republic of China, the concept of a professionally trained social worker is rejected on both ideological and pragmatic grounds. The local group, with its various actors bridging experience and age, is expected to provide the necessary assistance. In others, the general level of education remains low and training opportunities in universities are nonexistent. On-the-job training provides the only substitute for professional education. In the United States, where professional social work training has been most developed, the issue of the relevance to the provision of concrete services, especially to the low income population, remains as a critical problem. The interest in therapy based on "conversations with a purpose" continues at a very high level among graduate students in schools of social work, and there is a general antipathy to activities that are designed to provide concrete assistance to poor people looking for jobs, adequate shelter, or clothing or similar needs.

The irony contained in the advancement of social work into the realm of the professions throughout the world is that the new status granted to professional graduate social workers will create more opportunities to provide important services to the middle and upper classes either in voluntary agencies or through private practice. The United States experience may serve to provide some important warnings to other countries that wish to increase the effectiveness of the social service staff through university education.

As we close this retrospective appraisal, it is important to note that in two countries we have reports indicating that the national policy contains an assumption that different systems of social services should be designed for different races and that the services for people with white skin should be inherently superior to those given to persons with black skin. The differentiation is built into all aspects of the social service systems, including benefits to clients and education and salary for workers. This last instance can serve as a powerful reminder that social service architecture depends initially on the policies developed for social welfare in any particular setting and then ultimately rests on a foundation of values held by the majority of the citizenry in democratic lands or the values held by those who rule in nondemocratic countries. Without a commitment to the sanctity of human life and to improving the quality of life for all inhabitants, the architecture of service delivery will have little meaning. However, even with such a commitment, the problems of delivering such services within the resources available loom large and extremely difficult to overcome. We are pledged to using this medium to share the exploits and the failures of our colleagues throughout the world in the hope that some of the experiences reported here will prove helpful to others facing similar issues in other parts of our globe.

NOTES ON THE CONTRIBUTORS

JOSEFINA ACOSTA C., born in Colombia, has her M.S.W. from St. Louis University. After teaching high school in Colombia and Brazil, she became Director of Neighborhood Centers and then Assistant Director of the Welfare City Department of Bogotá She is currently Assistant Professor at the Universidad Nacional de Colombia, Social Work Department.

THOMAS BRENNAN is Professor of Social Administration and Director of the Department of Social Work at the University of Sydney. Born in England, he is an Honours graduate in Economics, Cambridge, and a Fellow of the Academy of Social Sciences, Australia. He has been Visiting Professor at the University of Hull in the United Kingdom, Director of Govan Social Survey at the University of Glasgow, and Director of Research in Social Science at the University of Swansea, Wales.

HENNING FRIIS, who holds a Master's of Economics from the University of Copenhagen, has been Social Science Advisor to the Danish Ministries of Social Affairs and Labour, Executive Director of the Danish National Institute of Social Research, and member of International Social Science Council. He has been consultant to Egypt, Ireland, India, Philippines, and most recently, Bangladesh. He is presently a member of the Board of Trustees, United Nations Institute for Training and Research.

ANDERS FROM is a Research Associate and Assistant Research Director at the Danish National Institute of Social Research. He has also been Assistant Lecturer at the University of Copenhagen, where he received his Master of Economics degree.

JOHN M. GANDY, Professor of Social Work at the University of Toronto, received his D.S.W. at this school. He has been Director of Planning of the Social Planning Council of Metropolitan Toronto and Director of Research for the Hyde Park Youth Project, Chicago, which demonstrated a coordinated approach to prevention and treatment of youth problems on a neighborhood basis. He has been on the board of the Ontario Welfare Council and the Volunteer Centre of Metropolitan Toronto. He has been awarded the National Health and Welfare Fellowship, the Senior Welfare Fellowship, the Laidlaw Fellowship, and the Dora Wilensky Memorial Fund.

ISADORA HARE, born and educated in the Republic of South Africa, has been living in the United States since 1974. A graduate of the University of the Witwatersrand, Johannesburg, she holds the degree of Master of Arts in Social Work, and was awarded Cum Laude for research in field instruction. She is currently employed as a School Social Worker in the Fairfax County Public Schools in the Washington, D.C., metropolitan area, and is a member of the CSWE and the NASW. She has been on the faculty of the University of the Witwatersrand and the School of Social Work and Community Planning at the University of Maryland. In 1973 she spent three months in Great Britain on a British Council bursary to study trends in social work education and practice in England and Scotland.

MARITA V. LINDSTROM was born in Helsinki, Finland. She received most of her education in the United States, where she received a B.S. from Empire State College, New York, and her Master of Social Work degree from Adelphi University. Presently she is serving as Faculty Advisor to the BSW candidates at Adelphi School of Social Work. Her previous activities include youth counseling and social work with alcohol abusers.

BRIAN McKENDRICK received his Master of Social Science in Social Work at the University of Natal. After several years with a multiracial child guidance clinic in Durban, he was appointed Director of WITSCO, a community organization agency in Johannesburg. He is on the staff of the School of Social Work, University of the Witwatersrand, Johannesburg, and is presently Assistant Director and Project Leader of a national survey on the selection and training of social work manpower in South Africa.

SUMIKO NAKAMURA, born in Tokyo, received a B.A. in English at Doshisha University and a B.A. in Sociology at Shorter College in Rome, Georgia. She received her M.S.S. from Adelphi University. Since her return to Japan she has been Deputy Chief of the Aichi

Women's and Minors' Bureau and Ministry of Labor in Nagoya and is currently at the Hea《
Office in Tokyo. This office is concerned with improving the status of women, protectin
and promoting the welfare of women and children.

LUZ E. RODRIGUEZ S. received her M.A. from the School of Social Service Administra‹
tion, University of Chicago, after receiving her undergraduate degree from the Universida《
de Panama. She has been Director of the School of Social Work at the Universidad d《
Panama and Professor of the School of Social Work at Catholic University, Dominica›
Republic. She has been president of the Panamanian Association of Social Workers an‹
president of the Latin American Association of Schools of Social Work. She has now retire《
and is doing voluntary work as President of the Union de Ciudadanas de Panama and th《
Social Welfare Council.

ALBERT ROSE, Professor and Dean of the University of Toronto School of Social Work
received his Ph.D. in Economics and Social Statistics from the University of Illinois. Hi‹
many community activities have included serving as President of the Canadian Associatio›
of Social Workers, Chairman of the Consultative Committee on Housing Policies for the Cit;
of Toronto, and Vice-Chairman of the Community Relations Committee, Canadian Jewis‹
Congress. He has been the recipient of the Canadian Centennial Medal from the Governmen›
of Canada and is an Honorary Life Member of the Community Planning Association o‹
Canada.

RUTH SIDEL is a graduate of Wellesley College and the Boston University of Social Work
She has worked with emotionally disturbed preschool children and has been Social Worl‹
Supervisor at Comprehensive Child Care Project associated with the Albert Einstein Colleg《
of Medicine in the Bronx. She spent part of 1971 and 1972 in the People's Republic o‹
China studying the role of women, child care facilities, and urban neighborhoo《
organization. She has written several books on China, including *Women and Child Care i*
China and *People, Politics and Ping Pong.*

MTSHENA SIDILE was born in Southern Rhodesia and received his B.S. from th《
University of South Africa. When he was 40 years old, he came to the United States, wher《
he received his M.S.W. at Adelphia University. He is currently an administrator at th《
Housing and Amenities Department in Bulawayo, Rhodesia. Three of his children have com《
to the United States on full scholarships for their undergraduate degrees.

NADA SMOLIC-KRKOVIC is Professor of Psychology, Social Work, and Gerontology an《
teaches Interdisciplinary Study of Social/Work at the University of Zagreb in Yugoslavia. H《
received his Ph.D. in psychology at the University of Zagreb.

DANIEL THURSZ is Dean and Professor of the School of Social Work and Communit;
Planning of the University of Maryland at Baltimore. He has served in this capacity sinc《
1967. Prior to that time he was the Associate Director of VISTA, the United State‹
Domestic Peace Corps, established as part of the Office of Economic Opportunity. He ha‹
held a number of important positions in social welfare and has been a leader in the Nation《
Association of Social Workers in the United States. Born in Morocco, Dr. Thursz ha‹
maintained close links with several centers of social welfare development throughout th《
globe.

BALBINA OTTONI VIEIRA received his degree from the Catholic University of Rio d《
Janeiro. He has been Chief of Social Services of the Hospital dos Servidodres de Estado i›
Rio de Janeiro and Consultant in Social Welfare of Service Social de Comercio. He ha‹
worked with the U.N.R.A. in Germany, has been consultant of Venezualian Children"
Bureau and Group Work Consultant at the Mutualité Agricole de France. He has also serve《
as President of the National Association of Brazilian Social Workers.

JOSEPH L. VIGILANTE is the Dean of the School of Social Work at Adelphi University i›
Garden City, New York, where he has served since 1962 in that capacity. Prior to joinin,
the Adelphi University faculty in 1955, Dr. Vigilante was a caseworker and a child welfar‹
worker in New York and Wisconsin. He has served as a consultant to a number of state an《
federal agencies. He has served on the national level with the National Association of Socia‹
Workers and is a member of the Board of Directors of the Council on Social Worl‹
Education.

SUBJECT INDEX